WILLIAM SHAKSPERE

A Study in Elizabethan Literature

BY

BARRETT WENDELL

ASSISTANT PROFESSOR OF ENGLISH AT HARVARD COLLEGE

AMS PRESS
NEW YORK

Reprinted from the edition of 1894, New York
First AMS EDITION published 1971
Manufactured in the United States of America

International Standard Book Number: 0-404-06905-3
Library of Congress Catalog Number: 79-127906

AMS PRESS INC.
NEW YORK, N.Y. 10003

NOTE

As this book has grown from lectures given, at Harvard College, to classes who were systematically reading the works under discussion, it has been impossible to avoid the assumption that a text of Shakspere is always close at hand.

Whoever is familiar with the subject must instantly perceive my constant obligation to the writings of Mr. Dowden and Mr. Furnivall. Just as helpful, though not obvious to the public, have been the manuscript notes on Shakspere kindly lent me by Messrs. Charles Lowell Young and Henry Copley Greene, of Harvard University; and by Miss M. T. Bennett, of Radcliffe College. The proof-sheets of an admirable essay on John Lyly by my colleague, Mr. George Pierce Baker, unhappily failed to reach me until after this book was printed.

B. W.

New Castle, N. H.,
    23 August, 1894.

CONTENTS

WILLIAM SHAKSPERE

I

INTRODUCTION

THE purpose of this study is to present a coherent view of the generally accepted facts concerning the life and the work of Shakspere. Its object, the common one of serious criticism, is so to increase our sympathetic knowledge of what we study that we may enjoy it with fresh intelligence and appreciation. The means by which we shall strive for this end will be a constant effort to see Shakspere, so far as is possible at this distance of time, as he saw himself.

Of one thing we may be certain. To himself Shakspere was a very different fact from what he now seems to the English-speaking world. To people of our time he generally presents himself as an isolated, supreme genius. To people of his own time — and he was a man of his own time himself — he was certainly nothing of the kind; he was no divine prophet, no superhuman seer, whose utterances should edify and guide posterity; he was only one of a considerable company of hard-working playwrights, whose work at the moment seemed neither more nor less serious

than that of any other school of theatrical writers.
Nothing but the lapse of time could have demonstrated
two or three facts now so commonplace that we are
apt to forget they were not always obvious.

First of all, the school of literature in which his
work belongs — the Elizabethan drama — proves to
have been one of the most completely typical phenomena in the whole history of the fine arts. It took
little more than half a century to emerge from an
archaic tradition, to develop into great imaginative
vitality, and to decline into a formal tradition, no
longer archaic, but if possible less vital than the tradition from which it emerged. In this typical literary evolution, again, Shakspere's historical position
happens to have been almost exactly central; some
of his work belongs to the earlier period of the
Elizabethan drama, much of it to the most intensely
vital, some of it to the decline. This fact alone —
that in a remarkably typical school of art he is the
most comprehensively typical figure — would make
him worth serious attention. The third commonplace invisible to his contemporaries, however, is
so much more important than either of the others
that nowadays it obscures them, and indeed obscures the whole subject. This most typical writer
of our most broadly typical literary school happened
to be an artist of first-rate genius. Canting as such a
phrase must sound, it has something like a precise
meaning. In the fine arts, the man of genius is he
who in perception and in expression alike, in thought

and in phrase, instinctively so does his work that his work remains significant after the conditions which actually produced it are past. Throughout the Elizabethan drama there were flashes of genius; in general, however, the work of the Elizabethan dramatists was so adapted to the conditions of the Elizabethan stage that, after the lapse of three centuries, its flashes of genius have faded into the obscurity of book-shelves, where they serve now chiefly to lighten the drudgery of men who study the history of literature. In the case of Shakspere, the genius was so strong and permeating that his work, from beginning to end, has survived every vestige of the conditions for which it was made. We are apt now to forget that it was made for any other conditions than those amid which, generation by generation, we find it.

If we would sincerely try to see the man as he saw himself, we must resolutely put aside these commonplaces of posterity. In their stead we must substitute the normal commonplaces of human experience. Shakspere, we know, was an Elizabethan playwright; and we know enough of the Elizabethan drama to form, in the end, a pretty clear conception of the professional task which was thus constantly before him. By both temperament and profession, too, Shakspere was a creative artist; and those of us who have had much to do with people who try to create works of art learn to know that in general the artistic temperament, great or small, develops according to pretty well fixed principles. Our effort to understand Shakspere, then, begins to define itself. We shall have done much if we can learn to see in him a man of normal artistic temperament, developing, in spite of its scale, in a normal way, under the known conditions which surrounded the Elizabethan theatre.

Such definite study of him as this has been possible only in recent years. Until rather lately one obstacle to it was insurmountable. To study the development of any artist, we must know something of the order in which his works were produced; and Shakspere's works have generally been presented to us in great chronological confusion. The first collection of his plays, a very carelessly printed folio, appeared in 1623. Here they were roughly classified as comedies, histories, and tragedies; under these heads, too, they were arranged in no sort of order. The book opens with the *Tempest*, for example, which is followed by the *Two Gentlemen of Verona;* yet nothing is now much better proved than that the *Two Gentlemen of Verona* is the earlier by above fifteen years. Again, the plays dealing with English history are printed in the order in which the sovereigns they deal with ascended the throne of England; yet, if we except *Henry VIII.*, which stands by itself, nothing is more certain than that *Henry VI.* is chronologically the first of the series, and *Henry V.* the last, with an interval of at least nine years between them. The general arrangement of the plays in the first folio, fairly exemplified by these instances, is still followed in standard editions of Shakspere. The resulting confusion of impression is almost ultimate.

During the past century or so, however, scholarship has gone far to reduce this chaos to order. On various grounds, a plausible chronology has arisen. Sixteen of the plays, and all of the poems, were published in quarto during Shakspere's lifetime. Entries in the Stationers' Register — analogous to modern copyright — exist in many cases. Allusions in the works of contemporary writers are sometimes helpful; so are allusions to contemporary matters in the plays themselves. More subtle, less certain, but surprisingly suggestive chronological evidence has been collected by elaborate analysis of technical style. It has been discovered, for example, that end-stopped verse, and rhyme are far more frequent in Shakspere's earlier work than in his later, and that what are called light and weak endings to verses occur in constantly increasing proportion during the last six or eight years of his writing. The plays have been grouped accordingly.[1] By some means or other, then, and in almost every case by means foreign to the actual substance of the works in question, foreign to the matters they deal with or to the mood in which they deal with them, a conjectural date — as a rule provisionally accepted by scholars — has been assigned to every work commonly ascribed to Shakspere.

Reading the plays and the poems in this conjecturally

[1] An adequate discussion of this matter is accessible to everybody in Dowden's *Primer of Shakspere*, pp. 32–46

chronological order we find in them something far removed from the pristine confusion of the standard editions. Once for all, of course, we must admit to ourselves that what results we thus find are not incontestable. As our chronology is only conjectural, so must be any inferences which we may draw from it. If these inferences be plausible, however, if they help us to find in Shakspere not only the supreme genius of English literature, but also a normal human being, greater than others, but not different in kind, we are fairly warranted in accepting them as a matter of faith. At least we may believe, though we may never assert, that they can help us in our effort to see Shakspere as he saw himself; and so to understand, to appreciate, to enjoy him better than before.

Our purpose, then, is to obtain a coherent view of the generally accepted facts concerning the life and the work of Shakspere. To accomplish this, we may best begin by glancing at the known facts of Shakspere's life. Then we shall briefly consider the condition of English literature at the time when his literary activity began. Then we shall consider in chronological order, and with what detail proves possible, all the works commonly assigned to him. Finally, we shall endeavor to define the resulting impression of his individuality.

II

THE FACTS OF SHAKSPERE'S LIFE

[All the known documents concerning Shakspere are collected in
Mr. Halliwell-Phillips's *Outlines of the Life of Shakespeare*. In Mr. F. G.
Fleay's *Life and Work of Shakespeare* is a masterly discussion of them.
Dowden's *Primer*, and Furnivall's Introduction to the *Leopold Shakspere* state the facts more compactly. In none of the authorities is it
always easy to separate facts from inferences. If Wilder's *Life*, Boston,
1893, were a bit more careful in detail, it would be perhaps the most
satisfactory, because the least complicated with conjecture.]

On April 26th, 1564, William, son of John Shakspere, was baptized at Stratford-on-Avon. John Shakspere, the father, had come from the neighboring
country to Stratford, where he was engaged in fairly
prosperous trade. In 1557 he had married Mary
Arden, a woman of social position somewhat better
than his own. In 1568 he was High Bailiff, or
Mayor of Stratford. Until 1577, indeed, the extant
records indicate that he was constantly looking up
in the world. In that year, they begin to indicate
that his circumstances were declining; in 1578 they
show that he had to put a mortgage for £40 on an
estate called Asbies. Meanwhile he had become the
father of five other children,[1] of whom four survived.

---

[1] Gilbert, b. 1566; Joan, b. 1569; Anne, b. 1571, d. 1579; Richard,
b. 1573; Edmund, b. 1580. Two older daughters had died in infancy.

Of William Shakspere's youth, then, we may be sure that it began in a well-to-do family of Stratford, increasing in numbers and prosperity; and that when he was about thirteen years old the prosperity came to an end.

On November 28th, 1582, when he was half-way between eighteen and nineteen years old, comes the first record which directly concerns him. A bond was given for his marriage to Anne Hathaway, a woman then in her twenty-sixth year, and of social position in no way better than Shakspere's. On May 26th, 1583, their first child, Susanna, was baptized. What inferences may be drawn from these dates have given rise to much discussion. In all probability they indicate a practice still common among respectable country folk, in America sometimes called "keeping company;" and are interesting chiefly as they throw light on the manners to which Shakspere was born. On February 2nd, 1585, his twin children, Hamnet and Judith, were baptized. In 1587, there is a record of his sanction, at Stratford, to a proposed arrangement concerning the Asbies mortgage which his father, who was now in prison for debt, had executed in 1578. This is literally all that is known of his early life at Stratford. Stories of how he went to school, how he saw plays, how he was at Kenilworth when Queen Elizabeth came there in 1575, how he was apprenticed to a local butcher, how he poached in Sir Thomas Lucy's park, have no authority. They are not impossible; there is nothing to prove them

From the actual facts, however, certain inferences may be drawn. At the age of twenty-three, he was the eldest of the five surviving children of a ruined country tradesman; he was married to a woman already about thirty, who had borne him three children; and he had no recorded means of support.

Five years later comes the next reference to him. On September 3d, 1592, Robert Greene, the dramatist, died. His last book, *Green's Groatsworth of Wit; bought with a Million of Repentaunce*, speaks rather scurrilously of the theatres where he had rioted away his life. In the course of it occurs this passage:

" Base minded men al three of you, if by my miserie ye be not warned: for unto none of you (like me) sought those burres to cleave: those Puppits (I meane) that speake from our mouths, those Anticks garnisht in our colours. Is it not strange that I, to whom they al have beene beholding: is it not like that you, to whome they all have beene beholding, shall (were ye in that case that I am now) be both at once of them forsaken? Yes, trust them not: for there is an upstart Crow, beautified with our feathers, that with his *Tygers heart wrapt in a Players hide*,[1] supposes he is as well able to bumbast out a blanke verse as the best of you: and being an absolute *Johannes fac totum*, is in his oune conceit the onely Shake-scene in a countrie. O that I might intreate your rare wits to be imployed in more profitable courses: & let these Apes imitate your past excellence, and never more acquaint them with your admired inventions. . . . It is pittie

[1] Cf. 3 *Henry VI*. Act I. Scene iv. 137.

men of such rare wits, should be subject to the pleasures of such rude groomes. . . . For other new commers, I leave them to the mercie of these painted monsters, who (I doubt not) will drive the best minded to despise them; for the rest its skils not though they make a jeast at them." [1]

From this passage, we may clearly infer that by the middle of 1592, Shakspere was a recognized writer of plays in London, that he was more or less involved in the theatrical squabbles of the time, that The Third Part of *King Henry VI.* was in existence, and that — at least to the mind of Robert Greene — he had plagiarized.

Within the year, Henry Chettle, the publisher of this posthumous diatribe of Greene's, published an apology for it, in the course of which he writes thus : —

" With neither of them that did take offence was I acquainted, and with one of them I care not if I never be : The other, . . . at that time I did not so much spare, as since I wish I had, . . . because my selfe have seen his demeanor no lesse civill than he exelent in the qualitie he professes : Besides, divers of worship have reported his uprightnes of dealing, which argues his honesty, and his facetious grace in writing, that aprooves his Art." [2]

It has been generally inferred that the two persons

---

[1] Shakspere's *Centurie of Prayse.* Second Edition, London. New Shakspere Society, 1879, p. 2.

[2] *Centurie of Prayse,* p. 4.

thus alluded to are the graceless Marlowe and the
excellent Shakspere.

On April 18th, 1593, about a week before his twenty-
ninth birthday, *Venus and Adonis*, his first published
work,[1] was entered in the Stationers' Register. During
the same year it was published in quarto, with Shakspere's name, by one Field, who was Stratford-born. It
proved highly popular; there were eleven quarto editions before 1630, and more than twenty allusions to
it during Shakspere's life-time have been discovered.

On February 6th, 1594, *A noble Roman history
of Tytus Andronicus* was entered in the Stationers'
Register, with no mention of Shakspere's name; it was
published, thus anonymously, in 1600. On May 9th,
1594, the *Rape of Lucrece* was entered; and it was
published within the year. From the terms of the
dedication, compared with those in the dedication of
Venus and Adonis,[2] it has been inferred that Shakspere had meanwhile become personally known to his
patron, the Earl of Southampton. The poem, though
popular, was less so than *Venus and Adonis;* there
were six quartos before 1624.

At Christmas time, 1594, the "servauntes to the
Lord Chamberlayne" acted twice at court; and Shakspere is mentioned as one of the members to whom
payment for these performances was made. Mr.
Fleay[3] shows reason to believe that he had belonged

---

[1] And is not this the whole meaning of the much-discussed phrase
in the dedication, "the first heir of my invention"?

[2] See p. 51.   [3] *Life,* pp. 8, 94.

to this company, under various patrons, since 1587, in which case he must have acted at court before; but this is the first distinct mention of his name. At Christmas-tide, 1594, " A comedy of *Errors* (like unto Plautus his Menœchmi ") was played at Gray's Inn. Clearly, by this time Shakspere was established in his profession. Just how he became so there is no record; the tales of his holding horses at the theatre-door, and so on, rest on no valid authority.

So far, then, the records show Shakspere first as a probably imprudent and needy youth, saddled with a family at twenty-three; and secondly, at thirty, as a fairly established theatrical man in London. In view of these facts, the next records [1] are significant. A conveyance of land at Stratford, dated January 26th, 1596, describes John Shakspere, the father, as " yeoman." In the Heralds' College, a draft grant of arms to this same John Shakspere, dated October 20th, 1596, describes him as a " gentleman." From the fact that this implied return of prosperity to the family has no other apparent source than the growing prosperity of the dramatist, it has been inferred that, like any other normal Englishman, Shakspere wished to inherit arms and to found a family. If so, another record, of the same year, is doubly pathetic; on August 11th, his only son, Hamnet, was buried at Stratford, in the twelfth year of his age.

The record of Shakspere's material prosperity, however, continues. In Easter Term, 1597, he bought

---

[1] *Leopold Shakspere,* p. ciii.

New Place, a mansion and grounds in Stratford, for £60; thereby becoming a landed proprietor. During the same year appeared the first quarto editions of his plays: namely, *Romeo and Juliet* in a very imperfect state and probably pirated, *Richard II.*, and *Richard III.;* his name, however, did not appear on any of the titlepages. Another indication of prosperity is that in November his father filed a bill in Chancery to recover the Asbies estate which he had mortgaged nineteen years before. At Christmas time *Love's Labour's Lost* was played before the Queen at Whitehall.

In 1598 this play was published, with Shakspere's name; so was the First Part of *Henry IV.;* so were fresh quartos of *Richard II.* and *Richard III.;* and the *Merchant of Venice* was both entered in the Stationers' Register and published.

In this year, too, a fragment of old correspondence gives us a glimpse of Shakspere. On the 24th of January one Abraham Sturley, a Stratford man, wrote to his kinsman Richard Quiney, who had gone to London on business, as follows: —

"Our countriman, Mr Shaksper, is willinge to disburse some monie upon some od yarde land or other at Shotterie . . . (Ur father) thinketh it a veri fitt patterne to move him to deale in the matter of our tithes. Bi the instruccion u can give him thearof, and bi the frends he can make therefore, we thinke it a fair marke for him to shoote att, and not unpossible to hitt."

Eight months later, on the 25th of October, Quiney wrote thus: —

" To my loveinge good ffrend & countreymann **Mr. Wm. Shackspere.** . . . I am bolde of you as of a ffrende, crave-inge yowr helpe with xxx li uppon Mr. Bushells and my securytee, or Mr. Myttons with me. . . . Yow shall ffrende me much in helping me out of all the debettes I owe in London, I thancke God, and much quiet my mynde, which wolde not be indebeted."

Some word of this letter seems to have been sent to Sturley, for on the 4th of November, Sturley wrote to Quiney, acknowledging

" ur letter of the 25 of October . . . which imported that our countriman Mr. Wm. Shak. would procure us monie, which I will like of as I shall heare when and wheare and howe; and I prai let not go that occasion if it mai sort to our indifferent condicions."

Later still, Richard Quiney's father wrote his son on the subject in person, perhaps a shade less confidently : —

" Yff yow bargen with Wm. Sha. . . . or receve money therefor, bring youre money homme that yow may."

Whatever these transactions were, Shakspere seems by this time to have presented himself to his fellow-townsmen at Stratford as a well-to-do man, and possibly a useful friend at court.

In 1598, furthermore, Shakspere acted in Ben Jon-son's *Every Man in his Humour*. But the most notable fact of the year for us is the publication of Francis Meres's *Palladis Tamia*.[1] In this book, which

[1] Or *Wit's Treasury*.

was entered in the Stationers' Register on September 7th, Shakspere is mentioned at least six times[1] as among the best of English authors. The most celebrated and familiar of these passages is the following, so obviously helpful in fixing the chronology of Shakspere's plays : —

"As the soule of *Euphorbus* was thought to live in *Pythagoras :* so the sweete wittie soule of *Ovid* lives in mellifluous & hony-tongued Shakespeare, witnes his *Venus* and *Adonis*, his *Lucrece*, his sugred Sonnets among his private friends, &c.

"As *Plautus* and *Seneca* are accounted the best for Comedy and Tragedy among the Latines ? so *Shakespeare* among yᵉ English is the most excellent in both kinds for the stage; for Comedy, witnes his *Gētlemē of Verona*, his *Errors*, his *Love labors lost*, his *Love labours wonne*, his *Midsummers night dreame*, & his *Merchant of Venice :* for Tragedy his *Richard the 2. Richard the 3. Henry the 4. King John, Titus Andronicus* and his *Romeo* and *Juliet*.

"As *Epius Stolo* said, that the Muses would speake with *Plautus* tongue, if they would speak Latin: so I say that the Muses would speak with *Shakespeares* fine filed phrase, if they would speake English."

At thirty-four, then, Shakspere had pretty clearly established himself as a poet, as a dramatist, and as an actor ; and, in the opinion of Stratford people, as a well-to-do, influential man of business and land-holder.

[1] *Centurie of Prayse*, 21–23.

In these characters the records maintain him with little change for above ten years to come. In 1599 two of his *Sonnets*, and three poems from *Love's Labour's Lost*, appeared in a volume called the *Passionate Pilgrim*, ascribed at the time to him, but otherwise probably spurious. In 1609 appeared the quarto of the *Sonnets* as we have them.

To pass from poems to plays, in 1599 appeared a fairly complete quarto of *Romeo and Juliet*. In 1600, *As You Like It*, *Henry V.*, *Much Ado About Nothing*, the Second Part of *Henry IV.*, the *Midsummer Night's Dream*, and the *Merchant of Venice* were entered in the Stationers' Register, and all of these except *As You Like It* were published in quarto, — *Henry V.* without his name; in the same year appeared anonymously the first extant quarto of *Titus Andronicus*. In 1602, *Twelfth Night* was acted; the *Merry Wives of Windsor* was entered and published; and in the same year were entered the First and Second Parts of *Henry VI.* and the *Revenge of Hamlet*. This is believed to be the version which appeared in quarto in 1603; the full text of *Hamlet* appeared in 1604. In 1607 *King Lear* was entered " as yt was played before the Kinges Majestie at Whitehall uppon St Stephens night at Christmas last." In the following year it appeared in two separate quartos, on the title-pages of which Shakspere's name is printed with very marked conspicuousness. In 1608, too, *Pericles* and *Anthony & Cleopatra* were entered. In 1609 *Troylus & Cressida* was entered and twice published; and

Pericles, too, twice appeared in quarto. This was the year, we may remember, in which the *Sonnets* appeared. From this time on, although a number of the foregoing plays were reprinted during his lifetime, no new work of his is known to have been either entered or printed until after his death; and the only one which appeared before the folio of 1623 was *Othello*, entered in 1621, and published in 1622. From these facts it would appear that his popularity as a dramatist was at its height in 1600; and that at least his activity diminished after 1609.

To pass from his works to his acting, he became, in 1599, a partner in the Globe Theatre, then just erected; and his company performed at court during Christmastide, in 1599, 1600, and 1602. It has been inferred by Mr. Fleay [1] that their absence from court in 1601 was connected with Essex's rebellion. It is possible that the play concerning Richard II., performed on the eve of that insurrection, was Shakspere's; if so, the Queen probably had reason to withhold her favor from him and his associates; but the matter is all conjectural. Queen Elizabeth died on March 24th, 1603. On May 19th, King James granted a license to Shakspere and others by name, to perform plays and to be called the King's Players. The company in question gave several plays at court each year until 1609; and in 1604, on the occasion of the King's entry into London, Shakspere, along with the other players, was granted four yards and a half of red cloth. During the years

[1] *Life*, 143–144.

2

in question, then, he was professionally at the height of his prosperity.

The records of his private affairs maintain this conclusion. In 1600 he brought an action for £7 against a certain John Clayton, and won it; in 1602 he bought one hundred and seven acres of land near Stratford, as well as other real property in the town; in 1604 there came another small action, and some large and small purchases of land. The records, in short, show him constantly and punctiliously thrifty; and as early as the purchase of 1602 he was legally described as " Wm. Shakespere of Stratford-uppon-Avon, gentleman." This description occurs a few months after he became the head of his family; for on September 8th, 1601, the year of the Essex conspiracy, his father was buried. In 1605, his fellow-player, Augustine Phillips, bequeathed him " a thirty-shilling piece in gold." On June 25th, 1607, Shakspere's elder daughter, Susanna, then twenty-four years old, was married to Dr. John Hall, a physician of Stratford; on February 21st, 1608, Elizabeth Hall, his grandchild, was baptized. Two months before, his youngest brother, Edmund, " a player," had died in London, and had been buried in S. Saviour's, Southwark. On September 9th, 1608, Shakspere's mother was buried at Stratford; on October 16th, he stood godfather there to one William Walker. These dry facts tell us something. Throughout the period of his professional prosperity he was demonstrably strengthening his position as a local personage at Stratford; and the chances seem to be that he came thither in person more and more.

From this time on, what records touch him personally show him chiefly at Stratford. In 1611, to be sure, the surprisingly detailed note-book of Dr. Simon Forman mentions performances of *Macbeth*, *Cymbeline*, and the *Winter's Tale*. In 1613, along with some older plays, the *Tempest* was performed at court; in the same year, when the Globe Theatre was burned, the fire started from a discharge of cannon in a play about Henry VIII., which may have been Shakspere's; and certainly in the same year he bought, and mortgaged, and leased, a house and shop in Blackfriars, London. What attracts one's attention more, however, is his presence in the country. In 1610 he bought more land from the Combes; in 1611 he subscribed to a fund for prosecuting in Parliament a bill for good roads; in 1612, described as " William Shackspeare, of Stratford-uppon-Avon, . . gentleman," he joined in a suit of which the object was to diminish his taxes; in 1614 he received a legacy of £5 from his Stratford neighbor, John Combe; in 1614, too, he was deep in a local controversy about the fencing of commons. Meanwhile there is said to be no record directly connecting him with theatrical life after 1609, when his publication ceased.

In view of this, the last paragraph of the Dedication of John Webster's *White Devil*[1] is in a way significant: —

[1] *Centurie of Prayse*, 100.

"Detraction is the sworne friend to ignorance: For mine owne part I have ever truly cherisht my good opinion of other mens worthy Labours, especially of that full and haightned stile of maister *Chapman:* The labor'd and understanding workes of maister *Johnson:* The no lesse worthy composures of the both worthily excellent Maister *Beaumont* & Maister *Fletcher:* And lastly (without wrong last to be named) the right happy and copious industry of M. *Shake-speare*, M. *Decker*, & M. *Heywood*, wishing what I write may be read by their light: Protesting, that, in the strength of mine owne judgement, I know them so worthy, that though I rest silent in my owne worke, yet to most of theirs I dare (without flattery) fix that of Martiall.

— non norunt, Hæc monumenta mori."

This was written in 1612. The first play of Chapman was published in 1598; the first of Heywood, in 1599; the first of Jonson and the first of Dekker in 1600; the first of Beaumont and Fletcher in 1607. Webster, probably a greater man than any of these, speaks of them all, in his first words, as traditional models. He groups Shakspere with them; and Shakspere had certainly begun his work, as a rival of Greene and Peele and Marlowe, years before any of these others except perhaps Dekker. In 1612 he was already, in a way, a tradition.

What little more is recorded of him belongs to the year 1616. On January 25th, his will was prepared. On February 10th, his younger daughter, Judith, married Thomas Quiney. On March 25th he signed his will. Just one month later, on April 25th,

1616, " Will. Shakspere, gent.," was buried in the church of Stratford.

All the rest of the story — how he died on his fifty-second birthday, how undue merry-making had something to do with it, how he made a doggerel epitaph for John Combe, and so on — is mere legend. Every known fact we have before us, except perhaps the fact that the editors of the *Centurie of Prayse*, who are a shade over-eager, have discovered more than a hundred[1] allusions to Shakspere between 1592 and 1616. At first sight, the record seems very meagre.

On reflection, though, it tells more of a story than at first seems the case. The son of a country trades-man who was beginning to improve his condition, Shakspere, in early youth, met with family misfor-tune, and made at best an imprudent marriage. Until the age of twenty-three, he was still in these circumstances. At twenty-eight he had established himself as an actor, a dramatist, and a poet in Lon-don. At thirty-two he had begun to help his father, and incidentally the family name of Shakspere, back into local consideration. At thirty-four he was a landed proprietor, a person who could be useful to country friends visiting London, and — at least in the opinion of Francis Meres — a first-rate literary figure. Till forty-five he maintained his professional position, constantly strengthening himself as a land-

[1] Including those published in *Fresh Allusions :* New Shakspere Society, 1886.

holder meanwhile. From forty-five to fifty-two, he was a country gentleman of Stratford. Prosaic enough this looks at first sight; but, to whoever will sympathetically appreciate the motives which have made Englishmen what Englishmen have been, it is not without its heroic side. We have had cant enough about snobbishness. A true-hearted Englishman always wants to die a gentleman if he can; and here, in the facts of Shakspere's life, we have the record of an Englishman, who, from a position which might easily have lapsed into peasantry, worked his way, in the end, to one of lasting local dignity.

III

LITERATURE AND THE THEATRE IN ENGLAND
UNTIL 1587

[The best popular history of English Literature is still Stopford Brooke's *Primer*. The best popular work on Elizabethan Literature is Saintsbury's; the best on the early drama is Addington Symonds's *Shakspere's Predecessors*. More satisfactory than any of these, as far as it goes, is Frederick Ryland's *Chronological Outlines of English Literature*. For whoever wishes more thorough treatment of the English stage, Mr. A. W. Ward's *History of English Dramatic Literature* is useful; and Mr. Fleay's *Chronicle History of the London Stage*, and *Biographical Chronicle of the English Drama* are very valuable.]

FROM the facts we have just considered, it is clear that in 1587 Shakspere was still at Stratford; and that by 1592 he was already so established a dramatist as to be grouped by Robert Greene with Peele and Marlowe. In the next year, 1593, the publication of *Venus and Adonis* brings him finally before us as a man of letters. The fact that, in 1587, the Earl of Leicester's players, the company with which he was later associated, paid a professional visit to Stratford, has led some people to surmise that when they returned to London they took him along. Whatever the facts were, we cannot be far wrong in assuming that the state of English Literature in 1587 fairly represents what Shakspere found, just as the state of things in 1612 fairly represents what Shakspere left.

His literary activity, then, his productive period, we may assume to be limited to twenty-five years, the last sixteen of the reign of Elizabeth and the first nine of the reign of James I. The state of our dramatic literature during this period, and to a great degree that of English poetry, may be adequately studied, for our purposes, in works generally assigned to him. To appreciate these, however, we must first glance at the state of English Literature which immediately precedes them.

Putting aside Chaucer, who was already as solitary a survival of a time long past as he is to-day, we may broadly say that during the first twenty-nine years of Queen Elizabeth's reign, English Literature contained and produced hardly anything permanent; a few lyrics, like Wyatt's *Forget not Yet*, or Lyly's *Cupid and Campaspe*, still to be found in any standard collection, may be said to comprise the whole literature of that period which has survived. In a traditional way, however, certain writers of the time remain familiar; without knowing quite what their work is like, people in general have a nebulous idea that the work exists, and at least formerly was of some importance. The earliest of these writers do not strictly belong to the time of Elizabeth at all. Both Sir Thomas Wyatt and the Earl of Surrey, who are commonly regarded as the pioneers of our modern literature, died in the reign of Henry VIII. Their writings, however, remained chiefly in manuscript until 1557, the year before the accession of Elizabeth. In that year, together with a considerable number of lyrics by other and later men, their songs and sonnets were published in Tottel's *Miscellany*. With that publication, modern English Literature, we may say, first became accessible to the general public.

By that time, as a hasty glance at the *Miscellany*, will suffice to show, the movement begun fifteen or twenty years before by Wyatt and Surrey had already progressed considerably. Wyatt was a gentleman, an ambassador, a statesman; Surrey, eldest son of the Duke of Norfolk, was a man of the highest rank and fashion. Wyatt, the elder by fourteen years, was by far the more serious character. The fact that nowadays they are commonly grouped together is due not so much to any close personal relation, as to the accident that their works were first printed in the same volume. It is justified historically, however, by the relation which their work bears to what precedes and to what follows. These courtiers, these men whose lives were passed in the most distinguished society of their time, found not only the literature, but even the language, of their native England in a state which, compared with the contemporary French or Italian, may fairly be called barbarous. Each alike did his best to imitate or to reproduce in English the civilized literary forms already prevalent on the Continent. Each, for example, translated sonnets of Petrarch; each made original sonnets after the manner of that master; and Surrey, among other things, was the first to use English blank verse, in a careful, and by no means ineffective, translation of two books of the Æneid. Each, in short, made a considerable number of linguistic and metrical experiments; and neither seems to have thought of publication. Manuscript copies of their verses were multiplied among their private friends. A fashion was started, until at last the ability to play gracefully with words became almost as essential to the equipment of an Elizabethan gentleman as the ability to ride or to fence. As a rule, however, these men of fashion followed the example of Wyatt and Surrey to the end. They improved the power and the flexibility of the language surprisingly; but they did not publish. In 1586, for example, Sir Philip Sidney died; the *Arcadia*, the first of his published works, did not appear till 1590. As late as 1598, too, we may remember that, according to Meres, the "sugred sonnets" of Shakespere, who was by no means a man of rank, followed the fashion in being reserved for his private friends. In 1587, then, one may safely say that for above thirty years a certain graceful poetic culture had been the fashion; that its chief conscious object — so far as it had any — was to civilize a barbarous language; that it delighted in oddity and novelty, and that it inclined to disdain publication.

There was no want of publication, however. The prose books of Roger Ascham, already rather antiquated, proved that a scholarly man could write very charmingly in English prose. Ascham was tutor to both Lady Jane Grey and Queen Elizabeth. He published a book on archery, and another on education, which are still pleasant to read; and he intended to write one on cock-fighting, which might have been more amusing than either of the others. Again, Foxe's great *Acts and Monuments*, traditionally called the *Book of Martyrs*, was, from 1563, as generally accessible as was the early version of the English Bible. Both of these naturally concerned themselves little with literary form; Foxe was so grimly in earnest that his views still affect the opinion held by English-speaking people concerning the Roman Catholic Church. Incidentally, however, he proved with what tremendous effect the English language might be used for serious narrative. There were increasing numbers of translations from the classics, too, of which the most generally remembered now are probably Golding's Ovid and North's Plutarch. There were popular translations, as well, of less serious foreign literature, of which the most familiar in tradition is Paynter's *Palace of Pleasure*, a collection of tales largely from Boccaccio. These translations, from classic tongues or from foreign, were alike in their object of supplying to a people whose curiosity was awakened material that should for the moment have the charm of novelty. Novelty, too, was what gave a charm hardly yet exhausted to those records of exploration and discovery which are best typified by

Hakluyt's *Voyages*. By these, also, a sentiment of patriotism was alike stimulated and gratified; a state of things, which, in a less stimulating form, was reproduced by such historical chronicles as those of Stowe and of Holinshed.

Decidedly the most notable publication for the moment, however, was one which in its day was the most popular book in English, and which was subsequently so completely neglected that for a century or more it was hardly known to be in existence. This was John Lyly's *Euphues*, first published in 1579, and four times republished within six years. In 1587, accordingly, its popularity had hardly begun to wane. Professedly a novel, this book has no plot to speak of, and does not pretend to develop character, or either fantastically or plausibly to describe any real or imaginary state of life. It does pretend to be aphoristic ; but the aphorisms it formulates are blamelessly obvious throughout. In none of the generally essential traits of popular fiction, then, does *Euphues* show a trace of such excellence as should account for its popularity. The secret of this is to be sought wholly in its formal style. This style, which is said by modern critics to be closely imitated from the Spanish, is probably the most elaborately, fantastically, obviously affected in the English language. To any modern reader, in spite of a certain prettiness of phrase and rhythm, it is persistently and emptily tedious ; to the Elizabethan public, on the other hand, it was clearly, for a good while, completely fascinating. It not only set a formal fashion of expression which was palpable for years in English prose, and is said greatly to have influenced actual conversation; it gave our language the word "euphuism," which remains to this day a generic term for saccharine literary affectation. When what seems mere affectation has such marked effect, it becomes historically important; to understand the period to which it appealed, we must make ourselves somehow feel its charm. In the case of *Euphues* this is not an easy task: actually to feel its charm is almost impossible. To appreciate wherein its old charm lay, however, is not so hard as at first one fears; from beginning to end, the book phrases everything — no matter how simple — in the most elaborately unexpected way that Lyly, who was perhaps the most ingenious writer known to English literature, could devise. The only kind of taste to which its far-fetched allusions, its thin juvenile pedantry, its elaborate circumlocutions, its endless balance and alliteration, can appeal is a taste which incessantly craves verbal novelty. Were there no other proof than the popularity of *Euphues* affords, there would be proof enough that, in 1587, the one thing which the literary and fashionable public of England most admired was a new, palpably clever turn of phrase.

If further proof were demanded, however, the next piece of evidence might be Spenser's *Shepherd's Calendar*, and his correspondence with Gabriel Harvey concerning English versifying. These two works, exactly contemporary with *Euphues*, were almost all that Spenser had as yet published. Not a line of the *Faerie Queene*, or of the *Amoretti*, or of the lesser verse by which he is now known, was as yet before the public ; nor was there yet in print a line of either Bacon, Marlowe, Sidney, Drayton, Ralegh, Daniel, Chapman, Hooker, Dekker, Middleton, Heywood, or Ben Jonson. Elizabethan Literature, as we now understand the term, was still a thing of the future.

To sum up this necessarily hasty review : in 1587, English Literature, which was between forty and fifty years old, consisted in the first place of increasingly successful efforts to reduce to literary form a hitherto barbarous language, and in the second, of such technical feats of skill with this new vehicle of expression as were bound by ingenious novelty to please both cultivated and popular fancy. Besides these, to be sure, it contained a fair amount of passable translation from classical and foreign authors, and an increasing amount of sometimes dry and sometimes vigorously effective narrative, generally historical. In a word, the curiosity of England was aroused ; whatever, in substance or in form, satisfied curiosity was welcome ; and among the more fashionable classes this passion for curious novelty took the form of inexhaustible appetite for verbal ingenuity.

So much for what was then recognized as literature, — what was circulated in manuscript among people of fashion, and what found its way, either

directly or surreptitiously, into print.   Along with this
there was beginning to flourish a distinct school of
literature which as yet had hardly been recognized
as such.   This was the theatre.   From time immemorial something like a popular drama had flourished
in England.   The earliest form in which we know it
is the Miracle Plays, which were popular dramatic
presentations,   often   in   startlingly   contemporary
terms, of Scriptural stories, originally produced by
the clergy, and always more or less under church
supervision.   These were followed by what are called
" Moralities," where actors personifying various virtues
and vices would go through some very simple dramatic action, usually enlivened by the pranks of
" Iniquity " or some other Vice.[1]   Then came similar
productions, called " Interludes," which   differed
from the Moralities only in pretending to deal with
less abstract personages.   The Miracle Plays, which
persisted at least well into the Sixteenth Century,
were generally performed on large portable stages,
wheeled through the streets like the " floats " in a
modern procession ; the actors were generally the
members of the local guilds, each one of which would
traditionally have in charge its own part of the Scrip-
ture story and its own travelling stage.   The Moralities and Interludes, on the other hand, which

[1] These old Moralities act better than you would suppose.   One
given verbatim not long ago, though acted by amateurs who were all
friends of the audience, had enough dramatic force to hold attention
like a good modern play.

required hardly any stage setting, might be played anywhere — in an inn-yard, in a gentleman's hall, in some open square. While sometimes performed by such occasional actors as always kept charge of the Miracle Plays, the Moralities and Interludes tended to fall into the hands of strolling players and such other half-artistic vagrants as are sure to exist anywhere. The mountebanks whom one may still see here and there, at country fairs or in the train of quack doctors, preserve, with little change, the aspect of things in which the English drama grew.

When the classical scholarship of the Renaissance began to declare itself in England, it attempted, as in other countries, to revive something resembling the Roman stage. In *Ralph Roister Doister* and in *Gammer Gurton's Needle* we have examples of efforts, at once human and scholarly, to civilize the English theatre. In *Gorboduc*, the first English work in which blank verse is used for dramatic purposes, we have a conscientious effort, on the part of scholarly people, to produce in English a tragedy which should emulate what were then deemed the divine excellences of Seneca. These efforts, essentially similar to those which until the present century controlled the development of the theatre in France, were very pleasing to the learned few ; witness the familiar passage about the theatre in Sir Philip Sidney's *Defence of Poesy*. On the other hand, there is little evidence that they ever appealed much to the popular fancy, which certainly persisted in enjoying the wholly unscholarly traditions of Miracles, Moralities, and Interludes. These permitted in matters theatrical a range of conventional freedom, — a serene disregard of limitations either of time or of place, a bold mixture of high matters and low, serious and comic, spiritual and obscene, — which, to any cultivated taste, was quite as barbarous as were the linguistic and metrical crudities reduced to formal civilization by the literary successors of Wyatt and Surrey. For a while it looked as if the theatre of the people would permanently separate itself from all serious literary tradition.

At least from 1576, however, there were regular theatres in London. To a modern mind, though, that very term is misleading. An Elizabethan theatre, a structure adapted to conventions which had arisen among strolling players, was very unlike a theatre of the present day. At least the pit was open to the sky; there was no scenery in the modern sense of the word; there was no proscenium, no curtain; and the more fashionable part of the audience sat in chairs on either side of the stage, smoking pipes after tobacco came into fashion, eating fruit, and, if they saw fit, making game of the performance. The actors, meanwhile, invariably male, — for no woman appeared on the English stage until after the Restoration, — appeared with what dignity they could between these two groups of spectators ; and whatever the period of the play they were performing, — classical, mediæval, or contemporary, — they always wore gorgeous clothes of recent fashion, perhaps discarded court finery bought second-hand, and the like. Altogether, the nearest modern approach to the stage conditions of an Elizabethan theatre is to be found in those of the Chinese theatres which may sometimes be discovered in the Chinese quarters of American cities. It was for such a stage as this that all the plays of Shakspere were written.

Decidedly before 1587, however, this unpromising place had begun to produce plays still of some interest, at least historically. Three names of that period are remembered in all histories of English Literature, — the names of Robert Greene, George Peele, and Christopher Marlowe. These men, all under thirty years of age, had all been educated at one of the universities, and were all black sheep. Greene, for example, is known to have deserted his wife, and to have lived with a woman named Ball, whose brother was hanged at Tyburn; Peele, whether rightly or wrongly, was, almost in his own time, made the hero of a crudely obscene jest-book; Marlowe was killed at the age of twenty-nine, in a tavern brawl. Yet, by 1587, all three of these men had produced plays of which any reader of Shakspere may form an idea by glancing at *Henry VI.*, *Richard III.*, and *Richard II.* There is much argument among critics as to whether a considerable part of *Henry VI.* may not actually have been written by one or more of the three, and as to whether *Richard III.* be not rather Marlowe's work than Shakspere's; while *Richard II.*, though generally admitted to be Shakspere's own, is undoubtedly written in Marlowe's manner. All three of these men combined good education with graceless lives and active wits. Historically they mark a fusion between the traditions of culture and those of the popular theatre. Far removed as their work is from the pseudo-classic tendency so much admired by Sidney, it is just as far removed from the crudely popular Interludes and Moralities; and in technical style — in freedom and fluency of verse — it is much better than anything before it. Some of Greene's lyrics are thoroughly good; at least in *David and Bethsabe*, Peele's work shows signs of lasting dramatic merit;[1] while Marlowe not only made blank verse the permanent vehicle of English tragedy, but actually expressed in dramatic form a profound sense of tragic fact.

Tamburlaine, to be sure, the first of Marlowe's tragedies, is assigned to this very year, 1587; and is commonly spoken of as if chiefly remarkable for its use of blank verse, finally delivering the stage " from jigging veins of rhyming mother-wits," and for such indubitably bombastic passages as " Holla! ye pamper'd jades of Asia!"[2]   In point of fact, however, it is still more notable for real power. This shows itself clearly in occasional passages, like the famous one on beauty :[3] —

---

[1] See particularly the notable scene of the drunken loyal Urias and the perfidious David.

[2] Part I. Act IV. sc. iii.   [3] Part I. Act V. sc. ii.

> "If all the pens that ever poets held
> Had fed the feeling of their masters' thoughts,
> And every sweetness that inspir'd their hearts,
> Their minds, and muses on admired themes ;
> If all the heavenly quintessence they still
> From their immortal flowers of poesy,
> Wherein, as in a mirror, we perceive
> The highest reaches of a human wit ;
> If these had made one poem's period,
> And all combin'd in beauty's worthiness,
> Yet should there hover in their restless heads
> One thought, one grace, one wonder, at the least,
> Which into words no virtue can digest."

Still more clearly, however, the lasting power of
Marlowe shows itself in his whole conception even of
Tamburlaine. If we will but accept the conventions,
and forget them ; if we will admit the monotony of
end-stopped lines and the sonorous bombast which
delighted the crude lyric appetite of early Elizabethan
playgoers; if we will only ask ourselves what all this
was meant to express, we shall find in *Tamburlaine*
itself a profound, lasting, noble sense of the great
human truth reiterated by the three later plays [1]
which Marlowe has left us. Like these, *Tamburlaine*
expresses, in grandly symbolic terms, the eternal
tragedy inherent in the conflict between human aspiration and human power. No poet ever felt this more
genuinely than Marlowe ; none ever expressed it more
firmly or more constantly. By 1587, then, the English
stage had already become the seat not only of very
animated play-writing, and of charming lyric verse,

---

[1] *Dr. Faustus*, the *Jew of Malta*, and *Edward II.*

but actually, though unobserved, of noble philosophic poetry.

It is with these men, and other men like them, that Shakspere is grouped by Robert Greene in the *Groatsworth of Wit*, which we remember belongs to 1592. Perhaps even more than theirs, however, the dramatic work of John Lyly marks the permanent divergence of English taste from the pseudo-classic principles commended by Sidney. Lyly's *Euphues*, as we have seen, was in its day the most popular book in the English language. It appeared in 1579; the next year appeared its sequel, *Euphues and his England*. Like the play-writing roysterers at whom we have just glanced, Lyly was a university man; unlike them, he seems to have had a strong tendency to respectable life. For some ten years after the success of *Euphues* there is evidence that he hung about the court, seeking office or some such advancement; and during these ten years, his literary work took a dramatic form. Written rather for court pageants, or for performance by choir-boys, than for the popular stage, Lyly's plays seem nowadays thin and amateurish; they quite lack the robust, unconscious carelessness of the regular Elizabethan theatre. Like *Euphues*, however, they are distinctly things of fashion; as such, they prove that, in theatrical affairs as well as in popular, fashionable taste had taken a definitely romantic turn. While Lyly threw classic form to the winds, caring as little for the unities as the wildest scribbler of Moralities, a thousand allusions and

turns of thought and phrase prove that he had read
pretty deep in the classics, and read for fun. He was
romantic in form, then, not for want of knowing better,
but as a matter of deliberate taste or policy. As such,
too, he was not only persistently euphuistic in style,
but he was also constantly experimental in matters of
mere stage-business. In his comedies, for example,
one finds, for the first time in English, such fantastically ingenious plays on words and repartee as
nowadays, reaching their acme in *Much Ado About
Nothing*, are commonly thought peculiar to Shakspere.
Again, perhaps influenced by the fact that all his
players were male, and consequently ill at ease in
skirts, he first introduced on the English stage the
device so repeatedly used by Shakspere of disguising his heroine as a man. Throughout, in short,
with frankly persistent ingenuity, these light, graceful, fantastic plays of Lyly's appeal, like the style of
Euphues, to a taste which delights above all else in
clever, apparently civilized novelty.

Such, in general, was the state of the English
stage in 1587. Committed to the still untrammelled
freedom of romantic form, it displayed in its fashionable aspect and in its popular alike every evidence of
appealing to an insatiable taste for novelty. The very
simplicity of its material conditions, however, combined
with the prevalent literary taste of the time to make the
actual novelties it offered to its public principally verbal. With none of the modern distractions of scenery
or of realistic costume, with hardly any mechanical help

to the temporary illusion which must always be dear to
a theatre-going heart, an Elizabethan audience found its
attention centred, to a degree now hardly imaginable,
on the actual words of the play.   While certain conventional kinds of drama, then, which may be discussed
best in connection with the actual works of Shakspere,
were beginning to define themselves, all had in common the trait of a constantly ingenious, experimental
phrasing, to be appreciated nowadays only when you
can force yourself into the mood of an every-day
theatre-goer who should enjoy a new turn of language
as heartily as a modern playgoer would enjoy a new
popular tune.   What now appeals to us in Marlowe's
Tamburlaine is the profound tragic feeling which
underlies it ; in its own day what made it popular was
the ranting sonorousness of its verse.

In all but purely lyric style, clearly enough, the
taste of 1587 was still rather childishly crude.   With
lyric verse the case was different.   The fashion of
verbal experiment, which had persisted since the
time of Wyatt, combined with the thin melody of
contemporary music not only to make words do much
of the essentially musical work of which modern song-
writers are relieved by our enormous musical development, but also to develop the positive lyric power of
the language to a degree which has never been surpassed.   Wyatt himself, we have seen, wrote *Forget
not Yet;* John Lyly wrote *Cupid and Campaspe.*
What delights one in these, and in the hundreds of
songs for which we must here let them be typical, is

not that they mean much, but that, with indefinable
subtlety, they are so exquisitely musical. To such
effects as theirs the public of 1587 was sensitive to a
degree now hard to imagine; the purity of a sense of
beauty new to a whole nation had not yet been cor-
rupted. By 1587, then, the Elizabethan lyric was
almost at its best. Fantastic as the statement seems,
though, it is probably true that the ultimate secret of
lyric beauty — the only permanent effect which Elizabethan literature had as yet achieved — is identical
with that which made *Euphues* so popular. The
lyric poet is technically the most ingenious conceivable juggler with words.

For all their common verbal ingenuity, however,
and their common, eager endeavor to carry out the
work begun by Wyatt and lastingly to civilize what
had seemed a wildly barbarous language, the pure
men of letters, for whom Sidney and Lyly may stand
representative, differed very widely in private consideration from the men of the theatre, such as Greene, or
Peele, or Marlowe. As a class the former were respectable or better; as a class the latter were disreputable.
For the moment fashion favored polite literary effort
to a degree unusual in human history; the theatre,
meanwhile, was what the theatre always has been
everywhere, — the centre not only of artistic activity,
but also of organized vice.

We touch here on a delicate matter, which of late
it has been the fashion to ignore. By rather deliberately ignoring it, however, most modern critics have

failed to make clear the actual circumstances in which
Shakspere found himself when he came to London.
Beyond doubt there were good and sturdy men connected with the Elizabethan stage, just as good and
sturdy people may always be found among stage-folk
everywhere. Beyond doubt, the remaining fragments
of Elizabethan dramatic writing, even if we throw out
of our consideration the works of Shakspere, comprise
much, indeed most, of the noblest poetry of their
time. Equally beyond doubt, however, the Elizabethan
theatre of 1587 was not a socially respectable place,
and Elizabethan theatrical people — the Bohemians
of a society where there was no alternative between
formal respectability and the full license of professional crime — were very low company.

As early as 1579, one Stephen Gosson, then an
ardent Puritan, dedicated to Sir Philip Sidney an
attack on the immorality of poetry and of the stage,
under the apt title, the *School of Abuse*. Sidney, who
had not authorized the dedication, evinced his dis-
pleasure by coming to the rescue with his *Defence of
Poesy*. Gosson was certainly scurrilous, and modern
critics have usually confined themselves to this aspect
of his work, which they attribute to the fact that he
himself had once been little better than one of the
wicked; it is said that he had unsuccessfully tried to
write plays. Sidney's *Defence* remains a beautiful, ele-
vated piece of English prose, full of a peculiar quality
which faintly suggests what the charm of Sidney's
actual personality must have been. For all this,

however, for all the snarling vulgarity of Gosson and
the noble amenity of Sidney, there is an aspect in
which Gosson rather than Sidney is in the right.
Wherever an organized theatre develops itself, one is
sure to find along with this centre of more or less
serious art an equally organized centre of moral corruption. Without the Elizabethan theatre, to be sure,
we could never have had Shakspere; yet the very
forces which produced Shakspere were producing at
the same time a growing state of social degradation.
To our minds, at a distance of three hundred years,
the Elizabethan theatre seems chiefly the source from
which has come to us a noble school of poetry. To
Elizabethan Puritans, to the very men whose blood
still runs in the veins of New England, the Elizabethan
poets were the panders who kept full those schools of
vice, the play-houses. Nor can all the patronizing
amenity of Sir Philip Sidney, blinding himself like
other apologists to what he did not choose to see, blind
us to the fact that the evils which Gosson so hatefully
attacked were real, lasting, and bound to be the price
which any society must pay for the enjoyment of a
professional stage.

In Gosson's time, too, this state of things affected
the personal life of theatrical people rather more
than usual. They were then just emerging from
the condition of strolling players. None of them
were yet rich enough to emerge, as Shakspere
emerged thirty years later, into a solidly respectable
social station. We have seen what sort of life Greene

lived, and Peele, and Marlowe.   Greene, like Marlowe,
died in a public-house, of which the hostess is said to
have crowned his body with a laurel wreath.   Rollicking, reckless, wicked these old playwrights were,
for all the beauty of their verse, all the nobility of
their perceptions.   They had their public with them,
to be sure ; if their plays succeeded, they might probably be better paid than any other men of their time
who had only their wits to live by.   Once paid,
however, they would do little better than riot away
their earnings in London taverns.

In view of this, a very familiar part of Shakspere's
writing seems freshly significant.   It was in 1596, we
may remember, that John Shakspere, for the first
time described as " gentleman," applied for arms ; and
in 1597 that Shakspere himself, by the purchase of
New Place, first became a landed proprietor.   To the
latter of these years, at latest, we must attribute the
first part of *Henry IV.*, which was entered in the
Stationers' Register on February 25th, 1597–98.   In
Henry IV. occur those vivid scenes concerning Falstaff and his crew on which our actual knowledge of
Elizabethan tavern-life is chiefly based.   It was in such
a tavern as makes classic the name of Eastcheap that
Marlowe met his end ; in just such a place that Greene
lived with the sister of Cutting Ball, hanged at Tyburn ;
in such a place, too, must have been cracked the bawdy
jokes of George Peele.   It seems hardly unreasonable,
then, to guess that Shakspere's wonderful picture of
the cradle of the Elizabethan drama may have been

made at the moment when prosperity at length allowed him to emerge into a more decent way of life. How ever this may be, there can be no doubt that, in 1587, any professional actor must perforce have found himself in such environment as surrounded Falstaff and Gadshill, and Peto, and Bardolph, and Mistress Quickly.

To sum up this cursory view of the state of English Literature and the English stage at the moment when Shakspere's professional life began: Formal English Literature, which had begun with the work of Wyatt, had accomplished only three things, all rather slight: it had reduced a barbarous language to something like a civilized form; it had supplied the newly awakened national curiosity with a good deal of compendious information; and it had at once stimulated and gratified an excessive appetite for verbal ingenuity, which delighted in the affectations of euphuism, and at the same time relished lyric verse of lasting beauty. Meanwhile, this kind of thing, though highly fashionable, did not pay particularly well; to all appearances not even John Lyly made any money to speak of. The theatre, on the other hand, had developed the popular trifles of strolling players into a fairly established and tolerably lucrative kind of drama, whose vigorously romantic tendency was much to the taste of fashionable and popular audiences alike. In the hands of Marlowe, this drama had already at least once been the vehicle of profound tragic feeling; yet Marlowe himself was

popular, not as a great tragic poet, but as a daring
verbal and formal innovator. The stage and literature alike, then, were chiefly notable for eager, experimental pursuit of novelty. They differed chiefly in
the fact that while literature, though respectable, was
merely fantastic, the stage, though increasingly human,
was very disreputable indeed.

Among works attributed to Shakspere, there are
several which, genuine or not, are certainly characteristic rather of the period than of the man. In the
beginning of what purports to be our study of Shakspere himself, then, we shall find ourselves in some
degree continuing our study of his time. There,
rather than here, seems the best place to consider
such phases of literature as appear in his poems, and
in the various kinds of drama — comedy, tragedy, and
history — which had begun to define themselves on
the stage. All we need now remember is that, at the
age of twenty three or four, Shakspere found himself,
with all his work still to do, in the environment at
which we have just glanced. As we study the development of his work, we shall incidentally glance, too,
at certain changes in theatrical conditions. What
our study should begin with is simply this environment with which he began.

Of the temperament of the man whose active life
began under these circumstances we have no record,
beyond what we may infer from his work. One very
familiar passage in his later writing, however, when
taken in connection with a familiar piece of contem-

porary gossip, seems at least suggestive of the possibilities which lay within him. The bit of gossip is a
random note preserved in the diary of one John Manningham, Barrister-at-Law of the Middle Temple, and
of Bradbourne, Kent. Writing in 1602 or 1603, with
no more authority than one " Mr. Curle," he tells a
story which very possibly is apocryphal, but which
certainly indicates in what manner of estimation
Shakspere was held after he had been fifteen years at
work : [1] —

"Upon a tyme when Burbidge played Rich. 3 there
was a Citizen gaene soe farr in liking with him, that before
shee went from the play shee appointed him to come that
night unto hir by the name of Ri: the 3.   Shakespeare
overhearing their conclusion went before, was intertained,
and at his game ere Burbedge came.   Then message being
brought that Rich. the 3ᵈ was at the dore, Shakespeare
caused returne to be made that William the Conquerour was
before Rich. the 3.   Shakespere's name William."

The familiar passage from Shakspere's own writing is the 111th sonnet, which was certainly written
within a few years of the same date. It gives at least
a plausible inner glimpse of a life whose outward aspect
might have justified Manningham's gossip : —

" O, for my sake do you with Fortune chide,
   The guilty goddess of my harmful deeds,
   That did not better for my life provide
   Than public means which public manners breeds.

[1] Centurie of Prayse, 45.

Thence comes it that my name receives a brand,
And almost thence my nature is subdued
To what it works in, like a dyer's hand:
Pity me then, and wish I were renew'd;
Whilst, like a willing patient, I will drink
Potions of eisel [1] 'gainst my strong infection;
No bitterness that I will bitter think,
Nor double penance, to correct correction.

> Pity me then, dear friend, and I assure ye
> Even that your pity is enough to cure me."

[1] Vinegar.

IV

THE WORKS OF SHAKSPERE

From now forth, we shall devote our attention chiefly to the works of Shakspere, in which we shall endeavor constantly to find traces of his artistic individuality. Though, like any technical term of criticism, the phrase sound canting, it has a real meaning. Any artist, in whatever art, whose work deserves serious attention, must either perceive or express the matters with which he deals — or better still both perceive and express them — in a way peculiar to himself. The artist's work need not be autobiographic; everybody knows, for example, that a most erratic man may write noble poetry, or an estimable young girl produce a novel which shocks her mother. Any work of art, however, must express something which the artist, either in experience or by imaginative sympathy, has perceived or known. If in the work of any artist, then, we succeed in defining traits not perceptible in that of others, we succeed, so far as these go, in defining his artistic individuality.

The generally accepted works of Shakspere consist of two rather long poems, a few short ones not distinguishable from his other lyrics, a collection of sonnets, and thirty-seven five-act plays, if we count separately the two parts of *Henry IV.* and the three of *Henry VI.* These works we shall generally consider in what appears to be their chronological order. Partly because the two long poems were undoubtedly his first publications, however, and partly because they are by far the most careful work of his earlier period, — and so the most seriously and consciously expressive, — we shall consider them first. The plays we shall try to arrange in their original order, placing the *Sonnets*, where they probably belong, in the midst of the dramatic work.

In reading this dramatic work, we must never allow ourselves to forget that it is not, like the poems and the sonnets, pure literature, addressed primarily to readers. From beginning to end it was written for an actual stage, at the general condition of which we have already glanced. So far, then, as we try to find the plays expressive of the artistic individuality of Shakspere, we must keep in mind that they are not mere writings, but texts intended to be recited by professional actors, under conditions long since obsolete, to popular audiences. Incidentally, then, while studying the work of Shakspere we must find ourselves continually studying the conditions and the development of the Elizabethan stage.

For this reason, our first glance at this stage could properly be hasty. As we shall find when we examine the first plays attributed to Shakspere, if not certainly his own, this stage had already begun to develop certain definite kinds of drama, tragic, historic, and comic. In a way, then, it is a fortunate chance that what seem beyond doubt the earliest of the plays are thought by many critics not to be genuine. From an uncertainty full of historical suggestion, and beyond question full of information concerning his artistic environment when his work began, we can proceed to certainties among which our earlier doubts may help us to define the traits which make Shakspere artistically individual.

For our purposes, we may conceive his complete work as grouping itself in four parts. The first includes his poems and the plays from *Titus Andronicus* to the *Two Gentlemen of Verona ;* the second includes the plays from the *Midsummer Night's Dream* to *Twelfth Night ;* between this and the third, as in some degree contemporaneous with both, we shall consider the *Sonnets ;* after them we shall consider the third group of plays, from *Julius Cæsar* to *Corio-lanus ; Timon of Athens*, and *Pericles, Prince of Tyre*, as transitional and peculiar, we shall glance at by themselves ; and finally we shall consider the fourth group of plays, from *Cymbeline* to *Henry VIII.*

V

VENUS AND ADONIS, AND THE RAPE OF LUCRECE

[*Venus and Adonis* was entered in the Stationers' Register on April 18th, 1593, by Richard Field, a publisher, who originally came from Stratford. It was published in the same year, with a dedication to the Earl of Southampton, signed " William Shakespeare." In this dedication, of which the terms suggest very slight acquaintance between poet and patron, occurs the familiar passage, " But if the first heir of my invention prove deformed, I shall be sorry it had so noble a god-father, and never after ear so barren a land, for fear it yield me still so bad a harvest." The poem seems to have been popular. Seven editions were published during Shakspere's life-time, and more than twenty allusions to it before 1616 have been discovered. Its source, to which it does not closely adhere, was probably Golding's translation of Ovid, published in 1567. Concerning its date, we can assert only that it was finished, in its present form, by 1593.

The Rape of Lucrece was entered in the Stationers' Register on May 9th, 1594. It was published in the same year, by Richard Field, with a dedication to the Earl of Southampton, from the terms of which it has been inferred that since the publication of *Venus and Adonis* the poet had had personal intercourse with his patron: " The love I dedicate to your lordship is without end; whereof this pamphlet, without beginning, is but a superfluous moiety. The warrant I have of your honourable disposition, not the worth of my untutored lines, makes it assured of acceptance." Prefixed to the poem is an " Argument," the only known example of Shakspere's non-dramatic prose. Five editions were published before 1616, and the *Centurie of Prayse* cites fourteen allusions to it meanwhile. Its precise source is not known; the story, at the time very familiar, occurs in Paynter's *Palace of Pleasure*. Concerning its date, we can assert only that it seems distinctly to have been subsequent to *Venus and Adonis*, and that it was finished, in its present form, by 1594.]

FOR our purposes, these two poems may be grouped together. *Venus and Adonis*, in its own day somewhat the more popular, still seems the more notable; in certain aspects the merits of *Lucrece* are undoubtedly more respectable. Together, however, these two poems, so nearly of the same period, represent a kind of Elizabethan Literature on which we have not as yet touched; together they reveal the same sort of artistic mood and power. In discussing them, then, we need not carefully separate them; and if most of our attention be centred on *Venus and Adonis*, we may safely assume that what we find true of that is in general terms true also of *Lucrece*.

From what we have already seen of Elizabethan Literature, we have assured ourselves that, at the time when these poems were written, polite literature was highly fashionable, and the stage in doubtful repute. From the recorded facts of Shakspere's life we ventured to make some guesses concerning his temperament which might lead us to suppose that, at any given moment, his serious interest would centre in reputable things. It seems reasonable, then, to infer that these poems, in all respects far more careful than his early dramatic writings, represent the kind of thing to which, at least for the moment, he would have preferred to devote himself. If so, he would probably have thought this purely literary work far more important than his better paid, but less elaborate, work for the stage.

The kind of pure literature represented by these poems is akin to what we have already considered.

From the time of Wyatt and Surrey forward, fashionable literature had shown the influence of the Renaissance in two ways. In the first place, starting with Wyatt's sonnets, it had constantly, and with increasing success, tried to imitate and to domesticate the formal graces of foreign culture. In the second place, starting perhaps with Surrey's translation of the Æneid, it had tried to inspire itself with the spirit of the classics, — for the moment as fresh to people who cared for literature as to-day, after three centuries of pedantry and editing, they seem stale, — and to reproduce in the native language of England something resembling their effect. To this latter tendency we owe such literature as the poems of Shakspere exemplify. What they attempt is simply to tell, in new and excellent phrase, stories which have survived from classical antiquity.

In this respect, as well as in some others, they have many points of likeness to much Italian painting of the preceding century. In each case, the artist — poet or painter — turned to the revived classics with a full appetite for pagan enjoyment; in each, he endeavored to tell in rich contemporary terms the stories he found there; in each, the phase of classical literature which appealed to his taste was chiefly the decadent literature of Rome. At first, it would seem as if the great popularity of Ovid were due half to his erotic license, and half to the fact that he wrote easy Latin. On further consideration, the question looks less simple. The liking of Renascent Europe

for the later classics is very similar to the liking of
our grandfathers for the Apollo Belvedere and the
Venus de' Medici, for Guido Reni and Carlo Dolce.
Freshly awakened artistic perception is apt to prefer
the graces of some past decadence to the simple, pure
beauty of really great periods.   Such final culture
as can separate good from bad, cleaving only to what
is best, is the fruit of prolonged critical earnest-
ness.   What these poems of Shakspere, and the others
of their kind, first evince, then, is a state of culture
alive to the delights of past civilization, but too young
to be soundly critical.

Choosing their subjects, accordingly, not from the
grander myths of Greece, but from the later ones of
Rome, the Elizabethan narrators of classic story proceeded to treat them in a spirit very different from
what generally prevails nowadays. A contemporary
of our own who should choose to relate anew some
familiar classic tradition would be apt to infuse into
it, if he could, some new significance, somewhat as
Goethe infused permanent philosophic meaning into
the mediæval legend of Faust.   The object of the
Elizabethan narrative poet, on the other hand, like
that of the Italian painters, was simply to tell the
story as effectively as he could.   He bothered himself
little about what it might signify ; he permitted himself the utmost freedom of phrase and accessory ; as a
rule, he never thought of employing any but contemporary terms.   Like his own stage, he dressed his
characters in the actual fashions of his own day ; if

he made them splendid and attractive, he had done his work. What originality he might show was almost wholly a matter of phrase. His plot he frankly borrowed; his style was his own, and the more ingeniously novel he could make it, the better. Like the other writers of the early Elizabethan period, he proves ultimately to have been an enthusiastic verbal juggler.

To understand Shakspere's poems, then, we must train ourselves to consider them as, in all probability, little else than elaborate feats of phrase-making. This does not mean that they are necessarily empty. A line or two from *Lucrece*, chosen quite at random, will serve to illustrate the real state of things: —

> " For men have marble, women waxen, minds,
>   And therefore are they form'd as marble will." [1]

Here is clearly a general truth about human nature, expressed with considerable felicity; and that is the aspect in which any modern reader would consider it. Here too, though, and equally plainly, is an alliterative, euphuistic antithesis between the hardness of marble and the softness of wax, resulting in a metaphor probably fresher three hundred years ago than it seems to day, but even then far-fetched; and that is the aspect in which the Elizabethan reader would have been apt to see it. What he would have relished is the subtle alliteration on *m* and *w*, the obvious antithesis, and the slight remoteness of the metaphor; so

[1] *Lucrece*, 1240.

far as he was concerned, the fact that the lines compactly express a general truth would have seemed, if meritorious at all, only incidentally so. We touch here on a state of things now rarely understood; it is more than probable that the lasting felicity of much Elizabethan poetry, and so of Shakspere's own, is largely accidental. Words and ideas are not easily extricable; whoever plays with either is sure to do something with the other. Nowadays it is the fashion to disdain verbal ingenuity, to look always rather at the thought than at the phrase; in Shakspere's time this state of things was completely reversed. As surely as our own thinkers sometimes blunder upon phrases, though, the Elizabethan phrase-makers — by Shakspere's time far more skilful in their art than our modern thinkers in their cogitations — oftener and oftener managed incidentally to say something final.

In deciding that the poems of Shakspere show him to be chiefly an enthusiastic, careful maker of phrases, and so incidentally of aphorisms, we declare him to have been, in temper and in method, Elizabethan; we do not individualize him. Our object throughout this study, however, is if possible to see him as an individual. To do this we may best compare his work with other work of the same period. The comparison is obviously at hand. In 1593, the year when *Venus and Adonis* appeared, Marlowe was killed. He left unfinished a poem called *Hero and Leander*, subsequently concluded by Chapman. By comparing Marlowe's poem with the poems of Shakspere, we may get some notion of Shakspere's literary individuality. What we have seen so far is true not only of Shakspere, but cf Marlowe too, and generally of their contemporaries ; what we shall try to see now is something more definite.

The effect of Marlowe's *Hero and Leander* is very distinct. Frankly erotic in motive, thoroughly sensuous in both conception and phrase, it never seems corrupt. Beyond doubt it is a nudity ; but it is among the few nudities in English Literature which one groups instinctively with the grand, unconscious nudities of painting or sculpture. Conscienceless it seems, impulsive, full of half-fantastic but constant imagination, unthinkingly pagan, — above all else, in its own way normal. One accepts it, one delights in it, one does not forget it, and one is not a bit the worse for the memory, in thought or in conduct.

Equally distinct is the effect of *Venus and Adonis*, whose motive resembles that of *Hero and Leander* enough to make it the better of Shakspere's poems for this comparison. No more erotic, rather less sensuous in both conception and phrase, it somehow seems, for all its many graver passages, more impure. It is such a nudity as suggests rather the painting of modern Paris than that of Titian's Venice. It is not conscienceless, not swiftly impulsive, not quite pagan, — above all, not quite normal. If one think only of its detail, it is sometimes altogether delightful and admirable ; if one think of it as a whole, — particularly at austere moments, — one be-

gins to wonder whether an ideal Shakspere, in maturer
life, ought not to have been a bit ashamed of it.
Surely, one feels, the man who wrote this knew perfectly well the difference between good and evil, and
did not write accordingly.

It is hard to realize that such a contrast of literary effect must come largely from differences in
style; yet obviously this is the fact. One chief distinction between Marlowe's poem and Shakspere's
is clearly that in the one case a number of words
were chosen and put together by one man, and in
the other by another. The cause of their notable
differences, then, may confidently be sought in specific
comparison of detail; if we can discover this cause
we shall have discovered something which clearly
distinguishes Shakspere from Marlowe, and so helps
us toward a notion of his individuality.

The first lines of *Venus and Adonis* describe
sunrise : —

> " Even as the sun with purple-colour'd face
> Had ta'en his last leave of the weeping morn,
> Rose-cheek'd Adonis hied him to the chase ;
> Hunting he loved, but love he laugh'd to scorn."

In *Hero and Leander* there is a similar description
of the same time of day [1] : —

> " Now had the Morn espied her lover's steeds ;
> Whereat she starts, puts on her purple weeds,
> And, red for anger that he stay'd so long,
> All headlong throws herself the clouds among."

[1] Second Sestiad.

In both descriptions there is conventional mythological allusion, in both the figurative language refers
to the purple hue often perceptible at dawn; yet despite this similarity, the difference of effect is almost
as marked as that of the poems they come from.
This difference is not all due to the greater compactness of Shakspere, who tells in two lines as much as
Marlowe tells in four; it is due still more to the fact
that of Shakspere's four lines all but the second
might, in real life, be literally true, while all four
lines of Marlowe deal with pure mythological
fancy.

The contrast thus indicated persists throughout.
Here is Marlowe's description of Hero's costume: [1]

> " The outside of her garments were of lawn,
>   The lining, purple silk, with gilt stars drawn;
>   Her wide sleeves green, and border'd with a grove
>   Where Venus in her naked glory strove
>   To please the careless and disdainful eyes
>   Of proud Adonis, that before her lies;
>   Her kirtle blue, whereon was many a stain,
>   Made with the blood of wretched lovers slain.
>   Upon her head she ware a myrtle wreath,
>   From whence her veil reach'd to the ground beneath :
>   Her veil was artificial flowers and leaves,
>   Whose workmanship both man and beast deceives."

Compare with this Shakspere's description of the
horse of Adonis [2] — in Shakspere's poem, we may
remember, no one is quite so thoroughly clothed as
Hero : —

[1] First Sestiad.   [2] Line 295 seq.

> " Round-hoof'd, short-jointed, fetlocks shag and long,
>   Broad breast, full eye, small head and nostril wide,
>   High crest, short ears, straight legs and passing strong,
>   Thin mane, thick tail, broad buttock, tender hide :
>   Look, what a horse should have he did not lack,
>   Save a proud rider on so proud a back."

Again, compare the similes and the action and the generalizations in the passages which follow. Here is Marlowe's description of the first meeting of Hero and Leander : —

> " It lies not in our power to love or hate,
>   For will in us is over-rul'd by fate.
>   When two are stript, long ere the course begin,
>   We wish that one should lose, the other win ;
>   And one especially do we affect
>   Of two gold ingots, like in each respect :
>   The reason no man knows ; let it suffice
>   What we behold is censur'd by our eyes.
>   Where both deliberate, the love is slight :
>   Who ever lov'd, that lov'd not at first sight ?[1]
>   He kneel'd ; but unto her devoutly pray'd :
>   Chaste Hero to herself thus softly said,
>   ' Were I the saint he worships, I would hear him ; '
>   And, as she spake those words, came somewhat near him."

And here is Shakspere's description of the last meeting[2] of Venus and Adonis. Having caught sight of him wounded,

> " As the snail, whose tender horns being hit,
>   Shrinks backward in his shelly cave with pain,
>   And there, all smother'd up, in shade doth sit,
>   Long after fearing to creep forth again ;

[1] Cited, we remember, in *As You Like It*, III. v. 83.
[2] Lines 1033–1068.

> So, at his bloody view, her eyes are fled
> Into the deep dark cabins of her head."

.   .   .   .   .   .

> [Then] " being open'd, threw unwilling light
> Upon the wide wound that the boar had trench'd
> In his soft flank ; whose wonted lily white
> With purple tears, that his wound wept, was drench'd :
>   No flower was nigh, no grass, herb, leaf, or weed,
>   But stole his blood and seem'd with him to bleed.

.   .   .   .   .   .

> "Upon his hurt she looks so steadfastly,
>   That her sight dazzling makes the wound seem three ;
> And then she reprehends her mangling eye,
>   That makes more gashes where no breach should be :
>   His face seems twain, each several limb is doubled ;
>   For oft the eye mistakes, the brain being troubled."

These examples are more than enough to indicate both the precise difference in the effect of
the two poems, and its cause. From beginning
to end, Marlowe is not literal, not concrete ; he
never makes you feel as if what he described were
actually happening in any real world. From beginning to end, on the other hand, Shakspere is constantly, minutely true to nature. While the action
of *Hero and Leander* occurs in some romantic nowhere, inhabited by people whose costume, if des-
cribable, is quite unimaginable, the action of *Venus
and Adonis* occurs in Elizabethan England, where men
know the points of horses. The absence from Marlowe's poem of all pretence to reality saves it from
apparent corruption ; in Shakspere's poem, incessant
suggestions of reality produce the contrary effect.

A very brief comparison of detail will show the technical means by which this difference is made apparent. Take two lines from Marlowe — one a simile, the other a generalization — and place beside them two lines of similar import from Shakspere: —

" When two are stript, long ere the course begin,"

writes Marlowe ;

" Or as the snail, whose tender horns being hit,"

writes Shakspere. In Marlowe's line, only one word — *stript* — is concrete enough to suggest a vivid visual image ; in Shakspere's line, there are four words — *snail*, *tender*, *horns*, and *hit* — each of which is as vividly concrete as the most vivid word of Marlowe's. Again,

" Who ever lov'd, that lov'd not at first sight ? "

writes Marlowe ;

" For oft the eye mistakes, the brain being troubled,"

writes Shakspere. In Marlowe's generalization, the words are simply general throughout ; in Shakspere's, they are so concrete as to amount to a plain statement of physiological fact.

This distinguishing trait — that, to a remarkable degree, Shakspere's words stand for actual concepts — pervades not only *Venus and Adonis*, but also *Lucrece*. It is more palpable in the former poem only because its effect there is so startlingly different from that produced by Marlowe's more nebulous vocabulary. It pervades not only the

poems, but the plays, too; beyond reasonable doubt
it is the trait which distinguishes Shakspere not only
among his contemporaries but from almost any other
English writer.

At first sight, this concreteness of phrase seems to
indicate extreme intensity of conscious thought, on
which conclusion have been based many worshipping expositions of the almost divine wisdom and
philosophy of Shakspere.   The conclusion cannot
be denied; it may, however, be reasonably questioned
even to the point of growing doubt as to whether
Shakspere himself, the Elizabethan playwright, could
have had much realizing sense of his own philosophy
and wisdom.   As we have seen, the literary fashion
of his time delighted above all things else in fresh, ingenious turns of phrase; in Shakspere's work, accordingly, fresh, ingenious turns of phrase abound.   As we
have seen, too, one cannot combine words and phrases
without also combining ideas; when language grows
definite, words and thoughts combine inextricably.
Such a phenomenon as Shakspere's style, then, may
well proceed from a cause surprisingly remote from
conscious intensity of thought; it may indicate nothing more than a constitutional habit of mind by which
words and concepts are instinctively allied with unusual firmness.   We all know palpable differences in
the habitual alliances of word and concept among our
own friends; we know, too, that these differences,
which often make uneducated or thoughtless people
appear to advantage, are a matter not so much of train-

ing, as of temperament. Of course the felicities of
phrase, and the incidental wisdom, which come from
such natural marriages of words and concepts are not
absolutely thoughtless; but the difference between
them and the feebler expressions of people whose
natural style lacks precision is often that while the
latter involve acute consciousness of thought, the
former involve little more than alert consciousness
of phrase. Take care of your words, if your words
naturally stand for real concepts, and your thoughts
will take care of themselves. Given such a natural
habit of mind as this in a healthy human being, given
too the immense skill in phrase-making which pervaded the literary atmosphere of Shakspere's time,
given an eager effort on Shakspere's part to make
phrases which should compare with the best of them,
and very surely the result you would expect is just
such a style as distinguishes *Venus and Adonis* and
Lucrece.

To dwell on this trait of style, even at the risk
of tedium, has been well worth our while. Palpable
throughout Shakspere's work, it is nowhere more
easily demonstrable than here, in the poems which
were clearly the most painstaking productions of
his early artistic life; for in the poems, admirable as they so often are in phrase, one can find
ultimately little else than admirably conscientious
phrase-making. Shakspere tells his stories with typical Elizabethan ingenuity; incidentally he infuses
them with a permeating sense of fact, astonishingly

different from the untrammelled imagination of Marlowe; yet plausibly, if not certainly, this effect is traceable to the instinctive habit of a mind in which the natural alliance of words and concepts was uniquely close.   Here, then, we have the trait which, above all others, defines the artistic individuality of Shakspere. To him, beyond any other writer of English, words and thoughts seemed naturally identical.

VI

THE PLAYS OF SHAKSPERE, FROM TITUS ANDRONI-
CUS TO THE TWO GENTLEMEN OF VERONA

I. TITUS ANDRONICUS

[*A Noble Roman Historye of Tytus Andronicus* was entered in
the Stationers' Register on February 6th, 1593–94. In 1598, Meres
mentioned *Titus Andronicus* as among Shakspere's tragedies. The
play, virtually in its present form, was published in quarto, without
Shakspere's name, in 1600. There was another anonymous quarto in
1611. Besides Meres's allusion to it, the *Centurie of Prayse* cites two
others during Shakspere's lifetime, neither of which mentions his
name. The second of these is in Ben Jonson's *Bartholomew Fair*,
which appeared in 1614 : " Hee that will sweare *Jeronimo* [1] or *Andronicus* are the best playes, yet shall passe unexcepted at, heere, as a man
whose Judgement shewes it is constant, and hath stood still, these five
and twentie, or thirtie yeeres." From this, as well as from its general
archaism, the inference has been drawn that the play belongs, at latest,
to 1589. As Shakspere was not in London before 1587, then, a reasonable conjectural date for it is 1588.

Its precise source is unknown. The story seems to have been
familiar. Possibly the play, as we have it, is a retouched version of
an older play called *Titus and Vespasian*, of which a German adaptation exists.

The genuineness of *Titus Andronicus* has been much questioned, on
the ground that it is unworthy of Shakspere ; the arguments in its
favor rest on Meres's allusion, and on the fact that it was included in
the folio of 1623. If Shakspere's, it is probably his earliest work.]

THE frequent doubt as to the genuineness of *Titus
Andronicus* gains color from the place where the
play is generally printed. In most editions of Shaks-

---

[1] Le., Kyd's *Spanish Tragedy*, circ. 1588.

pere it occurs between *Coriolanus* and *Romeo and
Juliet.* Thus placed, it seems little more than a monstrous tissue of absurdities, — a thing of which no
author who wrote such tragedies as the others could
conceivably have been guilty.

Read by itself, however, particularly at a moment
when one is not prepossessed by Shakspere's greater
work, it does not seem so bad. Crude as it is in
general conception and construction, free as it is from
any vigorous strokes of character, it has, here and
there, a rhetorical strength and impulse which sweep
you on unexpectedly. In the opening scene, for example, where Andronicus commits to the tomb the
bodies of his sons,[1] who have fallen in battle, his half-
lyric lament has real beauty : —

> " In peace and honour rest you here, my sons ;
>   Rome's readiest champions, repose you here in rest,
>   Secure from worldly chances and mishaps !
>   Here lurks no treason, here no envy swells,
>   Here grow no damned grudges ; here are no storms,
>   No noise, but silence and eternal sleep :
>   In peace and honour rest you here, my sons ! "

Or again, when Lavinia is brought to him, maimed
and ravished, his speech,[2] whoever wrote it, has a
rude power of its own : —

> " It was my deer ; and he that wounded her
>   Hath hurt me more than had he kill'd me dead :
>   For now I stand as one upon a rock
>   Environ'd with a wilderness of sea,
>   Who marks the waxing tide grow wave by wave,

---

[1] I. i. 150 seq.   [2] III. i. 91 seq.

> Expecting ever when some envious surge
> Will in his brinish bowels swallow him.
>
> .   .   .   .   .
>
> Had I but seen thy picture in this plight,
> It would have madded me: what shall I do,
> Now I behold thy lively body so ?
> Thou hast no hands, to wipe away thy tears;
> Nor tongue, to tell me who hath martyr'd thee:
> Thy husband he is dead; and for his death
> Thy brothers are condemn'd, and dead by this.
> Look, Marcus ! ah, son Lucius, look on her !
> When I did name her brothers, then fresh tears
> Stood on her cheeks, as doth the honey-dew
> Upon a gather'd lily, almost wither'd."

Whatever else this is, and there is plenty like it in
Titus Andronicus, it is good, sonorous rant.

As sonorously ranting, then, whether Shakspere's
or not, the play is a typical example of English tragedy at the moment when Shakspere's theatrical life
began.   If, in his earlier months of work, he tried
his hand at tragedy at all, he certainly must have
tried it at this kind of thing; for in substance, as well
as in style, *Titus Andronicus* typifies the early Elizabethan tragedy of blood.   The object of this, like
that of cheap modern newspapers, was to excite crude
emotion by heaping up physical horrors.   The penny
dreadfuls of our own time preserve the type perennially ; something of the sort always persists in theatres
of the lower sort; and it is perhaps noteworthy that
the titles, and in some degree the style, of these modern monstrosities preserve one of the most marked
traits of Elizabethan English, — extravagant allitera-

tion. Not only in extravagance of alliterative horrors, but also in serene disregard of historic fact, the lower literature of our own time preserves the old type. Both traits appear, too, in the romantic fancies of young children who take to literature. There has lately been in existence, for example, an appalling melodrama on the Massacre of St. Bartholomew, written at the age of ten by an American youth, wherein Charles IX., Catherine de' Medici, and Coligny figured along with a very heroic Adrien de Bourbon, who assassinated Charles, and, serenely ascending the throne, proceeded to govern France according to the liberal principles generally held axiomatic in the United States. It took no more liberty with French history than *Titus Andronicus* takes with Roman ; and both plays are of the same school.

In a way, such stuff seems hardly worth serious attention. At the very moment to which we have attributed *Titus Andronicus*, however, Marlowe was certainly developing the traditional tragedy of blood into a form which remains grandly if unequally significant in the *Jew of Malta*. Less than twenty years later, this same school of literature had produced *Hamlet* and *Othello*, and *King Lear*, and *Macbeth*. Even in them, many of its traits persist. Like their crude prototypes, they appeal to the taste prevalent in all Elizabethan audiences for excessive bloodshed, and stentorian rant. Until we understand that there is an aspect in which these great tragedies and this grotesque *Titus Andronicus* may rationally be grouped together, we shall not understand the Elizabethan theatre.

Whether Shakspere's or not, then, *Titus Andronicus* deserves a passing glance in any serious study of Shakspere. If his, as many of the soundest critics are disposed to believe, it deserves more; for, at least in the fact that it differs little from any conventional drama of its time, it throws light on his artistic character. Marlowe and Shakspere were just of an age. The year before that to which we have attributed *Titus Andronicus*, Marlowe had produced in *Tamburlaine* not only a popular play but a great tragic poem; in 1588, he produced another, the *Jew of Malta*. Whatever Marlowe touched, from the beginning, he instantly transformed into something better. Shakspere, meanwhile, if this play be his, contented himself with frankly imitative, conventional stage-craft.

II. HENRY VI.

[The First and Second Parts of *Henry VI.*, together with *Titus Andronicus*, were entered in the Stationers' Register, on April 19th, 1602, as transferred from Thomas Millington to Thomas Pavier. There is no specific mention of the Third Part until November 8th, 1623, when it was entered for publication in the folio. In their present form, all three parts first appeared in the folio of 1623.

No other version of the First Part is known. The Second Part is obviously a version of *The First Part of the Contention betwixt the two famous Houses of Yorke and Lancaster*, entered on March 12th, 1593–94, and published by Millington in the same year. The Third Part is a similar version of *The true Tragedie of Richard Duke of Yorke*, etc., published by Millington in 1595. Both of these quartos were republished in 1600. In none of these entries or publications, prior to 1623, is there any mention of Shakspere's name. Greene's allusion in 1592 is the only contemporary one directly connecting any of these plays with Shakspere. Nash, in the same year, alluded to the popularity of Talbot on the stage.

The question of the authorship of all these plays, as well as of the relation of the quartos to the folio, has been much disputed.[1]

The weight of opinion seems to favor the supposition that Greene, Peele, Kyd, and Marlowe had a hand in them, and that so far as Shakspere touched them it was by way of collaboration, interpolation, or revision.

Whoever wrote them, they are clearly conventional examples of Elizabethan chronicle-history, based for the most part on the chronicles of Holinshed, Hall, and Stowe. Their obvious crudities, as well as metrical tests, place them early; a reasonable conjecture might put them from 1590 to 1592.]

Titus Andronicus, we found, whether Shakspere's or not, throws light on the dramatic environment in which his work began. In *Henry VI.*, which for our purposes we may consider as a single play, we shall find a similar state of things; this three-part drama certainly makes clear two facts still new to us concerning the Elizabethan stage. The first is that, at least among the earlier playwrights, collaboration was habitual; the second is that chronicle-history — a kind of thing which has long been theatrically obsolete — is probably the most characteristic type of play produced by that stage. These matters we may well glance at before attending in detail to *Henry VI.*

Collaboration has always been more common in dramatic literature than in other kinds. One reason for this lies in the obvious difference between a play written for acting, and a book or what else addressed solely to readers. The author of a book can address

---

[1] See, for example, Miss J. Lee's paper in the New Shakspere Society's Transactions for 1876; and Fleay's discussion in the *Life and Works*, pp. 255–283.

his public, with no other intervention than that of printers and proof-readers, over whom, if he choose, he may exercise constant control. A play, on the other hand, can be put before the public, at least in the form which the author intends, only by the intervention of a number of trained performers; each of them, moreover, must not only intervene in all the visible complexity of his own personality, but he must furthermore be conditioned in his methods of expressing the author's meaning by the elaborate physical and mechanical circumstances of a theatre. A dramatic author, then, needs not only the equipment of an ordinary man of letters — grasp of subject and mastery of literary style — but also a knowledge of the resources and limits of the actual stage closely akin to the knowledge of the orchestra essential to a skilful composer of music. For this reason, few men of letters pure and simple have ever succeeded in writing an actable play; and those who have succeeded prove often to have done so only with the help of presumably humbler collaborators intimately familiar with the theatre.

When any school of dramatic literature is thoroughly developed, to be sure, as the Elizabethan drama became in Shakspere's time, or as the French has been in our own, theatrical people, and literary too, sometimes became accomplished enough to take the full burden of authorship on themselves. Even then, however, — as the mere mention of Beaumont and Fletcher, or a glance at the collected works of any modern French dramatist, will suggest, — collaboration is at least frequent; while in such an early stage of dramatic literature as prevailed when Shakspere's work began, collaboration will generally be the rule.

The stage for which Shakspere wrote, in fact, was a true stage, where plays were rated successful in accordance with their power of drawing audiences. Whoever suggested a touch in a play which should increase its power of attraction was welcome to any manager; and if four or five men working together made a play more attractive than one man working by himself, so much the better. As literature, of course, the play would probably suffer; but even to this day no successful manager troubles himself much about the merely literary aspect of plays which draw. It is more than probable, then, that like any other professional playwright of his time Shakspere began his work, and learned his trade, either by actual collaboration with more practised men, or by retouching plays which for one reason or another they had abandoned. The result of some such process would surely resemble *Henry VI.*

Just how such collaboration took place or resulted, of course, we cannot assert. In a familiar passage of *Henry VI.*, however, there is a line which we may reasonably guess to be an example. Greene, we remember, in his *Groatsworth of Wit*, strengthened his abuse of Shakspere[1] by parodying a line from the tirade of the captured Duke of York against the triumphant

[1] See p. 9.

Queen Margaret.   Here is the passage,[1] which occurs
both in the *True Tragedy* and in the folio : —

> " Thou art as opposite to every good
>   As the Antipodes are unto us,
>   Or as the south to the septentrion.
>   *O tiger's heart wrapt in a woman's hide !*
>   How couldst thou drain the life-blood of the child ? " etc.

The italicized line was imitated in 1600 by one Nich-
olson,[2] from which fact, as well as from Greene's
allusion and its own inherent rant, one may reasonably
infer that it was thought effective.   Now a glance at
the passage where it occurs will show that the sense
would be complete without it ; and what is more, that
the line differs both in concreteness of conception and
in general sound from the two lines immediately preceding, which are much in the manner of Greene
himself.   If Shakspere, touching up an old tirade of
Greene's, had introduced — for pure ranting effect —
a stray line of his own, we might have expected just
such a result as is before us.   The example, of course,
is completely hypothetical ; it will serve, however, to
suggest what Elizabethan collaboration was.

Collaborative, beyond doubt, though just where and
how we can never be sure, *Henry VI.* is still more
significant to us as an example of chronicle-history, a
kind of drama peculiar to the Elizabethan stage.   The
object of chronicle-history distinctly differed from any
which we now recognize as legitimately theatrical.

---

[1] 3 *Henry VI.* I. iv. 134–138.
[2] *Centurie of Prayse,* 33.

The tragedy of blood, as we have seen, was after all only an extravagant kind of juvenile sensationalism, whose object was to thrill an audience; the object of Elizabethan comedy, to which we shall come later, was the perennial object of comedy, — to amuse. The object of chronicle-history, on the other hand, though of course even this kind of play had to be incidentally interesting, was to teach a generally illiterate public the facts of national history.

As a rule, the lower classes of the time could not read. Even when they could, the history of England was not conveniently accessible; it was rather crudely digested in certain folio volumes, heavy in every sense of the word, and expensive. At the same time, immemorial dramatic traditions which survived from the miracle plays made the stage a normal vehicle of popular instruction, while the state of public affairs— when Mary Stuart was lately beheaded and the Armada still more lately dispersed — stimulated patriotic enthusiasm and curiosity. To this demand the theatre responded by producing a series of plays, from various hands, which together comprised pretty nearly the whole of English history. The most familiar of the series, of course, are the plays of Shakspere; but to go no further, there were an *Edward I.* by Peele, an admirable *Edward II.* by Marlowe, and an *Edward III.* sometimes thought Shakspere's own, to prepare the way for *Richard II.*

Throughout the series — in Shakspere's work as elsewhere — the writer of chronicle-history conceived his business in a way now foreign to anything theatrical. He did not trouble himself to compose a play in the modern sense of the word; there was no question of formally developed plot or situation. He simply went to Holinshed or some other conventional authority, read the narrative sufficiently for his purposes, selected — with disregard of detail, chronologic and other — what seemed to him theatrically effective, and translated his selections into blank verse dialogue. Incidentally, to be sure, as chronicle-history strengthened, particularly in the hands of Marlowe and Shakspere, there grew up in it some very vital characters. We may best understand Richard III. or Hotspur, however, if we realize that, from the dramatist's point of view, their very vitality is a part of his effort to translate into vivid theatrical terms a patriotic story which he found in ponderous, lifeless narrative.

Translation, then, rather than creation, even the most serious writer of chronicle-history must have thought his task. If he succeeded in translating Holinshed, or Hall, or Stowe, into a form which should entertain an audience while informing them, he did all he tried to do. When we consider the chronicle-histories as originally meant to be anything more than translations from narrative into presentably dramatic terms, we fail to understand them. So much is clear. Less clear, but equally true, is the fact that an Elizabethan dramatist at work on tragedy, comedy, or romance, really regarded his task as identical with his obvious task when he wrote chronicle-history. He never invented his

plot, if he could help himself; except in presenting his
material more effectively than it had been presented
by others, he never, for a moment, considered himself
bound, as modern writers of plays or fiction apparently
consider themselves bound, to be original. He turned
to novels, to poems, to stories, to old plays, as directly
as to chronicles. When he found anything to his purpose he took it and used it, with as little qualm of
conscience as a modern man of science would feel in
availing himself of another's published investigation.
Whatever the origin of his plot — history, novel, poem,
story, old play — the dramatist treated it not as a
creator, but as a translator.

So to *Henry VI.* As one generally reads it, — after
Henry V., a chronicle-history far riper in form, — it
seems grotesquely archaic. Approached by itself,
however, it proves more powerful than one expects.
To appreciate it, one must read fast, one must make
an effort not to notice but to accept the obsolete conventions of a theatre which, with no more sense of
oddity than Kingsley felt in making Hypatia speak
English, compressed into less than eight thousand
lines of bombastic dialogue forty-nine years of English
history. After all, these conventions, though obsolete,
are not actually more absurd than many of our own.
We can learn, if we will, not only to accept, but to forget them; and then, by placing ourselves so far as we
can in the mood of an Elizabethan playgoer, we may
get even from *Henry VI.* an impression of grand historical movement. The times the play deals with

were stirring and turbulent. Historic forces, of one
and another kind, were beyond the control of any individual; and in *Henry VI.*, after a while, one begins
to feel them, in all their maddening, tragic confusion.
One feels, too, one hardly knows how, the lapse of
time, the growth and the change which years bring.
Strangely, unexpectedly, one finds even in this crudely
collaborative old play the stuff of which real history
is made.

An accident which helps this effect is that, as a
mere piece of literature, the Second Part is distinctly
better than the First, and the Third nearly maintains
the level of the Second. In the total effect, then, the
comparative crudity of the First makes it seem long
past. Even this First Part, though, has a force of its
own. Take the very opening. After the extremely
human courtship of Henry V., which closes the preceding play, the consecutive and ranting laments
uttered by four uncles of the infant Henry VI., —

"Hung be the heavens with black!" and so on —

seem very absurd. We must remember, however, that
they follow the conventions of a stage very different
from ours, and that *Henry V.* comes about halfway
between. If, remembering this, and remembering,
too, the keen lyric appetite of the Elizabethan public,
we liken these laments to those of the modern lyric
stage, we see them in a different light. Sung in con-
cert, with impressive music, they might still make a
fine operatic quartette. Then, immediately, the tone

of these half-lyric speeches changes. Instantly comes
the discord of quarrel,—a quarrel which is to end, after
half a century of bloodshed, in the death of the unhappy Henry. This example typifies a fact which we
must keep constantly in mind. At least in its earlier
period, the Elizabethan stage tried constantly to produce, by purely dramatic means, effects which would
now be reserved for the opera. Without understanding this, we cannot quite understand what a play like
Henry VI. means. Appreciating the operatic nature
of the ranting declamation throughout, and of such
half-lyric passages as this opening quartette, we can
begin to feel what power the play has.

In the Second Part, for all its neglect of the great
dramatic possibilities inherent in the adulterous love
of Suffolk and the Queen, there are two passages better
than anything in the others. Both of these, in the
folio version, seem at least Shaksperean, if not certainly Shakspere's. The first is the death-scene of
Cardinal Beaufort; the second is the rebellion of Jack
Cade.

In the death-scene[1] we have a wonderfully vivid
picture of dying delirium, from which we would not
spare a word. In the *Contention* there is a mere
sketch of it, which would seem wholly like a careless
abridgment but for the change in a single line. In
the *Contention*, the speech which stands for the famous

"Comb down his hair; look, look! it stands upright,
Like lime-twigs set to catch my winged soul," etc.,

[1] *2 Henry VI.* III. iii.

is followed directly by a speech of Salisbury, —

> " See, how the pangs of death do gripe his heart."

In the folio, Beaufort's delirium is followed by a fervent prayer for him by the King, who is interrupted by Salisbury thus : —

> " See, how the pangs of death do make him grin ! "

That change — from " do gripe his heart" to " do make him grin " — may not be a deliberate change by Shakspere's hand, but surely nothing could be more like one. It has just the added concreteness of phrase, just the enormous gain in vividness, which distinguishes his style from any other.

Shaksperean, too, seem all the Cade scenes,[1] though clearly they existed in the *Contention*, and doubtless those that played your clowns spoke more than was set down for them. Though it be virtually in the *Contention*, however, the reasoning of the rioter who maintains Cade to be a legitimate Mortimer seems too like Shakspere's fun not to be his. Cade, we remember, declared that his princely father had been stolen in infancy and apprenticed to a bricklayer : the rioter confirms him [2] : —

> " Sir, he made a chimney in my father's house, and the bricks are alive at this day to testify it; therefore deny it not."

What makes the scenes seem Shaksperean, however, is not so much any matter of detail as the general

---

[1] 2 *Henry VI*. IV. ii.–viii.   [2] 2 *Henry VI*. IV. ii. 156.

temper which pervades them. Cade's mob, though far more lightly treated, is essentially the mob of *Julius Cæsar* and of *Coriolanus*. In an earlier, simpler form, it expresses what by and by we shall see to be a distinct trait of Shakspere. His personal convictions, of course, we can never know; as an artist, however, he was consistent throughout in his contempt — here laughing, but later serious — for the headless rabble: wherefore, very properly, Shakspere is nowadays taken to task by virtuous critics of a democratic turn.

In the Third Part of *Henry VI.* there are no passages so indubitably effective as those at which we have just glanced. As one reads the play hastily, however, one feels in it more than in the two others a definite tendency. From the opening quartette of lament breaking into discord, the First Part and the Second have been full of turbulent, confused disintegration. Here at last, in the Third Part, things good and evil, order and chaos, begin at last to range themselves; and slowly but surely defining itself as the embodiment of all the evil, we feel the personality of Glóster. The Third Part of *Henry VI.* tends straight to *Richard III.* In the *Richard III.* of our modern stage, indeed, some of the earlier scenes are actually taken directly from *Henry VI.*

Our discussion of *Richard III.*, however, must come later. For our present purposes we have traced the early chronicle-history far enough. Whatever part Shakspere had in *Henry VI.*, we have found the play, like *Titus Andronicus*, suggestive of the en-

vironment in which Shakspere's work began. It has
helped, then, to define our notion of the Elizabethan
stage. Essentially collaborative rather than individual,
frankly translative rather than creative in method,
designed quite as much to inform as to divert, often
more than half lyric in mood, the chronicle-history
is the most typical kind of Elizabethan drama. Assuming its conventions, we may find in *Henry VI.*
much that is permanently admirable, and some touches
which seem too good for any hand but Shakspere's.
What part he had in it, however, must remain doubtful. The real light it surely throws on his individuality amounts only to this: like *Titus Andronicus*,
if either play be in any degree genuine, it shows him
in his beginning frankly imitative and conventional.
His work is the work of a man patiently mastering
the technicalities of his art, not of one who instantly
impresses whatever he touches with that trait nowadays so much admired, — originality.

III. LOVE'S LABOUR'S LOST.

[*Love's Labour's Lost* was published in quarto, in 1598. On the titlepage we are informed that this version was "presented before her
Highness this last Christmas," and is "newly corrected and augmented
by W. Shakespere." It is mentioned by Meres; and the *Centurie of
Prayse* cites a slightly doubtful allusion to it in 1594. The source of
the plot is unknown. The weight of opinion makes this the earliest
play unquestionably assigned to Shakspere. It is conjectured from
internal evidence to have been written as early as 1589 or 1590, but to
have been revised in 1597 for the performance at court mentioned on
the titlepage.]

In its present form, *Love's Labour's Lost* is puzzling. There seems no reasonable doubt that it is a very early play, carefully revised for performance at court at a time when Shakspere had completely mastered his art. Just what is old in it and what new we have no certain means of judging; yet for our study of Shakspere's development we wish to consider not the revised play, but the original. While of course we can never be sure, however, we may reasonably guess that the correction and augmentation of 1597 was chiefly a matter of mere style, — a conclusion in which we are supported by the fact that out of some 1600 lines of verse nearly 1100 are rhymed. The shallowness of character throughout, too, and the obviously excessive ingenuity of plot and situation, as well as of phrase, are unlike Shakspere's later work. Assuming, then, that in general character *Love's Labour's Lost* is contemporary with the First Part of *Henry VI.*, but that in detail it is often seven or eight years later, we are warranted, for the moment, in neglecting matters of detail, and in considering the play very generally.

Thus considered, it groups itself immediately with *Titus Andronicus* and *Henry VI.* Disregarding the mere matter of style, — where Shakspere's concreteness of phrase appears throughout, — we find it essentially not an original work, but a vigorous comedy in the then fashionable manner of John Lyly. Lyly's comedies, and this too, are really dramatic phases of the Renascent mood which started, not in the translations of Surrey, but in the Sonnets of Wyatt. Beginning with a powerful effort to civilize the forms of a barbarous language, this movement, in little more than fifty years, had resulted in a literature which at once stimulated and gratified an insatiable appetite for graceful verbal novelty. In *Love's Labour's Lost* we have a capital example of this, running now and again into frank, good-natured burlesque of itself. Graceful as they are, these frothy, overwrought fantasies of phrase and character are nowadays puzzling; it is hard to realize quite how they could ever have been popular on the stage.

To appreciate this, we may conveniently recall a fact we detected in *Henry VI*. What seemed there mere bombast took on another aspect when we considered it not as primarily dramatic, but rather as operatic. On the Elizabethan stage, we found, mere turns of language and half-lyric cadences were conventionally used to express moods which in our own time would certainly prefer the completely lyric form of operatic compositions. Looked at in this light, *Love's Labour's Lost* grows more intelligible. In conception and in style alike, it expresses a state of artistic feeling which would now express itself in polite comic opera; its endless rhymes and metrical oddities, its quips and cranks, are really not theatrical at all; like Lyly's over-ingenious turns of phrase, they are the airs, the duets, the trios, the concerted pieces of a stage not yet fully operatic only for want of adequate development in the art of music. Nor is *Love's Labour's Lost* operatic only in detail: like modern comic opera, such essentially lyric work as this has no profound meaning; its object is just to delight, to amuse;

whoever searches for significance in such literature misunderstands it.

The excessive ingenuity of *Love's Labour's Lost*, which often makes it hard to read, makes it all the more worth the attention of whoever should minutely study Elizabethan style. The scope with which, in its final form, it at once exemplifies and burlesques the literary fashions and affectations of its day, is astonishing. The deliberate euphuism of Armado,[1] the sonneteering of the King and his courtiers,[2] the pedantry of the schoolmaster and the curate,[3] the repartee of the Princess and her ladies,[4] the pertness of the boy Moth,[5] the blunders of the clowns,[6] the outworn, but at the time not yet outstripped conventions of the Masque of the Worthies,[7] the permanent freshness of the closing song, the lyric ingenuity of every page, — all these, in their bewildering confusion, typically express the temper of a time when whoever wanted amusement was most amused by verbal novelty. Throughout, too, one can at last begin to realize how the ears of Elizabethan audiences were as eagerly sensitive to fresh, graceful, ingenious turns of phrase as modern ears are to catching melodies; and fresh turns of phrase Shakespere gave them here, to their heart's content, — now in contented conventional seriousness, the next minute in a frank, good-natured burst of burlesque, — with a paradoxical comprehensiveness thoroughly, if still superficially, individual.

[1] E.g. I. i. 232 seq.   [2] IV. iii. 26, 60, 101.   [3] E.g. V. i.
[4] E.g. V. ii. 1–78.   [5] E.g. I. ii.   [6] E.g. I. i. 182 seq
[7] V. ii. 523 seq.

From all this, one would naturally expect *Love's Labour's Lost* to be far from amusing on the modern stage. Within a few years, however, it has been acted with considerable success. The secret of vitality like this is not to be found in such matters as we have glanced at; it must be sought in something not merely contemporary, but of more permanent dramatic value. Several things of this kind are soon perceptible. In the first place, the play has an open-air atmosphere of its own, a bit conventional, to be sure, but romantic and sustained; you feel throughout that what is going on takes place in just the sort of world where it belongs. In the second place, there are various perennially effective situations, such as the elaborate concealment and eavesdropping by which the King and his lords discover that they have all fallen from their high resolves in common ;[1] and more notably still such as the elaborate confusion of identity, when the Princess and her ladies mask themselves to bewilder their disguised lovers.[2] In the third place, the elaborate repartee of the dialogue, particularly in the passages which make Biron and Rosaline so suggestive of Benedick and Beatrice, though very verbal, is very sparkling.[3] In the fourth place, the elaborate introduction of a play within a play,[4] broadly burlesquing a kind of literature which was passing out of fashion, must always have been

---

[1] IV. iii. 1–210.
[2] V. ii. 158–265.
[3] See II. i. 114–128 ; and cf. *Much Ado*, I. i. 117–146.
[4] V. ii. 523–735.

diverting, if only by way of contrast. Finally, to go
no further, the contrast of clowns and courtiers in
this very scene emphasizes what pervades the play, —
constant caricature of contemporary absurdity along
with frequent serious perpetration of the like.

To specify these details has been worth while,
because, as we shall see later, they constantly reappear
in the later work of Shakspere, who is remarkable
among dramatists for persistent repetition of whatever
has once proved dramatically effective. We might
have specified more such detail ; we might have studied
Love's Labour's Lost far more profoundly, defining
the various affectations it commits or satirizes, discussing whether this part of it or that was meant for
a personal attack on a rival company, and so on.
For our purposes, however, we have touched on the
play sufficiently. Contemporary, in a general way,
with *Titus Andronicus* and *Henry VI.*, and — perhaps because so palpably corrected and augmented
— vastly better than either of them, it groups itself
with them in our view of Shakspere as an artist.
When he began to write, comedy was more highly developed than tragedy or history. His first comedy,
then, was more ripe than his first work of other kinds ;
but like them it may be regarded, in the end, as a
successful experiment in the best manner of his time,
— not as a new contribution to dramatic literature.

IV. The Comedy of Errors.

[At Christmas time, 1594, a " Comedy of Errors (like to *Plautus* his *Menechmus*) " was played at Gray's Inn. Meres, in 1598, mentioned *Errors* among the comedies of Shakspere. The play was first entered in 1623, and published in the folio.

Its source is clearly the *Menechmi* of Plautus, probably in some translation, and one or two scenes from his *Amphitryon*. Modern critics generally agree in placing it, on internal evidence, before 1591, with a slight preference for 1589 [1] or 1590.]

In the three plays we have considered, assuming them to be at least partly Shakspere's, we found him, in his earliest dramatic work, by no means original. Instead of trying to do something new, he devoted himself to writing a tragedy of blood much in the manner of Kyd or Marlowe, to collaborating in a conventional chronicle-history in which various contemporary manners appear, and to making a comedy in the manner of Lyly. If we try to characterize this work by a single word, we can hardly find a better term than *experimental*.

As apparently an experiment, the *Comedy of Errors*, like the play we shall consider next, groups itself with what precede. Like the next play, however, — the *Two Gentlemen of Verona*, — it differs from the others in not imitating any one else. The first three experiments seem unpretentiously imitative ; the two following seem independent.

---

[1] 1589 is the latest year in which the allusion to France " making war against her heir — " III. ii. 127 — would have been literally true.

Clearly enough, the *Comedy of Errors* attempts to adapt for the Elizabethan stage — to translate into contemporary theatrical terms — a classic comedy. In a way, the effort is akin to that of the poems, which, as we saw, exemplified the phase of Renascent feeling which delighted not so much in the formal graces of foreign culture as in the humane spirit of ancient literature. While in the poems, however, Shakspere altered and adapted Ovid or whom else, with excessive verbal care, to the taste of the literary public, he altered Plautus, in the *Comedy of Errors*, for purely theatrical purposes. The resulting contrast is curious. The poems, in their own day far more reputable literature than any contemporary plays, became, from the very concreteness of their detail, rather more corrupt in effect than the originals from which they were drawn. At all events, they carry that sort of thing as far as it can tolerably go; for throughout, while dealing with matters which demand pagan unconsciousness, they are studiously conscious. The *Comedy of Errors*, on the other hand, — in its own day a purely theatrical affair, — Shakspere altered in a way which the most prim modern principles would unhesitatingly pronounce for the better. In Plautus, for example, the episode of the courtesan and the chain is frankly licentious; in Shakspere, it is so different [1] that without a reference to Plautus one can hardly make out why the lady in question is called a courtesan at all. This trait we shall find to be gen-

[1] III. ii. 169 seq.; IV. i., iii.

erally characteristic of Shakspere. Always a man of
his time, to be sure, he never lets the notion of propriety stand between him and an effective point; when
there is nothing to prevent, however, he is decent;
among his contemporaries, he is remarkable for refinement of taste.

This incidental refinement of plot is by no means
his only addition to the material of Plautus. The
second Dromio is Shakspere's, so is the conventional
pathos of Ægeon, so the effort to contrast the shrewish
Adriana with her gentler sister. The very mention
of these characters, however, calls our attention to
the most obvious weakness of the *Comedy of Errors.*
Except for conventional dramatic purposes, the characters throughout are little more than names; they
are not seriously individualized. A convenient rhetorical scheme of criticism sometimes states the prin-
ciple that any story or play must have a plot,—the
actions or events it deals with; and that as actions
or events must be performed by somebody, or happen
to somebody, somewhere, any play or novel must also
include characters and descriptions. A theoretically
excellent play, then, consists of an interesting plot,
which involves individual characters, in a distinct
local atmosphere. Applying this test to the *Comedy
of Errors,* we find a remarkably ingenious and well-
constructed plot, and little else. Characters and
background might be anybody and anywhere.

As a piece of untrammelled construction, as a plot
put together with what seems almost wilful disregard

of other complications, the *Comedy of Errors* most clearly shows itself experimental. In construction, to be sure, the play is theatrically as successful as any in the Elizabethan drama. Indeed, it sometimes approaches the niceties of the classic tradition; hardly anything else in Shakspere so nearly observes the unities. When we have sufficiently admired its construction, however, and the general ease and smoothness of its style, we have nearly exhausted it. Shakspere, in his mature years, is not so soon exhaustible. This very fact, apart from other evidence, would make us guess the *Comedy of Errors* to come early among his writings.

In the plot thus carefully composed, there are at least two features worth our notice. The first, at which we need merely glance, is the vigorous effect of dramatic contrast produced by beginning this prolonged farce with the romantic narrative of Ægeon's shipwreck and misfortunes and wanderings, and by ending it with the still more romantic discovery that the Abbess of Ephesus is the long-lost wife whom he has so faithfully mourned. The second, on which we may dwell a little longer, is the fundamental source of all the fun and trouble, — the elaborate, double confusion of identity. Confusion of identity, we remember, was one of the effective stage devices in *Love's Labour 's Lost;* but there it was merely a bit of episodic masking. Here it is the very essence of the plot. It is taken, of course, straight from Plautus; it remains effective in extravagant acting to this day.

Nowadays, however, and just as much in Shakspere's time, it could never have been plausible. In so extravagant a form as that in which we here find it, nothing could make it plausible except the actual conventions of the classic stage. There, we remember, the actors wore masks. Mask two of them alike, and no eye could tell at a glance which was which. No "make-up" on any modern stage which reveals human features, however, could possibly make two people look enough alike to warrant such theatrically effective confusion of identity as pervades the *Comedy of Errors*.

V. The Two Gentlemen of Verona.

[The *Two Gentlemen of Verona* was mentioned by Meres in 1598. Beyond a stray allusion in 1615 to making "a virtue of necessity," [1] there seems to be no other extant notice of it until its publication in the folio of 1623.

Its source is some English version of the *Diana* of Montemayor, a Portuguese poet.

On internal evidence modern critics generally agree in placing it early, — from 1591 to 1593 or so.]

Like all the plays we have considered so far, the *Two Gentlemen of Verona* seems experimental; like the *Comedy of Errors*, it is not imitative, but independent, and its experimental effect is caused chiefly by the abnormal development of one essential feature, to the neglect of the other two. Here the resemblance

[1] IV. i. 62.

ends. The essential feature abnormally developed in the *Two Gentlemen of Verona* is not the plot, but the characters. More than what precede, then, this play tends straight toward the unmistakably greater work to come.

At bottom, like all the rest, it is a dramatic version of narrative material. The kind of narrative here chosen for this translation is akin to what probably gave rise to *Love's Labour's Lost*. Substantially, both of these plays, like most of the following, amount to little more than such stories as are familiar in the *Decameron* and its numerous polyglot descendants. At least in English, the old translators of such fiction pretended, with true British cant, to didactic purpose.[1] Clearly, however, their real purpose was to amuse; and their efforts took the form of such unadorned plots as to-day suffice to stimulate the imagination of children, and sufficed three hundred years ago to stimulate anybody's. When translating such narrative into dramatic terms, then, a playwright found his attention centred elsewhere than when he was similarly translating chronicle-history. In that case, he was bound, while interesting his audience, to instruct them; for, after all, they received chronicle-histories rather in the mood of thoughtless students than in that of theatre-goers. The old chronicles, too, contained a great deal more matter than a dramatist could possibly use. With Italian novels the case was different. Often they were so

---

[1] See the Introduction to Paynter's *Palace of Pleasure*.

short as to need rather amplification than condensa-tion. The dramatist, then, was forced to invent something; and here, as much as when dealing with classic comedy, his object, like that of his original, was to be as entertaining as he could.

With such an object, we have seen, Shakspere experimentally introduced new factors into the plot of the *Comedy of Errors*, handling the plot throughout as carefully as he handled the verses of his poems. In the *Two Gentlemen of Verona* he let his plot take care of itself; but, without apparently conceiving his characters as very consistently individual, he enlivened them throughout, and thus incidentally gave their surroundings some definite atmosphere, by adding to the bare outline of his plot any number of subtle touches based on observation of real life.

These touches of character, which make you feel at any given moment as if these people were real, pervade the play. Typical ones may be found in the first scene between Julia and Lucetta,[1] so frankly repeated and improved in the *Merchant of Venice;*[2] in the mission of the disguised Julia to Sylvia,[3] so admirably improved in *Twelfth Night;*[4] and in the less beautiful but perhaps more final episode of Launce and his dog.[5] They are not only true to life; the observation, the temper, they imply has a distinct character of its own, — a character which anybody

[1] I. ii.   [2] I. ii.
[3] IV. iv. 113 seq.   [4] I. v. 178 seq.
[5] II. iii.; IV. iv.

familiar with the ripe work of Shakspere knows, without knowing why, to be peculiar to him. Here, at last, then, in the experimental detail of a romantic comedy, Shakspere first shows himself original. The vitality of detail in the *Two Gentlemen of Verona* gives it a vigor of effect previously unknown to the English stage.

This vigor of effect, however, is not so obvious as it would have been if Shakspere, in his later work, had been less economical of invention. Economy of invention — perhaps another name for professional prudence — made him more apt than almost any other known writer to use again and again devices which had once proved effective. Among mendacious proverbs, few are so completely false as that which declares Shakspere never to repeat; it were truer to say that he rarely did much else if he could help it. Whatever is notable in the *Two Gentlemen of Verona*, then, appeared later, and more effectively, in his more mature work. To people familiar with that mature work, this earlier version of its excellences must generally seem thin and weak. Considered where we have placed it, however, — after what has preceded, before what is to come, — it still produces an effect of great vitality.

There are two or three situations, also, which, when new, must have been effective on the stage. Perhaps the most effective of these come from Julia's disguising herself as a boy,[1] — a device which, as we

[1] II. vii.; IV. ii., iv.; V. iv.

have seen, must have been convenient in a theatre where female parts were played by boys, then, as now, not habituated to skirts. Less palpably effective, but still unquestionably so, are the scenes where Proteus plays false to Valentine.[1] The more one considers the fresh detail of this play, the cleverer it seems.

Detail once admired, however, the *Two Gentlemen of Verona* is by no means masterly. Not only is the plot hastily and clumsily put together, and therefore far from plausible, but the characters themselves are not generally conceived as consistent individuals. Their vitality is a matter of detail. Ethically they are incomplete, out of scale. From all this results an effect which, even in its own day, must have been unsatisfactory. At the end, our sympathy is clearly expected to be with both gentlemen, who are duly rewarded with such brides as romantic tradition expects them to live happily with ever after. In fact, we cannot sympathize with either of them. Proteus has behaved too outrageously to be rewarded at all; there is no reason for his change of heart; and there is no excuse for the conventional magnanimity of Valentine. For all its merits, the *Two Gentlemen of Verona* remains in total effect unplausible, experimental, artistically unsatisfactory.

---

[1] II. iv. 100 seq.; II. vi.; III. i., ii.; IV. ii. etc.

VI. SHAKSPERE ABOUT 1593.

Uncertain as our chronology must be, we may feel
tolerably assured that, whatever their actual dates,
and whatever subsequent revision they may have had,
the works now before us were substantially finished
by 1593.   With one or two possible exceptions,
furthermore, and exceptions which hardly alter the
general case, we may fairly assume that in 1593 Shakspere had accomplished little more.   It is worth while,
then, to pause for a moment, and define our impression of him at that time.   *Venus and Adonis*, we
remember, was published in that year, just about his
twenty-ninth birthday.   This first serious publication
may fairly be counted an epoch in his career.

In the course of six years at most, — the years from
twenty-three to twenty-nine, — he had certainly succeeded in establishing himself as an actor, in writing,
wholly or in part, at least seven noteworthy plays
which have survived, and in composing at least one
poem, of the highest contemporary fashion, which not
only succeeded in public, but attracted to him the
friendly patronage of a great nobleman.   When we
stop to consider how much, even of the works we
have now touched on, has remained in permanent literature, the achievement seems astounding.

When we turn to consider what English literature
had otherwise produced meantime, however, we find a
state of things almost equally notable.   In 1587, we

have seen, Elizabethan literature, as we now know it, hardly existed. In 1588[1] the "Martin Marprelate" controversy began. In 1589 came the first publications of Bacon and of Nash, and the first volume of Hakluyt's *Voyages*. In 1590 appeared *Tamburlaine*, the first publication of Marlowe; the *Arcadia*, the first of Sidney; and the first three books of Spenser's *Faerie Queene*. In 1591 came the first publications of Drayton and of Ralegh, Sidney's *Astrophel and Stella*, and two volumes of minor verse by Spenser. In 1592, along with publications by Constable, Greene, Gabriel Harvey, Lyly, Marlowe, and Nash, came Daniel's first publication, — the Sonnets to *Delia*. By 1593, then, Elizabethan literature was well under way; the period since 1587 had been one of unprecedented literary fertility.

The mental activity displayed in the early work of Shakspere, then, was a more normal fact than it would have been during almost any other six years of English history. During the same six years, too, Marlowe, who was just Shakspere's age, had been almost equally active. In 1593 he was killed. Except Shakspere, he proves, on the whole, the most notable literary figure of his day. By comparing his work, then, with the work which Shakspere accomplished during his lifetime we may most conveniently define our impression of Shakspere himself.

Tamburlaine, Marlowe's first extant play, is believed

[1] All notes of publication in this study are taken from Ryland's *Chronological Outlines of English Literature*: Macmillan: 1890.

to have been acted in 1587, when he was twenty-four
years old. It was followed by a Second Part, analogous to the Second Part of *Henry VI.*, by *Dr. Faustus*,
by the *Jew of Malta*, and by *Edward II.* There is a
fragment, too, of a play on the *Massacre at Paris*
(S. Bartholomew), and of another on *Dido*, as well as
a series of very loose translations from Ovid, and the
Hero and Leander which we have already considered.
Doubtless, too, Marlowe had a hand in other plays, —
perhaps in *Henry VI.* and *Richard III.* The works
we have mentioned, however, undoubtedly his, are
enough for our purpose.

Putting aside *Hero and Leander*, to which we have
given attention enough, we see at once that Marlowe's
completed work consisted of four blank-verse tragedies. In all of these the plots are not very carefully
composed, the characters — though broadly conceived
— are not minutely individualized, and the general
atmosphere is one of indefinite grandeur. In all four
there are many passages full of noble, surging imagination ; and many more which seem inferior. Yet the
total effect of any one of these tragedies, still more
the total effect of all four, is among the most impressive in English literature. From the beginning,
Marlowe, as an artist, was passionately sensitive to
the eternal tragedy which lies in the conflict between
human aspiration and the inexorable limit of human
achievement. In *Tamburlaine* this passionate sense
of truth is expressed in terms of a material struggle ;
in *Faustus* the struggle is spiritual ; in the *Jew of*

Malta it is racial; in *Edward II.* it is personal. Whether the struggle be with the limits of the conquerable earth, however, or with those of human knowledge, or with those of ancestral inheritance, or with our own warring selves, the struggle is forever the same. We would be other than we are; other than we are, we may not be. In all four of Marlowe's tragedies that great, true note vibrates. Knowingly or not, Marlowe expressed himself greatly. Dead in degradation before he was thirty years old, he must always remain a great poet.

In turning from this work to Shakspere's, we are instantly aware of a marked contrast, not wholly to Shakspere's advantage. If all four of Marlowe's tragedies expressed but one profound sense of truth, at least they expressed that one tragic fact in lastingly noble terms. So far, on the other hand, Shakspere's tragedy, and history, and comedy has expressed nothing more serious than is expressed in his poems, — a flexible eagerness to adapt himself to the popular taste. Experimental we have called his plays, and the word will equally apply to his poems. Clearly the first six years of Shakspere's work indicate no profound perception, no serious artistic purpose.

When we consider Shakspere's experiments, however, ranging over these first six years of his professional life, we are presently impressed by the fact that no two of them are alike. One is a tragedy of blood, one is a chronicle-history, one is a fantastic comedy after the manner of Lyly, one is

something resembling a pseudo-classic comedy, one is a
kind of romantic comedy which later Shakspere made
peculiarly his own, one is a fashionable erotic poem.
Clearly another trait besides lack of serious artistic
purpose distinguishes him from Marlowe; in view
of the comparative excellence of all these works, it
would be hard to find a more excellent versatility than
Shakspere's.

In our study of his poems, we dwelt enough on the
peculiarly concrete habit of thought which marked
him; we assured ourselves that in his mind words so
naturally stood for real concepts, that by merely playing with words he played unwittingly with thoughts,
too. His notable versatility proves to be a second
trait as marked and as permanent. In neither is there
so far a trace of conscious originality, such as one
feels must surely have underlain the passionate philosophy of Marlowe. Yet, in the *Two Gentlemen of
Verona* we found Shakspere at last as freshly original
as he had already been versatile. The originality there
displayed, however, was not a matter of philosophy,
not of generalization, not of wisdom. It was an originality of observation, and of humanly concrete statement; what he did was only to try a new theatrical
experiment, — to introduce into popular comedy gleams
of real human life hitherto unknown there. This
originality seems only half-conscious; it seems simply
the experimental adaptation to his professional work
of what he had learned by actual experience of life; as
such, it would very likely have seemed to him almost
accidental.

In three ways, then, although his accomplishment was not yet permanently great, Shakspere's power had displayed itself by 1593. In the first place, his mind was so made that words and concepts seemed one, and so his verbal gymnastics proved unwittingly wise; in the second place, whatever he turned his hand to he did as well as the next man, and he turned his hand to everything; in the third place, in experimenting with comedy he had stumbled on the fact and the use of his own great faculty of observation. None of these traits, however, are showy, none of the kind which either require or command instant recognition. To Shakspere, we may guess, they may well have seemed humdrum; and these six years little else than a prolonged apprenticeship. He had learned his trade; apart from this, he would probably have thought that he had accomplished nothing.

VII

I.

As the general uncertainty of our chronology must
indicate, the separation of some plays in this chapter
from those in the last is arbitrary. Its justification
must rest chiefly on two facts which broadly distinguish the groups : In the first place, while the interest
of the preceding plays is chiefly historical, the interest
of those to come remains intrinsic; apart from any
historical conditions they are often in themselves delightful. In the second place, while in the preceding
plays one finds at bottom hardly anything more significant than versatile technical experiment, one finds
throughout those to come constant indications of
growing, spontaneous, creative imagination.

In an artist of whatever kind, a period of vigorous
creative imagination declares itself after a fashion
which people who are not of artistic temperament
rarely understand. The artist does not feel that he
has something definite to say, — that he has a statement to make ; but when he is about his work, or
perhaps before, he is constantly aware of a haunting
mood which will not let him rest until he has some-

how expressed it. What that mood signifies in the scheme of the eternities he may as likely as not neither know nor care. All he need certainly know is that, without being able to tell why, he feels somehow with painful acuteness; what he cares for is chiefly to express his feeling in such manner as shall get rid of it. If he be a man of genius, his work under these conditions will be of lasting value; if not, it may be comically insignificant. To the artist, this is a matter of accident: to himself a man of genius is as commonplace as a plough-boy. The thing for us to remark, then, in this chapter and in the two following, is that throughout, to greater or less degree, the plays and the poems seem born of true artistic impulse, of that trait, uncomfortable to great folk and small, which at times, to any artistic temperament, makes the legends of inspiration seem almost credible.

As generally of lasting artistic value, then, — as palpably works of genius, — the writings to come must be read in a different mood from those which precede. To understand them we must not only train ourselves to appreciate how they impressed Elizabethans three hundred years ago; we must actually enjoy them ourselves. So essential is this, indeed, and so great the lasting enjoyment which, as we know them better, we may find throughout them, that in many moods to busy ourselves with them further seems wasted time, — worse still, it often seems like pedantic blindness to the constant delights which alone have made them permanent. In the end, however, if we assume in ourselves the full power of enjoyment, of artistic appreciation, and if we test it now and again by reading for pure pleasure the works which in our coming study we must discuss, we shall gain from our discussion the only thing which could really justify it, — an increased power of enjoyment. These general facts are nowhere clearer than in the *Midsummer Night's Dream.*

II. A MIDSUMMER NIGHT'S DREAM.

[The *Midsummer Night's Dream* was entered in the Stationers' Register on October 8th, 1600. During the same year it was twice published in quarto, with Shakspere's name. It was mentioned by Meres, in 1598.

The sources, none of them closely followed, are many and various. Among them are probably the life of Theseus in North's *Plutarch ;* Chaucer's *Knight's Tale, Wife of Bath's Tale,* and *Legend of Good Women ;* and perhaps Golding's *Ovid.* The fairy scenes have obvious relation to the actual folk-lore of the English peasantry. Besides, the sources of both the *Comedy of Errors* and the *Two Gentlemen of Verona* probably affect this play, too.

Conjectures as to the origin and date of the *Midsummer Night's Dream* vary. Some hold that the play was made, like Milton's *Comus,* for a wedding festival. The conjectures as to date, based on internal evidence, — verse-tests and allusions, — vary from 1590 to 1595, with a slight preference for 1594.]

The first, constant, and last effect of the *Midsummer Night's Dream* is one of poetry so pervasive that one feels brutally insensitive in seeking here anything but delight. Nowhere does Shakspere more fully justify Milton's words : [1] —

[1] *L'Allegro.*

" Then to the well-trod stage anon,
  If Jonson's learned sock be on,
  Or sweetest Shakespeare, Fancy's child,
  Warble his native wood-notes wild."

Nothing of Shakspere's, on the other hand, better confutes the saying which Drummond of Hawthornden attributes to Ben Jonson, that Shakspere wanted art. While it is undoubtedly true that, over and over again, Shakspere stopped far short of such laborious finish as makes the plays of Jonson, whatever else, so admirably conscientious, it is equally true that when Shakspere chose to take pains his technical workmanship was as artistic as his imaginative impulse. Few works in any literature possess more artistic unity than the *Midsummer Night's Dream*, few reveal on study more of that mastery whose art is so fine as to seem artless. Alike in spirit and in form, then, — in motive and in technical detail, — this play is a true work of art ; its inherent beauty is the chief thing to realize, to appreciate, to care for.

If we would understand why the *Midsummer Night's Dream* seems to belong in Shakspere's work where we have placed it, however, we must for a while neglect this prime duty of enjoyment, and consider the play minutely, attending first to the materials of which it is made, and then to the way in which it handles them.

Putting aside, as needless for our purpose, those various and scattered sources which are believed peculiarly its own, we may conveniently recall the fact that in the three comedies already considered we found certain devices and situations which seemed notably effective.[1] In *Love's Labour 's Lost*, among other matters, we noted a fresh, open-air atmosphere, a burlesque play performed by characters whose rudeness and eccentricity was in broadly comic contrast to the culture of their audience, and the perennially amusing confusion of identity. In that case, however, the confusion was reached by the unplausible device of masking. A stage mask, covering only the upper features, must leave the mouth free; consequently, it does not transform the wearer, and such blunders as the King's or Biron's require an audience conventionally to accept a disguise which really is none. Confusion of identity, however, thus found effective even when not plausible, was repeated and elaborately developed in the *Comedy of Errors*. Here, again, though, it lacked plausibility; the audience was asked to accept a degree of personal likeness attainable on the stage only by means of such masks as were worn by the Roman actors for whom the plot was originally made. To hasten on, we remarked, among other effective traits in the *Two Gentlemen of Verona*, the love-inspired treason of Proteus, and his instantaneous shifts of affection; though effective, however, these were neither plausible nor sympathetic. To go no further, here are a number of stage devices, already used experimentally by Shakspere with probable success, but never in a way which could give

[1] See pp. 86, 91, 96.

either writer, spectator, or reader serious artistic satisfaction.

In the *Midsummer Night's Dream* all these are reproduced, but none experimentally. Each has its place in a composition so complete that at sensitive moments one shrinks from dissecting it; and all are plausible. The scene is laid in a mythical world far enough from reality to make the wood-notes seem that of its inevitable atmosphere. The situation of the burlesque play is reproduced with a firmer hand; and this time the burlesque interlude has a plot, of which we shall see more later.[1] The love treason is transferred from a tolerably cool man to an emotionally overwrought girl; thereby, while retaining all its theatrical effect, it becomes at once far less deliberate and far more sympathetic.[2] While Proteus tells Valentine's secret to the Duke, too, Helena tells Hermia's only to her lover. Finally, both confusion of identity and protean changes of affection [3] are made plausible, like very dreams themselves, by bodily transference to a dream-world, where the fairies of English folk-lore play endless tricks with mortals and with one another, making their fellow-beings fantastically their sport.

These instances are enough to show why we may reasonably call this play, in Shakspere's development, a first declaration of artistic consciousness. A confusion of pleasant motives, already used in unsatis-

[1] See p. 116.

[2] Cf. *T. G.* III. i. 1–50 with *M. N. D.* I. i. 226 seq.

[3] Cf. *T. G.* II. iv. 192 seq. with *M. N. D.* II. ii. 103 seq.; III. i. 132 seq., etc.

factory form, may be guessed to have gathered in his mind. Whoever has had a gleam of artistic experience — such as the haunting line, for example, which belongs inevitably in some unwritten sonnet — knows that such spirits as these can be laid only by expression. There need be no didactic purpose here; in one sense there need hardly be purpose at all. If we imagine that the Shakspere we have already defined was thus possessed by creative impulse, we imagine enough to account for the *Midsummer Night's Dream*.

So much for the artistic motive of the play. Turning to the technical art by which this is made manifest, we may conveniently consider it in the three aspects which we have earlier seen to be essential to any narrative or dramatic composition: plot, character, and atmosphere, or background.

To a modern reader, the plot of the *Midsummer Night's Dream* seems to concern itself chiefly with the doings of the fairies, who are so constantly charming, and of the clowns, who are so constantly amusing. Even to-day, however, a sight of the play on the stage reveals at once that, so far as plot is concerned, these matters are accessory; that the real centre of the plot is the love-story of the four Athenians. The artistic purpose of all the rest is simply to make this plausible. With this purpose, the play begins with a statement of the condition of affairs in the romantic Athens of Theseus, — not a real world, but a world no further removed from reality than plenty of others which we are accustomed conventionally to accept on the stage. Thence, and not from the actuality of real life, we proceed through the extravagant buffoonery of the clowns — the most grotesque of human beings, but still grotesquely human — to the dreamland of the fairies. This dreamland, after all, is little further removed from the romantic introductory Athens of Theseus than that Athens itself was from the world where it found us. Once in dreamland, the fantastic extravagances of the main plot — in their earlier forms so far from credibility — are kept constantly plausible by the superhuman agencies which direct them ; and these in turn are kept plausible by the incessant intermingling and contrast with the fairies of the equally extravagant, but still fundamentally human clowns. Then, after some three acts of this, the morning horns of Theseus break the dream ; the fairies vanish ; we come back to our own world through the romantic Athens of Theseus, with which we began. The fifth act recapitulates, almost musically ; the final scene of the fairies is not a part of the action, but an epilogue, a convention frequent in the Elizabethan theatre. The fairy scenes, then, — the accessories by means of which the main plot is made artistically plausible, — are themselves made plausible first by deliberate removal from real life; and secondly by deliberate contrast with a phase of real life hardly less extravagant than they. The constructive art here shown is admirable.

At first, too, this constructive art seems original. On consideration, however, it proves to be only an adaptation of a convention common on the Elizabethan stage. Though among Shakspere's works an Induction is found only in the *Taming of the Shrew*, Inductions — which made the main action a play within a play — were very frequent throughout the early drama. We shall have more to say of them when we come to the *Taming of the Shrew*.[1] Here it is enough to point out that the first act of the *Midsummer Night's Dream* is, essentially, a very skilful development of the conventional Induction.

The plot of the *Midsummer Night's Dream*, then, is far superior to anything we have met before. When we come to the characters we find a state of things less favorable to our notion that the play should be placed here in Shakspere's artistic development. Certainly less individual than those of the *Two Gentlemen of Verona*, these characters seem almost less so than those of *Love's Labour's Lost*. Taken by themselves, for example, the Athenians of the court of Theseus seem hardly more individual than the Ephesians of the *Comedy of Errors*. Considered not by themselves, however, but rather as one of three clearly defined groups, their aspect changes; they stand in marked and strongly dramatic contrast to two other groups, as distinct from one another as from the Athenian courtiers, — the clowns and the fairies. In answer, then, to those critics who, largely on the score of individualized character, would place the *Midsummer Night's Dream* earlier than the *Two Gentlemen of Verona*, we may say that,

[1] See p. 159.

like the other plays considered in the last chapter, the latter is intrinsically experimental, while the former is intrinsically artistic ; and that three broadly generalized groups of character, whose mutual relations are skilfully adjusted, fit the general artistic motive of the *Midsummer Night's Dream* far better than could more individual characters whose individuality should make them a bit unmanageable. In the *Two Gentlemen of Verona*, furthermore, the individual touches were rather matters of experimental detail than of creative imagination. The contrast defines a general truth : Because a writer can individualize character, it does not follow that he can master and manage his own individual creatures. In the perfectly manageable vagueness of character here, then, we have fresh evidence of how careful Shakspere's art may have been. As we have seen, if our chronology be not all wrong, his power developed slowly. Here, then, we may at least guess that the state of things shows him in a truly artistic mood, too wise even to attempt things at all beyond his certain power.

In one scene, though, the juvenility of character seems too great for any such explanation ; this is in the child-like squabble between Hermia and Helena.[1] On the stage, to be sure, it is still funny ; but the fun is crude : grown girls, we feel, never squabble quite in this way. Properly to appreciate the scene, we must remember the circumstances for which it was written : there were no female actors, — a fact which goes far to atone for the coarseness of female

[1] III. ii. 282–344.

character common throughout the lesser Elizabethan drama; Helena was written to be played by a big boy, Hermia by a small one.

If we be inclined to wander in our delight with the atmosphere of the *Midsummer Night's Dream*, a fact like this should recall us to ourselves. Dainty as its atmosphere is, specific too as distinguished from any other in literature, the play itself could never have seemed to its writer only the beautiful poem which it chiefly seems to us. He made it for living actors, — men and boys. The fairy atmosphere was to be conveyed to his audience not only by the lovely lines which remain as fresh as ever, but by the bodily presence of child-actors, whose actual forms should revive among the spectators the familiar old fancies of the little people. Such fancies, far from what arise nowadays as we contemplate in the *Midsummer Night's Dream* the stout legs of a middle-aged ballet, could be more than suggested on the stage of Shakspere's time. It was a stage whose conventions allowed Macbeth and Banquo, fifteen years later, to make their entrance on wicker hobby-horses, with dangling false legs[1]; whose conventions permitted Cleopatra to wear laced stays, which she orders cut in a moment of agitation.[2] On such a stage, the pink limbs of chubby children — and the lesser fairies who serve Bottom have no lines which might not be taught a child of three or four[3] —

[1] See p. 309.   [2] *Antony and Cleopatra*, I. iii. 71.
[3] III. i. 166 seq. ; IV. i.

might have seemed almost actually the fairy fancies which remain the folk-lore of Northern Europe.

Here and there, among modern peasantry, such folk-lore still survives, much as it was when Shakspere wrote. The contrast between his way of dealing with it and ours is typical of the change in the times. He asked himself, as an artist, how it might serve his artistic purpose; and using it accordingly, he made it the lasting type of cultivated romantic tradition. If Spenser's fairies never quite lived, and Drayton's have long been forgotten, Shakspere's will always remain the lasting little people of the English ages. Men of our time treat the old stories differently, asking not what may be done with them, but what they mean. In the legends of the little people, some wise contemporaries of ours fancy that they can trace lingering race-memories of the dwarfish aborigines of Europe. When our own ancestors drove them back toward the northern snows, these scholars guess, some may have lingered in caves and burrows, emerging at night, brutishly grateful to whoever was kind, mischievous to whoever plagued them. So, perhaps, there are modern minds who may get from the *Midsummer Night's Dream* more satisfaction in pointing out that the name of Oberon is a version of that of the dwarf king Alberich — himself doubtless some prehistoric Eskimo — than in giving themselves over to the delights of Oberon's dreamy realm.

As students not of science, but of literature, however, we should never lose sight of these delights.

Our study has compelled us to analyze in this play something besides its beauty. If we would understand Shakspere, however, its beauty, not its anatomy, is what we must think of first, last, and always. Its beauty is what Shakspere must have cared for and thought of. As a true creative artist, indeed, he was probably less conscious of its mechanism than our study has made us. An artist who has real creative impulse generally works by an unwitting instinct, with a truth which makes his work both significant and organic; sometimes it seems as if a critically conscious artist could never create like one who believes himself to work untrammelled, to say things as he says them, because, without troubling himself as to why, he feels sure that just thus they should be said. Some mood like this seems to underlie the famous criticism of Theseus on this very fairy story. By appreciating that, after all, we may best appreciate the *Midsummer Night's Dream*: [1] —

> "I never may believe
> These antique fables, nor these fairy toys.
> Lovers and madmen have such seething brains,
> Such shaping fantasies, that apprehend
> More than cool reason ever comprehends.
> The lunatic, the lover and the poet
> Are of imagination all compact:
> One sees more devils than vast hell can hold,
> That is, the madman : the lover, all as frantic,
> Sees Helen's beauty in a brow of Egypt :

[1] V. i. 2–17.

The poet's eye, in a fine frenzy rolling,
Doth glance from heaven to earth, from earth to heaven,
And as imagination bodies forth
The forms of things unknown, the poet's pen
Turns them to shapes and gives to airy nothing
A local habitation and a name."

III. ROMEO AND JULIET.

[An imperfect and probably unauthorized quarto of *Romeo and Juliet* was published anonymously in 1597. A tolerably complete quarto, also anonymous, appeared in 1599; there was a third quarto in 1609. The play is attributed to Shakspere by Meres; and the *Centurie of Prayse* cites an allusion to it as Shakspere's in 1595.

The story, a very old one, occurs in various forms and languages. The immediate sources of the play are two English versions of a French version of a novel by Bandello: *Romeus and Juliet*, a long poem by Arthur Brooke, published in 1562; and Paynter's *Palace of Pleasure*.

Conjectures as to date range from 1591 to the second quarto. The general opinion seems to be that there was an early play, perhaps collaborative, which Shakspere slowly rewrote at intervals. The play, in its present form, may be reasonably placed near the *Midsummer Night's Dream*, about 1594 or 1595.]

One reason for grouping together the *Midsummer Night's Dream* and *Romeo and Juliet* lies in the fact that the story of the latter is virtually the same as that of *Pyramus and Thisbe*. As in *Love's Labour's Lost*, Shakspere at once practised and burlesqued the absurdities of fashionable style, so here he seems a bit later to treat this tragic tale in two distinct moods: in one, he makes of it a play which, whatever

its date, is generally admitted to be his first great
tragedy ; in the other he turns it into a burlesque
which emphasizes every point of the tragedy where
the sublime verges on the ridiculous. Another thing
which groups the plays together is Mercutio's lyric
interlude about Queen Mab,[1] — a passage so fatal to
modern actors, who try to make it a part of the
action. Clearly, however, the relation of *Romeo and
Juliet* to the *Midsummer Night's Dream* is even more
debatable than we found the relation between that
play and the preceding comedies.

The relation of *Romeo and Juliet* to its sources, on
the other hand, — to matter distinctly not Shaksperean, — is very close indeed. Most of us know the
play so well, and think of it so constantly as Shakspere's from beginning to end, that a direct comparison
of some familiar passages and their sources is worth
while. It will show more palpably than any similar
comparison of less familiar matters how completely
an Elizabethan dramatist looked upon his task as
mere translation.[2] Two examples will serve our purpose : the first is that which Shakspere translated
into the familiar character of the Nurse, so often
talked about as peculiarly his own ; the second is that
which he translated into the soliloquy of Juliet when
she drinks the sleeping-draught. These are broadly
typical not only of *Romeo and Juliet* throughout, but
also of Shakspere's plays in general, and indeed of
the whole Elizabethan drama.

[1] I. iv. 53–95.   [2] See p. 76.

In Paynter's version of the story [1] there is nothing
more than mention that Juliet's governess, an old
woman, was the go-between for the lovers ; and this
is said to be all that exists in either the French version or the Italian.   Brooke, on the other hand, introduces the following passage : [2] —

" To Romeus she goes of him she doth desyre,
   To know the mean of mariage by councell of the fryre.
   On Saterday, quod he, if Juliet come to shrift,
   She shall be shrived and maried, how lyke you noorse this drift ?
   Now by my truth (quod she) gods blessing have your hart;
   For yet in all my life I have not heard of such a part.
   Lord, how you yong men can such crafty wiles devise,
   If that you love the daughter well to bleare the mothers eyes.
    .   .   .   .
   Now for the rest let me and Juliet alone :
   To get her leave, some feate excuse I will devise anone
   For that her golden locks by sloth have been unkempt :
   Or for unwares some wanton dreame the youthfull damsell
      drempt,
   Or for in thoughts of love her ydel time she spent:
   Or otherwise within her hart deserved to be shent.
   I know her mother will in no case say her nay:
   I warrant you she shall not fayle to come on Saterday.
   And then she sweares to him, the mother loves her well :
   And how she gave her suck in youth she leaveth not to tell.
   A pretty babe (quod she) it was when it was yong :
   Lord, how it could full pretely have prated with it tong.
   A thousand time and more I laid her on my lappe,
   And clapt her on the buttocke soft and kist where I did clappe.

---

[1] Both Paynter's version and Brooke's were published by the New
Shakspere Society, ed. P. A. Daniel, in 1875. They occur also in
Hazlitt's *Shakspere's Library*.

[2] *Romeus and Juliet*, 631 seq.

And gladder then was I of such a kisse forsooth:
Then I had been to have a kisse of some olde lechers mouth.
And thus of Juliets youth began this prating noorse,
And of her present state to make a tedious long discoorse.
For . . when these Beldams sit at ease upon theyr tayle :
The day and eke the candle light before theyr talke shall fayle.
And part they say is true, and part they do devise:
Yet boldly do they chat of both when no man checkes theyr
   lyes."

That marvellously Shaksperean creation, the Nurse,
it turns out, was conceived and brought forth, thirty
years before Shakspere's time, by Arthur Brooke.

Now for that marvellously Shaksperean piece of
psychology, when Juliet drinks the potion. Here is
Paynter's version : [1] —

"*Iulietta* beinge within hir Chambre having an eawer
ful of Water standing uppon the Table filled the viole
which the Frier gave her: and after she had made the
mixture, she set it by hir bed side, and went to Bed.
And being layde, new Thoughtes began to assaile her, with
a concept of grievous Death, which brought hir into such
case as she could not tell what to doe, but playning incessantly sayd, 'Am not I the most unhappy and desperat
creature, that ever was borne of Woman? . . my distresse
hath brought me to sutch extremity, as to save mine honor
and conscience, I am forced to devoure the drynke whereof
I know not the vertue : but what know I (sayd she)
whether the Operatyon of thys Pouder will be to soone or
to late, or not correspondent to the due time . . ? What
know I moreover, if the Serpents and other venomous and
crauling Wormes, whych commonly frequent the Graves

[1] Daniel, p. 130; Hazlitt, p. 244.

and pittes of the Earth wyll hurt me, thynkyng that I am deade? But howe shall I indure the stynche of so many carions and Bones of myne auncestors which rest in the Grave, yf by Fortune I do awake before Rhomeo and Fryer *Laurence* doe come to help me?'"[1]

All directly from the French, this is substantially repeated by Brooke. At this point, then, we may turn to his version, which goes on a little more fluently than Paynter's: —

" And whilst she in these thoughts doth dwell somewhat to long,
  The force of her ymagining anon dyd waxe so strong,
  That she surmysde she saw, out of the hollow vaulte,
  (A griesly thing to looke upon) the carkas of Tybalt;
  Right in the selfe same sort that she few dayes before
  Had seene him in his blood embrewde, to death eke wounded
    sore
  And then when she agayne within her selfe had wayde
  That quicke she should be buried there, and by his side be
    layde,
  All comfortles, for she shall living feere have none,
  But many a rotten carkas, and full many a naked bone ;
  Her dainty tender partes gan shever all for dred,
  Her golden heares did stand upright upon her chillish head.
  Then pressed with the feare that she there lived in,
  A sweat as colde as mountaine yse pearst through her tender
    skin,
  That with the moysture hath wet every part of hers :
  And more besides, she vainely thinkes, whilst vainely thus she
    feares,
  A thousand bodies dead have compast her about,
  And lest they will dismember her she greatly stands in dout."[2]

[1] Cf. *Romeo and Juliet*, IV. iii. 14 seq.
[2] *Romeus and Juliet*, 2377 seq.

Paynter's conclusion of the translation is perhaps the more memorable : —

" And feelyng that hir forces diminyshed by lyttle and lyttle, fearing that through to great debilyty she was not able to do hir enterpryse, like a furious and insensate Woman, with out further care, gulped up the Water wythin the Voyal, then crossing hir armes upon hir stomacke, she lost at that instante all the powers of hir Body, restyng in a Traunce."

In Juliet's soliloquy, Shakspere introduces two touches not in these original versions : her business with the dagger, and her doubt of the Friar's honesty. Apart from these, he merely condenses and translates these grotesque old narratives into permanent form ; for example : [1] —

" O, if I wake, shall I not be distraught,
  Environed with all these hideous fears ?
  And madly play with my forefathers' joints ?
  And pluck the mangled Tybalt from his shroud ?
  And, in this rage with some great kinsman's bone,
  As with a club, dash out my desperate brains ?
  O, look ! methinks I see my cousin's ghost,
  Seeking out Romeo, that did spit his body
  Upon a rapier's point : stay, Tybalt, stay !
  Romeo, I come ! this do I drink to thee."

With less citation, it would have been hard to emphasize the two facts which these typical passages should make clear : in the first place, they show how Elizabethan dramatists generally dealt with the

[1] IV. iii. 49 seq.

original sources of their plays, — tragic, comic, and historic alike; in the second place, they prove the remoteness of *Romeo and Juliet*, even in psychologic detail, from what it is commonly thought to be, — a pure creation of Shakspere's brain.

Turning now from substance to style, we may find in the style of *Romeo and Juliet* many traits by no means peculiar to Shakspere among Elizabethan writers. A glance at Romeo's speeches anywhere in the first act,[1] or at any of Mercutio's,[2] will reveal plenty of such quips, and cranks, and puns as we found in *Love's Labour's Lost*. Throughout the play, too, we continually come on lyric passages, as distinguished from dramatic. For one thing, rhymes are frequent. Again, such a speech as Mercutio's about Queen Mab[3] can be understood only when we compare it to interpolated songs in modern comedies; it is simply a charming, independent piece of lyric declamation. So, when Romeo accosts Juliet[4] we have a formal sonnet; nor can blank verse disguise the essentially lyric quality of the Epithalamium;[5] or of the Morning Song;[6] or of the fugue-like quartette of lament over the unconscious Juliet.[7] The more one studies the play, in short, the more curiously archaic the style often seems; it is really an example of the Euphuistic fantasy prevalent in early Elizabethan literature.

[1] E. g. I. i. 177 seq.
[2] His dying pun is familiar; III. i. 102.
[3] I. iv. 53 seq.
[4] I. v. 95–108.
[5] III. ii. 1–33.
[6] III. v. 1–36.
[7] IV. v. 43–64.

While this literature is obsolete, however, *Romeo and Juliet*, in spite of its fidelity to obsolete sources, survives among the most popular plays on the modern stage. The reason why is not far to seek. Shakspere has infused the whole play with creative imagination. On the numberless beauties of detail, which make us half forget its eccentricities, we need not dwell; the great lyric charm of *Romeo and Juliet* is not its chief merit. As a composition, as a complete conception, the play is masterly.

Fundamentally the plot is that of a conventional tragedy of blood. Mercutio, Tybalt, Paris, Romeo, and Juliet, — not to speak of Lady Montague, — come to violent deaths; and the last scene takes place in a charnel-house, which, in the stage setting of the time, might well have been strewn with heaps of bones. On horror's head horrors accumulate as much as anywhere; but whereas in the old tragedies of blood the horrors came from nowhere, in this case they are the legitimate effects of uncontrollable causes. For example, the play opens after a manner still conventional, with a scene between servants, the object of which apparently is only to occupy the first few minutes. But watch what these servants do: One bites his thumb. A fight ensues. Tybalt enters and takes part. Before blood-letting on either side has given his temper a chance to cool, the fight is officially stopped. While his passion, thus aroused, still runs high, he discovers Romeo at the Capulet feast, where Romeo's presence seems to him a studied insult. Restrained by old Capulet, he grows more angry still. As soon as he meets Romeo in public, he openly insults him. Mercutio steps in, and is killed. Romeo avenges him. So the tragedy proceeds ; were it not for that first thoughtless thumb-biting of the servants, we see, nothing could have fallen out in quite this way. The thumb-biting is one of the direct causes which by a growing series of effects lead straight to the final catastrophe. Few plots anywhere are so carefully composed.

The individuality of the characters, meanwhile, constant and consistent throughout, is not so emphasized as to distract attention from the plot. Rather the very coherence of plot on which we have just touched is secured by the fact that the temperaments of the separate characters interact as they would in life. It is because Tybalt and Mercutio, for example, are the kind of men they are, that they come to their ends in a way which involves the fate of Romeo and Juliet. Throughout the play one feels instinctively that here, at last, the creative imagination of Shakspere had begun to make his own fictions as real as human beings.

We can hardly conclude, however, that this matter presented itself to him as seriously as we are disposed to think of it. After all, what a writer feels, in the position we here suppose to have been Shakspere's, is not so much profound psychologic wisdom as intuitive knowledge that the people he is describing must be what they are, and must act or think as they do. So far as his conscious intervention with them goes, indeed, it may rather impair than improve their vitality. In *Romeo and Juliet*, for example, there is one statement which, perhaps fantastically, might be taken for evidence — as far as it goes — that Shakspere was not consciously treating his characters so seriously as posterity has supposed. This concerns Juliet's age. In Brooke she is sixteen years old. Why Shakspere should make her two years younger has given rise to much speculation, about the prematurity of Italian youth and the like. Perhaps this speculation is very wise. More probably, however, at least to some of us, the reason why Shakspere's Juliet is fourteen seems to lie in a single pun, at the time of Juliet's first appearance : [1]

> " *Lady Capulet :* She's not fourteen.
>   *Nurse :*   I 'll lay fourteen of my teeth, —
>   And yet, *to my teen be it spoken* I have but *four*, —
>   She is not fourteen."

Clearly no other numeral in the teens could make that slight joke at once so sonorous, so precise, and so funny. *Fifteen* makes a bad pun with *five ; sixteen* sounds short and sibilant; seven, eight, or nine teeth are enough to make a decent showing. Right or wrong, too, this simple reason for Juliet's age — so very remote from modern artistic seriousness — is exactly the sort of reason which would generally have affected a writer of the period to which we have attributed *Romeo and Juliet*.

[1] I. iii. 12 seq.

A similar state of things pervades the atmosphere of the play. In actual detail, much of it is English. In total effect, it is so Italian that one may read *Romeo and Juliet* with increasing surprise and delight in Verona itself. Such an effect comes generally by no deliberate process of study, but rather from a spontaneous feeling in the artist that thus things ought to be.

In spite, then, of its closeness to its origins, in spite, too, of so many contemporaneous vices of style, *Romeo and Juliet* seems as original as it seems vital. In Brooke and Paynter there is no plausibility; in Shakspere's play there is such veracity of conception that a thousand trivialities of style in no way impair its place in world-literature. *Romeo and Juliet* is a great work of art; and first among Shakspere's works it expresses a great emotional truth, — a lasting, tragic fact of human experience.

A creative artist is not so apt to comprehend the moral significance of what he creates as are his critics, particularly after the lapse of two or three centuries. It is more than likely that a writer in Shakspere's position may not actually have realized even what we have already touched on. It is most unlikely that he should have realized what makes *Romeo and Juliet* so permanently human. The tragedy it deals with, the tragedy of youthful love, is inevitable. Such love must pass; in real life, if fate do not cut it short in all its purity, it must lapse into some maturity far different from itself — calm domesticity, per-

haps, or adulterous passion. The very fate of Romeo
and Juliet, then, a real fate, full of that sense of the
inevitable which must pervade true tragedy, proves,
on consideration, not only broadly typical, but, for all
its sadness, inherently happy. It preserves heroically
permanent an emotional purity which in prolonged
life could not have survived.

Our sympathy with this is all the warmer because
the superficial poignancy of the tragedy has a pathos
which anybody can feel, without a bit of analysis.
Despite all these merits, though, — its tragic pathos
which appeals to everybody ; its veracity of conception, its sentiment, its poetry which appeal to the
ripest culture, — *Romeo and Juliet*, as a play, seems
in the end only a story told for its own sake by an
artist whose creative imagination was at last astir.
One finds in it no fundamental sense of mystery,
no cloud-piercing vision leading upward the eyes of
the elect, no self-revealing impulse. What Shakspere actually did, in short, reduces itself to this:
With laboriously mastered art, and with a creative
impulse not traceable in his earlier work, he gave
permanent vitality to matters which in other hands
had shown only possibilities of life. From what
seemed the material for a tragedy of blood, he
made a great tragic poem, — not philosophic in its
motive, like the tragedies of Marlowe, but more lasting even than they in its human truth. This he did,
too, after a manner which we shall learn to recognize as his own. With the least possible departure

from his sources, with the utmost economy of invention, and despite endless affectations of style which have been fatal to the work of his contemporaries, he translated Brooke and Paynter into this great tragedy which we all know. To himself it very probably seemed only a play in which he somehow felt more hearty interest than of old. To us, however, it seems rather a play throughout which we feel the spontaneous impulse of his creative imagination. From beginning to end, we can see now, the tragedy is permeated with that deep, lasting sense of fact which makes us so often think of Shakspere not as an author but as a creator.

IV. RICHARD III.

[*Richard III.* was entered in the Stationers' Register on October 20th, 1597. It was published anonymously in quarto during the same year; the next year came a second quarto with Shakspere's name; there were three other quartos during his lifetime. The popularity thus evinced is confirmed by the fact that, besides Meres's allusion, the *Centurie of Prayse* cites eight others during Shakspere's life, two of which refer it directly to Shakspere, and four of which mention, as familiar, Richard's last line, "A horse! A horse! My kingdom for a horse!"

Its source is Holinshed, and perhaps an earlier play, now lost.

In spite of its long connection with Shakspere, its authorship has been disputed on internal grounds. On internal evidence it is commonly assigned to 1593 or 1594.]

Whoever wrote *Richard III.*, the play so clearly belongs to the same series of chronicle-histories with *Henry VI.* that, as we have seen, the modern version of it which still holds the stage contains actual scenes, as well as speeches, from the latter play. Were it not still popular on the stage, indeed, one would be disposed to group it rather with the experimental plays of the last chapter than with the more masterly plays of this. Its vitality, however, so far as it goes, is not accidental. While, as a whole, the play follows the conventions of the old chronicle-history so closely that, in its original form, it cannot hold the attention of a modern audience, it contains, in its central figure, a character as vitally human, if not as complex, as any that Shakspere created.

On the archaism of so much of the play is based part of the doubt as to its authorship. The poet who could make the *Midsummer Night's Dream*, it is felt, or *Romeo and Juliet*, could not have perpetrated the absurdities which half impair the dramatic power of the scene where Gloster stops a royal funeral in the street, to make perfidious love to the widowed chief mourner;[1] nor could he have made three royal widows sit on the ground, lamenting through a hundred lines like Irish keeners.[2] Again, some critics feel, the simplicity of villainy embodied in the character of Richard is too inhuman, after all, for such a master of psychology as Shakspere had already proved himself. More likely, to such a state of mind as theirs, this whole play is really Marlowe's, or perhaps collaborative.

The force of these criticisms is evident. To avoid

[1] I. ii.   [2] IV. iv.

them — to give *Richard III.* a definite place in our notion of Shakspere's development — we must remind ourselves in the first place of the state of dramatic literature in 1593, and in the second place of what we have assumed Shakspere to have done since that year.

As we saw when we studied *Henry VI.*, chronicle-history, the most typically Elizabethan kind of drama, remained archaic in form and in purpose at a time when at least in purpose tragedy had become modernly comprehensible, and comedy had become so in both purpose and form. To a modern mind, the obsolete, rather operatic than dramatic, methods which have made Shakspere's *Richard III.* give place on the stage to Colley Cibber's vulgar version, are plain marks of weakness. To one familiar with the older chronicle-histories, they are simply a continuation, with added artistic purpose, of the conventions which the theatre of their time accepted.

To analyze in detail the art of *Richard III.* would for our purposes involve too long a delay. The result of it any one can feel. The character of Richard, for all the simplicity of his villainy, is as human as any in fiction ; again and again, as you read his lines, you find yourself accepting them as if they were actual human utterances. The world in which this human being moves, on the other hand, is almost as unreal, in its archaic conventionality, as that of the Moralities and the Interludes ; and so are many of his own speeches.[1] It is as if a modern, realistic

[1] E.g. I. i. 30, 145–154.

portrait were painted on such a golden background as one finds among thirteenth-century Italians. Despite this incongruity, however, so palpable on the modern stage as to be dramatically impossible, a mere reader of the play is hardly aware that anything is wrong. Like an Elizabethan theatre-goer, he accepts the half-lyric old conventions, and finds his attention centred on the vivid vitality of the central figure. Here he finds completed the tendency which, in the Third Part of *Henry VI.*, he had already perceived.[1] In Gloster is finally concentrated all the evil, all the disorder which had been desolating England from the moment when discord rose over the coffin of Henry V. In Gloster, when all this evil is finally ripe, it meets its just end with the victory of the first Tudor sovereign, whose granddaughter still reigned when *Richard III.* was written. Readers, even to-day, accept *Richard III.* as a great tragic poem; actors as a superb one-part play.

What seemed its lack of art, then, proves rather to have been its lack of complete emergence from archaic convention. Even this, however, does not explain its place in the work of Shakspere. Richard III., as a character, we have seen, certainly has such vitality as can come only from creative imagination in its maker; but, compared with the plays we have assigned to about the same period, *Richard III.* — for all its mere theatrical effectiveness — is extremely crude.

[1] See p. 81.

In this very fact, sometimes used as an argument against its genuineness, or at least against our conjectural chronology, we may find a strong argument in our favor. The *Midsummer Night's Dream* carried English comedy to a point as yet unapproached; so, at least in the matter of human plausibility, *Romeo and Juliet* carried English tragedy; and we saw reason for believing that these two plays belong to the same period. Whatever any writer's genius, such effort as is involved in either of these plays is exhausting, — still more exhausting is such effort as is involved in both. Given this fact, and given the comparative lack of development in chronicle-history, we could not rationally expect a chronicle-history from the same hand to show anything like a ripeness parallel to that of the ripening comedy and tragedy. At most, we could expect it to show growing signs of imaginative vitality; and these are just what we find in *Richard III.*

The state of things thus suggested — that when Shakespere was doing one kind of work with exceptional vigor his work of other kinds shows far less departure from conventions — we shall find throughout his career. For our purposes, it is the chief thing to note concerning *Richard III.*

V. RICHARD II.

[*Richard II.* was entered in the Stationers' Register on August 29th, 1597. It was published anonymously during the same year; and again the next year, with Shakspere's name. In these quartos the deposition scene — IV. i. 153-318 — is omitted. It appears first in a quarto of 1608; and remains in the fourth quarto, of 1615. Apparently it belongs to the original play, and was suppressed as politically objectionable. *Richard II.* was mentioned by Meres. There seems to have been another play on this subject which was perhaps the one played on the eve of Essex's rebellion in 1600-1.

The source of *Richard II.* is Holinshed, which is closely followed.

On internal evidence, the play is commonly assigned to about the same period as *Richard III.* Probably it is the later of the two.]

Like *Richard III., Richard II.* must for our purposes be regarded as a chronicle-history written at a moment when Shakspere's best energies were concentrated on comedy and tragedy. As we should expect, its method is essentially conventional, — nothing is done or said exactly as it would have been in real life. The story, in short, is translated from Holinshed into a dramatic form plainly influenced by Marlowe's, whose *Edward II.* this play closely resembles. For all this, *Richard II.* differs from Shakspere's earlier chronicle-histories in two respects: it has distinct unity of purpose, — its scenes and incidents are carefully selected, and organically composed; and it is so complete in finish that its numerous beauties of detail are not salient. In other words, while Shakspere's earlier chronicle-histories may be regarded as experiments, *Richard II.*, without palpable originality, uses a mastered archaic method for the expression of a definite artistic purpose.

Of course, Shakspere was not inventing. Unless we constantly discard the notion of invention, we cannot understand chronicle-history. Actual historical facts, however, impress historians who are also artists in specifically emotional ways; and such emotions even modern writers of history, if they be artists, try to express. This is what Shakspere has done in *Richard II.*; and if *Richard III.* remind one of some modern figure painted on a thirteenth-century background, *Richard II.*, consistent throughout, reminds one more vividly still of the quaintly life-like portrait of Richard himself enthroned in golden glory, still to be seen in the choir of Westminster Abbey.

In many places, Shakspere follows Holinshed's actual words with a closeness which makes the superb sound of Shakspere's language amazing; this is notable, for example, in the heralds' speeches, at the lists at Coventry.[1] When Shakspere invents his speeches, too, as in the scene where for eleven consecutive lines the dying Gaunt puns on his own name,[2] or in the scene where Richard, just deposed, goes through sixteen lines of sentimental euphuism with a mirror,[3] Shakspere's method is as archaically conventional as ever. This conventionality, however, is no more salient than the actual beauties which surround it; such for example, as Gaunt's noble speech about England,[4]

---

[1] I. iii. 104–116.   [2] II. i. 73–83.
[3] IV. i. 276–291.   [4] II. i. 40–66.

or as Carlisle's wonderful narrative of the death of Norfolk: [1] —

> " Many a time hath banish'd Norfolk fought
>   For Jesu Christ in glorious Christian field,
>   Streaming the ensign of the Christian cross
>   Against black pagans, Turks, and Saracens ;
>   And toil'd with works of war, retired himself
>   To Italy ; and there at Venice gave
>   His body to that pleasant country's earth,
>   And his pure soul unto his captain Christ,
>   Under whose colours he had fought so long."

Conventionalities and beauties alike, each seems exactly in place. What is more, while none even of the beauties are inevitably human utterances, each generally helps to define the character who utters it ; for while the conventionality of phrase in *Richard II.* prevents the characters from seeming exactly human, they have distinct individuality. Carlisle, brave, loyal, simple, is an ideal English gentleman ; York, always honest, is weak and dull ; Bolingbroke, supple, intriguing, yet somehow royal, reminds one curiously of Louis Napoleon ; Richard himself, in his feeble, delicate complexity, is the most individual of all. Amiable, almost fascinating, he is fundamentally unable to keep fact in view ; with graceful sentimentality he is always wandering from plain matters of fact to fantastic dreams and phrases. Euphuism, so inapt when we stop to criticise it in Gaunt or Bolingbroke, becomes in Richard strongly

[1] IV. i. 92-100.

characteristic. Winning in the irresponsibility of private life, such a character when clothed with the dignity of royalty becomes a public danger. The fatal incompatibility of the character and the duties of Richard II. involves the tragedy which pervades this play.

For besides being a chronicle-history, and a master-piece of its archaic kind, *Richard II.* is a really tragic prologue to the series of chronicle-histories which it opens. Thus we generally think of it, neglecting its position in the literature of its time. To define this, we should compare it with its obvious model, the *Edward II.* of Marlowe. In this tragedy — so profoundly tragic that one inclines to forget its real character as chronicle-history — there are passages more human than anything in Shakspere's play. Shakspere, for instance, has no lines which touch one like Edward's speech amid the squalid horrors of his dungeon : —

> " Tell Isabel the queen, I look'd not thus,
> When for her sake I ran at tilt in France,
> And there unhors'd the Duke of Cleremont."

The entire death-scene of Edward is finer than that of Richard. As a whole, however, *Edward II.*, while at times more vitally imaginative than *Richard II.*, shows far less mastery of art. If more imaginative, it is much less evenly sustained. The trait of *Richard II.* in the development of Shakspere begins to define itself. At a moment when he was making permanent tragedies and comedies, which occupied his best energy, he was also making the old conventions of chronicle-history serve to express, in a thoroughly mastered archaic form, his growing sense of fact.

VI. KING JOHN.

[*King John* is the only one of Shakspere's plays never entered in the Stationers' Register. Apart from its mention by Meres, there is no definite trace of it until its publication in the folio of 1623.

Unlike Shakspere's other chronicle-histories, it is founded, not on the chronicles themselves, but on an earlier play, *The Troublesome Raigne of John King of England*, etc., published in 1591. This was reprinted in 1611, with the name " W. Sh." on the titlepage. In all probability, however, the attributing of this earlier play to Shakspere is merely the trick of a dishonest publisher.

From internal evidence *King John* has been conjecturally assigned to 1595 or 1596. Critics generally agree in placing it somewhere between *Richard II.* and *Henry IV.*]

Less careful, less constantly sustained than *Richard II.*, *King John* often impresses one as queerer, more archaic, more puzzling than any other of Shakspere's chronicle-histories. This impression, of course, may be chiefly due to the accident that in most editions of the series it is printed first, and so that one is apt to read it with no preparation for its conventions. As we shall see, however, there are reasons enough in the play as it stands to make it seem at first sight more strange than what we have already considered, and yet, on inspection, to prove it a distinct step forward in the development of chronicle history.

One cause for its oddity of effect lies in its origin. Instead of translating directly from the chronicles, Shakspere clearly did not trouble himself about them at all; but only adapted a clumsy old play to the improving conditions of the stage. At the time, the subject of this play was accidentally popular. Though tradition generally confirms history in declaring John to have been the worst king England ever had, tradition and history equally agree in preserving a suspicion that he came to his end by poison, administered by an ecclesiastic who had been enraged beyond measure by John's attacks on the vested property of the Church. When England broke away from the church of Rome, then, John, by an obvious distortion of tradition, became something like a Protestant hero. In the early editions of Foxe's *Book of Martyrs* there is a full page of illustrations, showing how the wicked monk, duly absolved to begin with, took the poison from a toad, put it in the king's wine-cup, tasted the liquor to disarm suspicion, died at the same time with the king, and had masses regularly said for his traitorous, murderous soul. This view of things was presented, among others, in the *Troublesome Raigne*.

The old play, thus for the moment popular, was in two parts. In adapting it, Shakspere reduced it to the limits of a single performance. However he may have improved it in many ways, he managed in

one way to make it decidedly less intelligible than
before. In the *Troublesome Raigne* there are a number of ribald scenes where the Bastard sacks religious
houses, and incidentally discovers there a state of
morals agreeable at once to the principles of Elizabethan Protestants and to the taste of Elizabethan
audiences. This proceeding so excites the clergy
that they compass the king's death. In Shakspere's
play, this whole matter is compressed into two short
passages : —

1.[1]   "*K. John.* Cousin, away for England! haste before :
        And, ere our coming, see thou shake the bags
        Of hoarding abbots ; imprisoned angels
        Set at liberty : the fat ribs of peace
        Must by the hungry now be fed upon :
        Use our commission in his utmost force.
            Bast. Bell, book, and candle shall not drive me back,
        When gold and silver becks me to come on."
2.[2]   "*Bast.* How I have sped among the clergymen,
        The sums I have collected shall express."

The poisoning of the king, then, comes without very
obvious cause. In this respect, the old play is the
better.

Nor is this the only instance in which Shakspere did
not improve things. Shakspere's Constance, in general, however her rhetoric may be admired, certainly
rants ; like so many passages in the earlier chronicle-
histories, her long speeches belong rather to grand
opera than to tragedy proper. The Constance of the

[1] III. iii. 6–13.   [2] IV. ii. 141–142.

Troublesome Raigne, on the other hand, though less eloquent, is more human. Compare, for example, the last appearance of Constance in the two plays: it is when her heart has been broken by the capture of Arthur. Here is her last speech in the *Troublesome Raigne* : —

> " *Lewes.* Have patience, Madame, this is chaunce of warre :
> He may be ransomde, we revenge his wrong.
>   *Constance.* Be it ner so soone, I shall not live so long. "

In *King John* this pathetic utterance is expanded into five speeches, which comprise above fifty lines of tremendous declamation, beginning: [1] —

> " No, no, I will not, having breath to cry:
>   O, that my tongue were in the thunder's mouth !
>   Then with a passion would I shake the world;
>   And rouse from sleep that fell anatomy
>   Which cannot hear a lady's feeble voice," etc.

Whatever Shakspere's Constance may be at heart, she is not always so human in expression as the Constance of the *Troublesome Raigne*.

In general, however, Shakspere's play is by far the better. To find such instances as we have just glanced at, one must seek. Taking the two plays as a spectator or a hasty reader would take them, they differ in effect much as *Romeo and Juliet* differs from *Titus Andronicus*. The old play has so little vitality of imagination that it is hardly ever plausible; *King John*, on the other hand, is

[1] III. iv. 37 seq.

full of touches which, when we once accept the
old conventions, waken characters and scenes alike
into something far nearer real life than we have
yet found in chronicle-history. Character after character emerges into consistent individuality.   Best
of all, of course, is the Bastard, who from a rather
lifeless comic personage becomes one of Shakspere's
own living men. Arthur, whose situation and fate
recall those of the young princes in *Richard III.*,
is at once so human and so pathetic that many modern critics are set to wondering whether the tender sense of boyish charm and parental bereavement
hereby revealed may not have been awakened by
the illness and death in 1596 of Shakspere's only son.
Elinor is thoroughly alive, too;[1] so is the intriguing
Cardinal Pandulph;[2] so is Hubert, whose scenes
with the King and with Arthur remain dramatically
effective;[3] so is King John himself; and so often, in
spite of her rant, is Constance. In no earlier chronicle-
history, for example, is there anything like so human
a touch as in the scene where Elinor tries to entice
Arthur from Constance:[4] —

> "*Eli.*   Come to thy grandam, child.
>   *Const.* Do, child, go to it grandam, child ;
>   Give grandam kingdom, and it grandam will
>   Give it a plum, a cherry, and a fig ;
>   There 's a good grandam."

In the *Troublesome Raigne* there is no hint of these
speeches. They are all Shakspere's.

[1] See I. i.   [2] See III. iv. 112 seq.
[3] III. iii. 19 seq.; IV. i.   [4] II. i. 159 seq.

As concrete an example as any of what Shakspere has done in *King John* may be found in the very opening line. The *Troublesome Raigne* opens with a formal speech by Elinor : —

> " Barons of England, and my noble Lords ;
> Though God and fortune have bereft from us
> Victorious Richard scourge of infidels," etc.

In general manner, this is very much like the opening of *Richard II.* : —

> " Old John of Gaunt, time-honour'd Lancaster," etc.

Shakspere's *King John*, on the other hand, opens with an improved version of the forty-first line of the *Troublesome Raigne*, the line with which the action begins : —

> " Now say, Chatillon, what would France with us ? "

By the eighth line, the passionate temperaments of John and of Elinor have been revealed by two characteristic outbursts [1] for which the *Troublesome Raigne* affords no suggestion. The example is sufficient : what has happened in *King John* is what happened in *Romeo and Juliet*. Creative imagination, to all appearances spontaneous, has made real, living people out of what had previously been stage types.

In this very fact lies the reason why *King John* generally impresses one as more archaic, or at least as more queer, than *Richard II.* Such a phrase as Richard's

> " Old John of Gaunt, time-honour'd Lancaster,"

[1] I. i. 5, 6.

could never have been uttered by any real man; such a phrase as John's

"Now say, Chatillon, what would France with us?"

might be uttered by anybody still. In *Richard II.*, then, the consistent conventionality of everything makes us accept the whole play if we accept any part of it. In *King John* the continual confusion of real, human vitality with the old quasi-operatic conventions combines with the general carelessness of construction to make each kind of thing seem more out of place than it would seem by itself. Like any other transitional incongruity, *King John* is often harder to accept than the consistent conventions from which it departs. Its very excellences emphasize its faults and its oddities.

In *King John*, then, we find Shakspere's creative energy awake, much as we found it in *Romeo and Juliet;* and somewhat as we found it in the *Midsummer Night's Dream*, in *Richard III.*, and in *Richard II.* From the fact that *King John*, while in some respects as vital as any of these, is less careful, we may infer that this creative energy was growing more spontaneously strong. Clearly, though, it has not here produced a work which for ripeness of development can compare with the comedy or the tragedy already before us. To understand this slowness in the development of chronicle-history, we may conveniently turn to the next play in our study. If our chronology be right, *King John* belongs to the same period as the *Merchant of Venice.*

VII. The Merchant of Venice.

[The *Merchant of Venice* was entered in the Stationers' Register in
July, 1598. It was twice published in quarto during 1600. It was
mentioned by Meres, and one passage was perhaps paraphrased in a
play called the *Wily Beguiled*, written in 1596 or 1597.

The actual sources of the *Merchant of Venice* remain doubtful. The
weight of opinion seems to hold that Shakspere rewrote an older play,
now lost, which was probably founded on the *Pecorone* of Ser Giovanni
Fiorentino. In any event, the stories here combined are very old, and
might have come to Shakspere's attention in various ways.

While the date of the play cannot be fixed with certainty, we may
be fairly sure that it was written later than the plays we have considered hitherto, and certainly before 1598. The weight of opinion seems
to favor 1596]

If the *Merchant of Venice* be nearly contemporary
with *King John*, we can readily see why the advance
made in the latter play is less marked than we might
have expected; for like the comedy and the tragedy
which we guessed to have absorbed the energy which
might have developed chronicle-history into something riper than *Richard III.* or *Richard II.*, the
Merchant of Venice must have demanded, in the writing, the better part of its maker's attention. The
reason why *King John* remains archaic, then, we may
guess to be that at the time of its writing Shakspere's chief energies were directed elsewhere.

For, whatever its origin, the *Merchant of Venice* is
a permanently good play, still effective on the stage.
A modern audience accepts it and enjoys it as heartily
as ever. When we stop to consider the plot, to be sure,

we discover a state of things which to say the least is surprising. We have been asked to believe that in ducal Venice, where business was doing on the Rialto, a respectable merchant, whom Tintoretto might have painted, made a serious contract with a Jewish neighbor, by the terms of which the Jew might legally murder him; and that meanwhile a spendthrift Venetian gentleman borrowed from this same merchant a considerable sum in good Venetian coin, for the purpose of pressing his suit to an heiress, whose hand was to be given, as a matter of course, to whoever should select among three locked boxes the one which contained her portrait. Thus stated, the plot of the *Merchant of Venice* appears as childishly absurd as any in all nursery tradition. Thus stated, however, — though the statement is literally true, — it startles one a bit; for, whether we see or read the play, we have not only been asked to accept this nonsense; we have unhesitatingly accepted it. Shakspere's art has made it plausible.

The technical construction of the plot has of late been greatly admired. Without more accurate knowledge of the sources, to be sure, we cannot assert just what Shakspere did, and what was done by other hands. It seems probable, however, that to Shakspere's instinctive tact we owe the variation from the original plot, to which, so far as plot goes, the plausibility of the Merchant of Venice is chiefly due. In the older story, the lady of Belmont is a piratical and widowed siren, who persuades passing merchants to stake their vessels against her hand that they will possess her person, and then drugs them at supper. The substitution for this crude incident of the delicately fantastic story of the caskets is distinctly characteristic of Shakspere, among Elizabethan dramatists. Most of his contemporaries would greatly have relished the original situation. Shakspere, on the other hand, while never prudish and always willing to make licentious jokes, seems to have been remarkably free from a taste for unmixed obscenity. Compared with other men of his time, he shows decided purity of mind. Whether he actually made it or not, then, the change from the old plot is such as he would have been apt to make.

It is this change, more than anything else, which makes the *Merchant of Venice* plausible. As an artist, of course, Shakspere's task was to distract attention from the absurdity of his plot. This, we have seen, he accomplished. He did so largely by constantly keeping before his audience two separate though closely intermingled atmospheres : first, that of a romantic Venice such as Paul Veronese might have painted ; secondly, that of the still more romantic, actually utopian, Belmont, such as was involved in the story of the caskets. His composition here somewhat resembles that of the *Midsummer Night's Dream*. He adapts and develops for his purposes the conventional devices of an induction. Belmont is as unreal, though not so fantastic, as the fairy wood of Athens ; yet the unreality of Belmont is necessary to make plausible the romantic extravagances of Venice. Shakspere begins, then, by a scene in Venice where everything might conceivably be true. Though a suggestion of Portia occurs in the first scene, there is no allusion to the caskets. Then the scene shifts to Belmont, where Portia and Nerissa talk long enough to be readily accepted by any audience before the caskets are mentioned at all. With that mention begins the utopian atmosphere. When we have accepted that, the bond of the pound of flesh seems far more in the order of things than if we had come to it straight from real life; yet even then it is reserved until the one hundred and fiftieth line of the following scene. From that time on, romantic Venice and utopian Belmont are more and more intermingled, until in the last two acts one hardly knows which is which. The last act — a lyric epilogue which removes us from the excessive improbability of the trial scene — leaves us in a realm of utopian fancy. Different as the effect of this romantic play is from that of the fairy comedy, the device by which it is secured is clearly the old induction-like device of leading us gradually from credible things to incredible.

Nor is this the only instance of Shakspeare's characteristic economy of invention. In the *Two Gentlemen of Verona* [1] we remember among other effective things the catalogue of lovers discussed between mistress and maid; the disguise of the heroine as a man, with consequent confusion of identity; and the robust low

[1] See p. 94.

comedy of Launce and Speed. In the *Merchant of Venice* all these are reproduced and developed. The change in the catalogue of lovers is a distinct improvement. In the first instance the mistress proposed the names and the maid commented on them, which was amusing but rude; here the maid proposes the names and the mistress comments, which is both amusing and — at least according to Elizabethan notions — consistent with good manners.[1] Launce and Speed are reproduced in Launcelot Gibbo and his father, — a much better contrasted or at least more varied pair. The disguised heroine, on the other hand, is not only repeated but trebled. There are but three women in the *Merchant of Venice;* and all three assume male costume — as complete a concession to the taste of audiences as you shall find in all dramatic literature.

What really makes the *Merchant of Venice* so permanently effective, however, is not so much these well-tried devices, which after all prove chiefly that the play is constructed with careful theatrical intelligence. It is rather that along with this care appears the trait which we have clearly seen growing in *Romeo and Juliet*, in *Richard III.*, and in *King John.* From beginning to end, the characters of the *Merchant of Venice* are so individual and so human that one's attention centres wholly on them. As readers or as spectators we become convinced that these people are real; in consequence we accept everything else as a matter of course. Appreciating who and what the

[1] Cf. *Two Gentlemen of Verona*, I. ii. with *Merchant of Venice*, I. ii.

characters are, we never stop to remark what absurd things they do.

Of course, this profoundly human conception is presented by conventional means as remote as possible from modern realism. More than two-thirds of the play is in verse, and much of the prose might as fairly be termed poetry. What this poetry expresses, however, are simple human emotions. Take the very opening scene. In beautifully fluent verse, growing free from the affectations and the aggressive ingenuity of Shakspere's earlier work, we are reminded of the familiar fact that a man of affairs, rather deeply involved, gets very anxious without knowing quite why. The vigorous verse — a conventional means of expression as remote as music from actual human utterance — we enjoy and forget. What we remember is that we have been put agreeably in possession of a state of things as true in Nineveh or in Wall Street as in commercial Venice, — a state of things incessant wherever men do business. Readers of Shakspere are apt to neglect, in discussing him, the obsolete conventionalism of his intrinsically noble and beautiful methods. Try to locate a blank-verse dialogue, with interspersed lyrics, in a modern stock-exchange, though, and you will find how differently Shakspere would have had to express himself had he written now. It is well for literature that he was free to use the grand conventions of Elizabethan style in setting forth his permanently human conceptions of character.

Just how these characters were conceived, of course,

no one can assert. What one knows of the way in which fiction grows nowadays, however, would warrant at least a confident guess that they were conceived by no conscious process of psychologic analysis. Writer after writer, whose actual works are of the most varying merit, agree that when they were writing the passages where their characters seem most alive, the characters generally got beyond their control, — doing and saying things which the writers never intended. The plays we have lately considered, and many still to come, agree in suggesting that some such process of spontaneously creative imagination was more probably at work in Shakspere's mind, than was any such consciously constructive method as people of small artistic experience are apt to infer from his results.

Whatever his method, there can be no doubt that it resulted in a presentation of character which may fairly be called sympathetic. In this play we instinctively sympathize with everybody. Baldly stated, Bassanio's purpose of borrowing money to make love to an heiress whose fortune shall pay his debts, is by no means that of a romantic hero; no more is Antonio's expectoratory method of manifesting distaste for the Hebrew race. As Shakspere puts these things, however, we accept them as unreservedly as we accept the graces of Portia. This heroine remains among the most charming in Shakspere, — an exquisite type of that unhappily rare kind of human being who is produced only by the union of high thinking and high living. She is so distinctly a person of quality that certain critics have surmised her to indicate a definite improvement in Shakspere's social position. What is perhaps more notable is that the conception of such a character involves in its creator a trait not needful to the conception of the characters we have met hitherto, — at least a sympathetic understanding of the fascination which a charming woman, with whose faults and errors you are unacquainted, can exercise. Whether anybody was ever in fact quite so altogether delightful as Portia remains in fiction, may perhaps be questioned. That many a worthy, and unworthy, woman has seemed so to adoring men is beyond doubt. About the only fault which one can fairly find with her is the fault she shares with all the other delightful people in the play. One and all, with whom our sympathy is clearly expected to go, treat Shylock, who nowadays is made almost equally sympathetic, in a manner which any modern temper must deem cruelly inhuman.

Shylock, like everybody else in the play, is presented as a human being. Distorted though his nature be by years of individual contempt and centuries of racial persecution, he remains a man. With the exception of his first "aside" in the presence of Antonio,[1] there is nothing to prevent us from taking his proposal of the monstrous bond as something like a jest on his own usurious practices; and for all his racial hatred, he seems, like many modern Hebrews, anxious for decent and familiar treatment

[1] I. iii. 42–53.

by the people among whom he lives. The treatment he receives from the very Christians he has obliged, who apparently decoy him to supper that his daughter may have a chance for her thievish escapade, naturally arouses all the evil in him. His revenge, if not admirable, is most comprehensible. Not so, to modern feeling, is the contemptuously brutal treatment which he receives from the charming people with whom we are expected to sympathize fully.

To understand this, at least as it was meant, we must forget the Nineteenth Century, and revive at least two dead sentiments which in the time of Elizabeth still survived : the abhorrence of usury, and the abhorrence of the Jewish race which for centuries had been fostered by the Church. Usury, of course, remained in our own time, if indeed it be not still, a technical crime ; but except in some palpably monstrous form it has never impressed any sane living man as intrinsically evil. The only people nowadays who object to the practice of lending money at interest are such envious, hateful, and malicious folk as happen to have none to lend ; and generally even the taking of illegally high interest is regarded not as an essentially wicked act, but as a technically ; as a *malum prohibitum*, like smuggling, rather than as a *malum in se,* like robbery or murder. In Shakspere's time, this feeling was quite reversed ; people had been taught, by a thousand years of bad ecclesiastical economy, that whoever took interest on money was essentially as

vile as a woman who should sell herself. To such
a state of mind, Shylock's frank avowal that he takes
interest[1] amounts to such a cynical profession of rascality as might now once for all repel sympathy from
a vicious female character. Again, to the mediæval
mind — and in many respects the Elizabethan mind
remained mediæval — the Jew had been represented
by centuries of churchly teaching as the living type
of a race who had deliberately murdered an incarnate God. Nothing less than a tremendous decay
of dogmatic Christianity could possibly have permitted
the growth of such humane sentiments toward Jews
as generally prevail to-day.

An imaginative effort to revive these old sentiments, and thus to place ourselves in the position of
an Elizabethan audience, helps us in some degree to
understand the treatment of Shylock. As Shylock is
now presented on the stage, however, his fate remains repellent — by no means the sort of thing we
expect in a romantic comedy where virtue and vice
get only their deserts. We can hardly help feeling
that, despite his misfortunes and his faults, the
grandly Hebraic Jew of the modern stage is treated
outrageously; yet we cannot feel that any such sentiment could probably have been intended by an
Elizabethan dramatist. To get at the bottom of the
trouble, we must consider the stage history of "the
Jew that Shakspere drew."

No records of any performance of the *Merchant of*

---

[1] I. iii. 70–103.

Venice have been discovered earlier than 1701. In that year a much altered version of it, made by the Marquis of Lansdowne, was produced in London. The Shylock of this version was a broadly comic personage, with the huge nose and red wig of the traditional Judas. Forty years later, in 1741, Macklin revived Shakspere's play, and played Shylock in something resembling the modern manner. From that time to this, for above a century and a half, Shylock has looked not like a Jew, but like a Hebrew. Very clearly, the Lansdowne tradition of broad, low comedy does not fit Shakspere's lines. Shylock, as a character, is a great, serious Shaksperean creation, which may be psychologically studied almost like a real human being. In this psychologically sympathetic age, we are given to this sort of study; in literature, at all events, we consider rather what people actually are than what they look like. We neglect the various bodily forms in which character may manifest itself; no cant is more popular than that which disdains appearances. Such cant was as foreign to Shakspere's time as any other form of sentimental philanthropy; to an Elizabethan audience, what looked mean was for that very reason essentially contemptible. Though no actual records support the conclusion, then, it seems more than probable that the real Shylock of Shakspere's stage combined the old traditions with the new, — that in make-up, in appearance, in manner, he was meanly "Jewy;" while the tremendous creative imagination of the dramatist made him at heart sympathetically human. Only under such circumstances could the fate of Shylock be artistically tolerable.

At all events, we have certain side-lights on the matter. Elizabethan England was childishly brutal; to-day, indeed, England sometimes seems more robustly unsympathetic than America. In actual lunacy, as the *Changeling* of Middleton will show, the England of Elizabeth saw not something horrible, but rather something conventionally comic — much as drunkenness is still held comic on the stage. In physical suffering it often saw mere grotesque contortion: witness the frequency of thrashing in old comedy. And even to-day, we are less sincerely beyond these things than we sometimes admit. After all, what repels our sympathy in the *Merchant of Venice* is, not so much the actual treatment which Shylock receives as the grandly Hebraic aspect of the personage whom we see receive it. Substitute for this figure a meanly cringing one, like the pimps and pawnbrokers who still compose the Jewish rabble, and, for all Shakspere's sympathetic psychology, Shylock will seem to get little else than his deserts. If this be true nowadays, it would be vastly more true in an age so foreign to our fine philanthropy as the brutally childish England of Elizabeth; and some such childishly unfeeling conception was probably the real conception of Shakspere. As an artistic playwright, he could not have meant our sympathy to go with

Shylock; yet no rendering of Shylock which makes the man look noble enough to be seriously sympathetic could ever have failed to command sympathy. There are few facts in the Elizabethan drama which more strongly emphasize the remoteness from ourselves not only of Elizabethan England, but also of Shakspere, the Elizabethan playwright.

This view of Shakspere we must always keep in mind. As we come to these more lasting of his works, we are prone to forget it. In the *Merchant of Venice*, for example, we cannot but find, along with what we have already glanced at, a constantly growing beauty, gravity, significance of mere poetry; everywhere, in short, we feel Shakspere's grasp of life growing firmer, his wisdom deeper. We are tempted to guess that all this is not merely temperamental, but profoundly, philosophically conscious. We may generally be preserved from this temptation, however, by such constant consideration of fact as in this chapter we have insisted upon. Among the hypotheses about this play, the simplest is this: A stage playwright of that olden time set himself the regular task of translating into effective dramatic form an archaically trivial old story. In the course of some nine years of practice he had so mastered his technical art, theatrical and literary alike, and had so awakened his own faculty of spontaneously creative imagination, that he made his version of the story permanently plausible. He did more; like any masterly artist, he introduced into his work touch after touch of

the kind which makes works of art endlessly suggestive to ages more and more foreign, in thought and in
feeling, to the age which produced them.   The *Merchant of Venice*, then, is full of implicit wisdom, and
beauty, and significance.   That Shakspere realized all
this, however, does not follow.   Critics who declare a
great artist fully conscious of whatever his work
implies are generally those who least know how
works of art are made.

VIII. The Taming of the Shrew.

[The *Taming of the Shrew*, in its present form, appeared first in the
folio of 1623.   There is no certain allusion to it at any earlier date.

On May 2nd, 1594, however, " A pleasant conceited history called
the *Tayming of a Shrowe*" was entered in the Stationers' Register.
This, which was published in quarto during the same year, is evidently
the source, if not the original version, of the comedy finally ascribed to
Shakspere.   Who wrote the earlier play, how much of the final
play may be pronounced Shakspere's, and to what period we may
assign his work on it, have been much discussed with no certain result.

It seems probable that the play as we have it is the work of several
hands, revised by Shakspere somewhere about 1597.]

If the *Taming of a Shrew* be Shakspere's, and such,
at least to a considerable degree, we may assume it until
further adverse evidence appears, it is in various ways
different from any of his work which we have as yet
considered.   In the plays discussed in the last chapter, Shakspere seemed plainly to be trying his hand,
with marked versatility, at various experiments.   In
the plays hitherto discussed in this chapter, he has

seemed the master of his vehicle, which with more or less artistic seriousness he has used to express the various moods into which his various subjects have thrown him. In this play one finds far less definite artistic motive than in those which we have lately read; yet at the same time one finds such easy mastery of dramatic technique that the *Taming of the Shrew* remains among the most popular light comedies on the English stage. The play is a rollicking farce, so full of fun that, whether we read or see it, we accept its assumptions. When we stop to consider, we are surprised to find these involving that archaic view of conjugal relations which permits the husband, provided his stick be not too big, to enforce domestic discipline by whipping. All of which is at once less serious than the artistic plays we have dealt with, and more skilful than the experimental.

One reason for this peculiar effect may lie in the fact that while most of the plays we have lately considered are almost certainly Shakspere's throughout, a large part of the *Taming of the Shrew* is thought to be by others. The old *Taming of a Shrew* was in all probability by somebody else, though by whom we cannot be sure. The passages about Bianca and most of the other minor characters are very likely by some intervening hand. This leaves to Shakspere himself little more than the characters of Sly, Katharine, and Petruchio, with occasional touches throughout, — a state of things quite in accordance with the habitual collaboration of the Elizabethan theatre.

Collaborative or not, however, the play has a distinct effect of its own, which is by no means one of palpable patchwork. Its plot, to begin with, is swift and constant in action, and quite firm enough still to hold the attention of any audience. Even if the play were not by Shakspere at all, too, it contains one feature, unique in the work ascribed to Shakspere, but common in the drama of his time, which would be well worth our attention. This is the Induction, which makes the main action a play within a play. Probably intended to be followed by improvised remarks between scenes, it was almost certainly intended to be balanced by a formal epilogue, or conclusion, in which Sly should fall asleep as lord, and wake up as tinker. Eccentric as such a device seems nowadays, it is very suggestive of the conditions of the Elizabethan theatre; it clearly exemplifies, too, the old convention which Shakspere developed into the artistic removal from real life of whatever in the *Midsummer Night's Dream* or in the *Merchant of Venice* was at first blush incredible.

Inductions, interpolated comments by the personages thereof, and final conclusions, were common on the Elizabethan stage. A glance at the works of Greene or of Peele, or at Beaumont and Fletcher's *Knight of the Burning Pestle*, will show how general this sort of thing was. Impracticable on our own stage, it was exactly fitted to the conditions of the stage by which all of Shakspere's plays were produced. On either side of that stage, we remember, in the place now occupied by proscenium boxes, were seats where the more fashionable part of the audience sat, themselves a brilliant feature of the spectacle afforded to the more vulgar company in the pit or the gallery. Among these people of quality, the actors in the Induction could seat themselves while the main play went on, forming a natural system of intermediates between audience and play — actually part of both. When the audience was banished from the stage, such a proceeding became impracticable. Finally the whole system merged into the rhymed prologue, which has disappeared in turn. It is interesting to us chiefly as a fresh reminder that the stage for which Shakspere made his plays was a totally different thing from the stage to which we are accustomed.

In itself, to be sure, the Induction of the *Taming of the Shrew* is comical. So is the real play. Neither, however, possesses very individual traits; both deal, after the manner of their day, with such incidents as compose the stock plots of Italian novels, at that time generally popular.

To pass to the characters of the *Taming of the Shrew*, we find them, with three exceptions, merely conventional stage figures, of the sort which figured in Shakspere's earlier experimental work. These exceptions are those on which we have already touched, — Sly in the Induction, and in the play Katharine and Petruchio. At least contrasted with the other characters, these seem almost Shaksperean in vitality. Certainly the queerly matched pair, for all their extrav-

agance of humour, — in the Elizabethan sense of the
word as well as in ours, — have a vitality which
blinds us to the outrageously archaic state of their
matrimonial relations, much as the vitality of the
characters in the *Merchant of Venice* blinds us to the
absurd conditions which surround them.   It is idle to
pretend, however, that even the most human characters in the *Taming of the Shrew* come anywhere near
the full vitality frequent in the better plays which
have preceded.

To a great extent, one may say the same of the atmosphere.   This is conventionally Italian, and plausible enough for its purpose.   Certainly, though, it is
little more.   Conceivably one might imagine in this
environment the personages of the *Two Gentlemen of
Verona;* by a stretch of imagination, one might possibly
imagine here some stray personages from *Romeo and
Juliet* or from the *Merchant of Venice.*   Even these,
however, would seem out of place; while the personages of the Italian plays to come could no more appear
in the Italy of Petruchio than Petruchio himself could
appear unaltered in real life.

Altogether, the more one considers this perennially
amusing play, the less substantial one finds it; after
all, it proves to be only a hack-made farce.   It is
a good farce, however; though fun is the most evan-
escent trait of any literary period, it is lastingly funny;
and, considering that in all likelihood it proceeds from
at least three distinct hands, it has surprising unity of
diverting effect.   Such unity of effect can hardly be acci-

dental. There is no reason for not attributing it to the practised and skilful hand of Shakspere, revising and completing the cruder work of others.

Pleasant as we may find all this, there is no denying that the *Taming of the Shrew*, far from carrying comedy to a point beyond that which it had already reached in Shakspere's hands, is probably less effective, — or at least less artistically serious, — than anything, of any kind, which we have considered since the *Two Gentlemen of Verona*. At first glance, this seems to count strongly against our chronology. To understand it, as a little while ago to understand *King John*, we must consider along with this rollicking farce the other work which modern chronology assumes to be contemporary with it. Here the contemporary play is *Henry IV.*

IX. HENRY IV.

[For our purposes the two parts of *Henry IV.* may be considered together.

The First Part was entered in the Stationers' Register on February 25th, 1598. It was published during the same year, and was four times republished during Shakspere's lifetime.

The Second Part was entered in the Stationers' Register on August 23rd, 1600. It was published during the same year. No other quarto of it is known. There is reason to believe, however, that it was written before the publication of the First Part. In the quarto of 1600, for one thing, the name *Old* is prefixed to one of Falstaff's speeches, while throughout the First Part Falstaff's name is substituted for that of Oldcastle; from which we may fairly infer that the Second Part was written before the change of name from Oldcastle to Falstaff occurred.

The sources of both parts, as well as of *Henry V.*, are Holinshed and an old play, published in 1598, called the *Famous Victories of Henry the Fifth*, etc.

Meres mentioned *Henry IV.* as one of Shakspere's plays. Various other allusions to the play during Shakspere's lifetime indicate that the characters of Falstaff, Shallow, and Silence were generally familiar.

Modern critics agree in conjecturally assigning the whole play to 1597 or 1598.]

Henry IV. may be assigned, more confidently than usual, to the years immediately following that to which we assigned the *Merchant of Venice.* To the earlier of these years we assigned the *Taming of the Shrew*, which thus appears to be, like *Richard III.* or *King John*, the off-hand work of a moment when Shakspere's chief energies were absorbed by another kind of writing. Taken together, too, the years 1597 and 1598 were undoubtedly those in which Shakspere's dramatic work began to be published, the years when arms were granted to his father, the years when he began to buy land, the years when Meres's allusion proves him to have become a recognized man of letters, and the years when the correspondence of Sturley and of Quiney shows that his fellow-townsmen thought him a person of consequence in London. We may fairly conclude, then, that *Henry IV.* was at least among the plays which he was making when, after ten years of professional work, his power was beginning to bring him both fortune and reputation.

It becomes interesting, then, to inquire what, if any, is the leading trait of this *Henry IV.*, the play which more than any other marks the emergence of Shakspere into full contemporary recognition. This trait is plain. More than any of the plays we have considered hitherto, *Henry IV.* is completely plausible. Whenever or wherever one read it, one puts it down with a sense that one has been in contact with actual life. This total impression absorbs all memory of the medium by which this actual life has been brought to us. We forget details, of construction, of style, even of character; we are conscious only of a profound impression that we have seen real people, who have done real things.

Surprising as this effect is, a little closer inspection of the text makes it more so still. On the titlepage of the earliest quarto, as well as in the Stationers' Register, the name of Falstaff is quite as conspicuous as that of the King. "With the humorous conceits of Sir John Falstalffe," reads the titlepage; and the line is purposely so removed from the preceding ones as instantly to attract any eye. Clearly, *Henry IV.* has two parts, throughout: the first deals with such actually historical matter as became familiar in the earlier chronicle-histories; the second is an independent comedy of manners, with no historical basis at all. These two parts are united by little more than the figure of the Prince — to say the character of the Prince were almost misleading, for his conduct and speeches in the historical scenes differ completely from his conduct and speeches in the comic. What is more, the two parts differ similarly throughout: the historical preserves with little change the long declamatory

speeches, and the highly conventionalized incident, of
the old chronicle-history; the comic part is almost
literal in its humorous presentation of low London
life.   Such incongruity, to be sure, was no new thing;
we find something like it in the *Famous Victories*,
something like it, too, in the *Troublesome Raigne;* and
the old miracle-plays are full of it.   The surprising
thing about *Henry IV.* is that its incongruity, unlike
that of these older plays, troubles us no more than the
constant incongruity of real life.   When not disposed
to be very critical, we accept it without question.

As we begin to study the play, one reason for this
plausibility transpires.   Marked as the incongruity of
the two parts at first appears, it proves, on inspection,
to be a matter of little more than diction.   Inimi-
tably human as Falstaff's scenes seem to a reader,
they are not composed in a manner which could be
effectively presented on a modern stage.   Like the
scenes where the King figures, they are rather a series
of long speeches, not interwoven but strung together,
than a strictly dramatic composition.   In our time
they lend themselves more readily to reading than to
acting.   The infrequency of Falstaff on the modern
stage is probably due not so much to the fact that few
can act him, as to the fact that in order to be actable under our present dramatic conditions, his lines
would have to be rewritten.   From end to end, in
short, *Henry IV.* is composed not as a modern play,
but as a typical old chronicle-history.

What makes it so plausible, then, is not that it

discards old conventions. Nobody anywhere, for example, is more frankly rhetorical than the King;[1]
Hotspur dies[2] as blatantly as John of Gaunt died;[8]
even Falstaff himself and the Prince declaim with a
disregard of action as complete as Mercutio's when he
introduces his lyric description of Queen Mab. In
mere form, *Henry IV.* is as conventional as it can be.
What makes it seem otherwise is that here, as in the
Merchant of Venice, these obsolete conventions are
used, with the confidence of full technical mastery,
to express conceptions of human character which
throughout are consistently vital. In our sense of
this great feat of creative imagination, we never stop
to consider the means by which it is accomplished;
we forget the vehicle, we are aware only of the conceptions it conveys. Ultimately, then, the lasting difference of effect between the *Merchant of Venice* and
Henry IV. resolves itself into the accidental difference between their subjects. What the living people
in the *Merchant of Venice* do proves on consideration
childishly incredible; what the living people do in
Henry IV. is substantially historical. It is the fundamental truth of chronicle-history combining with
Shakspere's intense power of creative imagination,
already declared in fantastic comedy, which makes
Henry IV. a new thing in literature.

A new thing in literature it undoubtedly is, though;

---

[1] E. g. 1 *Hen. IV.* I. i.; 2 *Hen. IV.* III. i. 1–31.

[2] 1 *Hen. IV.* V. iv. 77–86.

[8] *R. II.* II. i.

and a thing not destined to be fully developed until our own century. Its deliberate intermingling of vigorous fiction with the general outline of acknowledged history, reawakens into actual life a long-past world. The archaism of its form and manner allies it to the older work of Greene, of Peele, of Marlowe; it remains chronicle-history. The full vitality of its conception allies it rather to the novels of Walter Scott; chronicle-history though it be, it is at the same time our first, and by no means our least, example of historical fiction.

In the presence of so great a feat of creative imagination as this, — a feat which gives us a kind of art hitherto unknown, — we naturally feel ourselves eager to seek, if we may, for some glimpse of how the feat presented itself to the man who performed it. On this point there is something resembling evidence. Certainly the most notable character in *Henry IV.* is Falstaff, and there remain indications of how Falstaff grew.

The original name of this character is known to have been Oldcastle. The change of name is thought to have been made in deference to members of the Oldcastle family,[1] who naturally did not relish the revival of their ancestor in precisely this form. Though Falstaff as we have him, then, be a pure fiction, at least his name — and in some slight degree the tradition it stood for — originally had historic basis. Sir John Oldcastle, Lord Cobham, was a gen-

---

[1] See the epilogue to 2 *Henry IV.*

tleman of the time of Henry V., whose liberal principles got him into trouble with the Church ; the King
abandoned him to the mercy of the Church, which
burned him at the stake for such heresy as later
would have been called Protestantism.   In Elizabeth's
time, accordingly, Oldcastle was a Protestant, or rather
a Puritan, hero, duly commemorated at great length in
Foxe's *Book of Martyrs*.   A passage from this narrative tells how when he was bidden to confess himself
to the Church, before going to trial and execution, he
refused to make any other confession than a public
one to God : [1] —

"And with that he kneeled down on the pavement,
holding up his hands towards heaven, and said: 'I shrive
myself here unto thee, my eternal living
God, that in my frail youth I offended thee,
O Lord! most grievously in pride, wrath, and
gluttony, in covetousness, and in lechery.   Many men
have I hurt in mine anger, and done many other horrible
sins; good Lord, I ask thy mercy.'   And therewith weep-
ingly he stood up again, and said with a mighty voice:
'Lo, good people! lo ; for the breaking of God's law and
his great commandments, they never yet cursed me, but,
for their own laws and traditions, most cruelly do they
handle both me and other men ; and therefore, both they
and their laws, by the promise of God, shall be utterly
destroyed.'   (Jer. ii.)."

Lord Cobham confesseth him-self unto God.

From his own words, then, we may believe that
the Puritan hero, in his unregenerate state, had been

[1] Foxe: *Acts and Monuments*: London, 1841: iii. 330.

guilty of pride, wrath and gluttony, covetousness and lechery, hard fighting, and many other hòrrible sins. To speak very generally, so had the Falstaff of *Henry IV*.

In Shakspere's time Oldcastle was a familiar figure on the stage. There still exists an old play bearing his name, which was once ascribed to Shakspere. This play, to be sure, commonly presents him as a Protestant hero; now and then, however, he disguises himself, to escape persecution, in a manner which must have been comic. There are various traces elsewhere of a broadly comic Oldcastle in some old play, — for example, an allusion to "the rich rubies and incomparable carbuncles of Sir John Oldcastle's nose." In the *Famous Victories*, too, Oldcastle appears among the boon companions of the riotous Prince, and makes one speech which suggests Falstaff's temper : [1]

> " If the old king my father was dead,"

says the Prince,

> " We would all be kings."

> " Hee is a good olde man,"

answers Sir John Oldcastle.

> " God take him to his mercy the sooner."

What reminds one of Falstaff in that speech is not only its temper, but the religious allusion. In his second speech, for example, Falstaff says, —

[1] Facsimile of Qu. 1598, p. 17.

" God save thy grace, — majesty I should say, for grace thou wilt
    have none." [1] ·

In the same scene [2] is this more familiar speech,

" Now am I, if a man should speak truly, little better than one of
    the wicked."

Later in the play [3] comes his well-known utterance,

" Thou knowest in the state of innocency Adam fell; and what
    should poor Jack Falstaff do in the days of villany ? "

And in the wonderful tale of his death [4] the Hostess
says,

" He was rheumatic, and talked of the whore of Babylon; "

to which the Boy adds that

" a' saw a flea stick upon Bardolph's nose, and a' said it was a
    black soul burning in hell-fire."

Shakspere's Falstaff, in short, talks a great deal of
Puritan cant.

From these facts, and from the well-known tendency of artistic folk to satirize lax or erratic godli-
ness, there is reason to infer that the traditional
Oldcastle of the stage, and so the original conception
of Falstaff, was such a satire on Puritanism as one
finds in Middleton's *Chaste Maid in Cheapside*, in
Ben Jonson's *Bartholomew Fair*, in *Hudibras*, or in
the Reverend Mr. Stiggins of the *Pickwick Papers*.

Clearly, however, the Falstaff of *Henry IV.* is no
such personage as this. How the change came, we
can never quite know; but whoever is familiar with

---

[1] 1 *H. IV.* I. ii. 18.   [2] Line 105.
[3] III. iii. 185.   [4] *Henry V.* II. iii. 40–43.

the way in which good fiction grows, can make a
pretty sure guess. In a little play lately written for
private acting there was a character so consistent as
to excite the admiration of the actor who played it.
A certain subtle slowness of mind underlay every
speech ; and at last, when the personage grew warm
with wine, his drunkenness was of a kind which involved this mental habit. The actor thereupon com-
plimented the author on his skilful psychology ; when
presently it appeared that the author had not even
been aware that his personage got drunk at all —
he had only felt sure that of course when the fellow
in question spoke he must perforce speak the words
written down. This whole process of remarkably
consistent creation, in short, had been completely unconscious. The case is typical. Imagine it to be as
true of Falstaff as it is of the smaller creatures whose
growth we may still watch in detail. Intended for a
burlesque Puritan, the fat knight begins to speak and
move of his own accord. By an inevitable process of
spontaneous growth, he gathers about himself a new,
fictitious world, more real if anything than the historical world amid which it is placed. As must constantly
be the case, in short, with the work of artists whose
creative imagination is fully alive, the conception out-
grows its origin ; it develops not into a conventional
type, but into an individual character of unique vitality.
Long before Falstaff was himself, Oldcastle and Puritanism must have been forgotten ; until, at last, with
complete truth as well as manners, Shakspere could

write that " Oldcastle died a martyr, and this is not the man." [1]

Whatever his process of growth, Falstaff is certainly among the most human figures in English literature. What is more, the world surrounding him, and particularly the Eastcheap tavern, are more like actual every-day life than almost anything else in Shakspere. What Shakspere generally expresses is profound knowledge of human nature; here we have also a vivid picture of Elizabethan manners. In this aspect, the Falstaff scenes of *Henry IV.* have an added interest, historical and biographical alike. As has been said before, there was no Bohemia in Shakspere's England : whoever was not regular in life had to be hand and glove with thieves and cut-throats ; and, to go no further, the known history of Greene and of Marlowe is enough to prove that the environment so vividly set forth in the tavern scenes of *Henry IV.* is that from which proceeded the early masterpieces of the Elizabethan drama. In Shakspere's own life, too, we have seen that *Henry IV.* marks the moment of emergence from Bohemian obscurity into permanent personal respectability. The inference is fair, then, that this great spontaneous picture of the cradle of our stage marks the time when Shakspere himself had grown beyond it, yet was still near enough to realize all its features. Only at such moments, perhaps, are complete conceptions of actual experience possible. [2]

Falstaff and his world, however, by no means ex-

---

[1] 2 *H. IV.* Epilogue.   [2] See p. 43.

haust the creative energy of *Henry IV.* In another way, the same trait so pervades all the historical passages that, to a degree rare anywhere, we can constantly feel the great movement of historical forces. For one thing, mark how this play and *Richard II* are bound together by the lines: —

> "Northumberland, thou ladder by the which
> My cousin Bolingbroke ascends my throne."[1]

The example typifies how all the evil which broke loose in Richard's time is in the air. Men here are in the hands of fate, working itself out on a scale far beyond any human lifetime. In private affairs, too, as well as in public, one feels forces beyond human control; a student of heredity, for example, might note with approval how clearly the sons of Bolingbroke display, each in his own way, the lax sense of honor which marked the youth of their father. It is the Bolingbroke blood which makes Prince John of Lancaster equivocally entrap his enemies,[2] and which makes the Prince of Wales, for all his ultimate heroism, so cruelly untrue to his boon companions.[3] *Henry IV.*, in short, can properly give rise to endlessly grave, and perhaps pregnant, philosophizing.

So may actual life. What conclusions may be drawn concerning the ultimate meaning of actual life may hardly be discussed here. One thing, however, is certain. The nearer any great work of art approaches

---

[1] *R. II.* V. i. 55 ; 2 *Hen. IV.* III. i. 70.
[2] 2 *H. IV*, IV. ii.   [3] 1 *H. IV.* I. ii. 219 seq.

not the details, but the proportions of actual life, the nearer the imagination of its maker approaches in its scheme the divine imagination which has made our infinitely mysterious world, the more end-lessly suggestive that work of art must always be. To the artist, however, all this meaning is often as strange as to one who meets for the first time the work in which it lies implied. What the artist knows is often no more than a blind conviction that thus, and not otherwise, the mood which possesses him must be expressed. Those who find in the great artists consciously dogmatic philosophers are gener-ally those who are least artists themselves.

In *Henry IV.* we have sought out traits which, more than probably, Shakspere himself never realized. What he must surely have realized need have been no more than this: Setting to work at a stage-play, of the old chronicle-history school, he found his power of creative imagination so spontaneously alert that by the mere process of letting his characters do and say what they inevitably would, he made the most successful chronicle-history which had as yet appeared on the English stage. That he had done more, — that he had changed chronicle-history into historical fiction, and that he had created characters which should become the household words of the world, — he need never have guessed. A cool study of the play as it stands makes this opinion the most probable. The Second Part seems more hasty than the first; it was very likely hastily made to meet a popular demand which the First had excited. Nowadays, too, as we have seen, both parts so abound with the obsolete conventions of chronicle-history that they would surely act ill. As stage-plays, then, — and for stage-plays Shakspere surely meant them, — they are things of the past. So constantly vital is the imagination which pervades them, however, that as readers we of later days never think of the dead conventions at all. We accept them for just what they are, — only means of expression; by their means we come face to face with the imaginative conceptions of a master's mind. In our sense of the ultimate human plausibility of these conceptions, the fruit of a union between creative imagination and a solid basis of historical fact, we properly lose all sense of the means by which this end is wrought.

X. THE MERRY WIVES OF WINDSOR.

[The *Merry Wives of Windsor* was entered in the Stationers' Register on January 18th, 1602. It was published, in a very imperfect quarto, during the same year. The relation of this quarto to the final version of the play has been much discussed; probably, though it professes to be a work of Shakspere as it was performed " before her Majestie," it is pirated and incomplete. There was another quarto in 1619. The tradition that the play was written in a fortnight at the express command of the Queen, who desired to see Falstaff in love, cannot be traced beyond 1702. Nor can the comparative chronology of this play and *Henry V.* be definitely settled. Mr. Fleay believes the *Merry Wives* to be a revision of an old play called the *Jealous Comedy*.

The plot appears to be based on certain novels translated from the Italian, to be found in Hazlitt's *Shakespeare's Library*.

A conjectural date, commonly accepted, is 1598 or 1599.]

Whatever the origin of the *Merry Wives of Windsor*, and whatever the history of its final text, the play is clearly related to both *Henry IV.* and *Henry V.* On the titlepage of the quarto this fact appears at a glance : —

"A Most pleasaunt and excellent conceited Comedie, of Syr *John Falstaffe*, and the merrie Wives of *Windsor*. Entermixed with sundrie variable and pleasing humors, of . . Justice *Shallow*, . . With the swaggering vaine of Auncient *Pistoll*, and Corporall *Nym*."

Falstaff, of course, appears in both parts of *Henry IV.* ; Shallow and Pistol in the Second Part; Pistol again, and Nym, in *Henry V.* The conclusion that the *Merry Wives* must therefore be subsequent to *Henry V.*, however, is not necessary ; for as *Henry V.* was certainly published in 1600, two years before the quarto of the *Merry Wives*, the mention of Nym on this titlepage may merely be a reference to the general popularity of the character. Which version of Nym was first written, nobody can tell. The one thing of which we may feel sure is that all these characters were popular.

Accordingly there has now and again been effort seriously to identify the personages in the *Merry Wives of Windsor* with those who bear the same names in the chronicle-histories. This effort has met with small success. While Falstaff, and Bardolph, and the Hostess, and Pistol, and the rest remain the same people in scene after scene of *Henry IV.* and *Henry V.*, they seem somehow different in the *Merry Wives*. The truth is probably that, as they appear in this jolly comedy, they are identical with their other selves only in a very general way, which freshly emphasizes the archaism of Shakspere's theatre. Nowadays, when Thackeray, or Balzac, or Anthony Trollope introduces in one book a character which has appeared in another, we expect to find the various aspects of the character consistent; each imaginary individual is assumed to have the same sort of identity which real people have. In literature of an older kind, on the other hand, there are what we may call generic personages: the Harlequin and the Pantaloon of pantomime, for example; the Sganarelle of Molière; the Lisette and Frontin of Eighteenth Century comedy; the Vice of the old English Moralities. Wherever these personages appear, their make-up is the same, and so are their general traits. Over and over again, however, they appear, under incompatible circumstances; and all one ever expects is that in any given play, or what else, the personage shall be for the moment consistent. It is in this old, conventional way, rather than in the modern, literal sense, that the personages of the *Merry Wives of Windsor* are identical with those of the chronicle-histories. Their identity is one of type, of aspect, of name, not of history; it is an identity which belongs to a far earlier period of serious literature than our own. Nowadays one finds such types chiefly in the detectives and the desperadoes of penny dreadfuls.

This generic quality of the characters in the *Merry*

12

Wives of Windsor is somewhat obscured by their decided individuality, by the vigorous humor of their conception, and by the thoroughly English quality of their environment. To take a single example, the school-boy who makes a mess of his Latin grammar[1] is a perennially funny sketch of adolescent English-speaking flightiness : whoever has had pupils must always relish it. The way in which the oddities of foreign speech are burlesqued, too, in Sir Hugh Evans and Doctor Caius,[2] makes the other personages seem the more English by contrast. This solitary comedy in which Shakspere lays his scene in England, seems as thoroughly national as any of the chronicle-histories. True to English life in so many details, then, and with characters as vital and as jolly in conception — for all their extravagance — as anything we have met in comedy, the *Merry Wives* always seems peculiarly English.

Very clearly, however, when we stop to consider the swift, intricate, amusing plot, we find there several traits which are not English at all. In the first place, the general scheme of the plot is conventionally Italian, and the underlying assumption — that an attempt at seduction is capital fun — is far more congenial to Continental than to plain English ways of thought. In the second place, the whole action tends toward the masque of the fairies in the fifth act, itself at once a revival of the device which had already proved effective in *Love's Labour's Lost* and in the *Midsummer*

---

[1] IV. i.   [2] E.g. III. i.

Night's Dream, an admirable little type of what the Elizabethan masque was, and a dramatic convention as remote from real English life as is the ballet of the modern stage. The *Merry Wives of Windsor*, in short, is not really English at all; it is rather a vigorous translation into English terms of an essentially foreign conception, accomplished with a skill rivalled only in *Box and Cox*, — perhaps the one modern adaptation from the French which does not betray its foreign origin.

As a broadly humorous presentation of conventionalized characters, conducting themselves — for all the English flavor of their environment — in a manner substantially agreeable rather to Continental than to English ideas, the *Merry Wives of Windsor* seems a far less serious work than either *Henry IV.* or the riper comedies and tragedy which have preceded. It may be taken, to be sure, a little more seriously than we have as yet taken it. For one thing, in spite of considerable disguise and confusion of identity, the stock devices of the older comedy, the fun here turns chiefly on an equally lasting and far more human device, — on the self-deception of the fatuous Falstaff, and of the jealous Ford. Self-deception, as funny a thing as mistaken identity, has its roots not in the accidents but in the essential weakness of human nature ; we shall find it later the chief comic motive of Shakspere, and later still a tragic one, too. In the second place, the main situation of the plot here — the effort of a man of rank to seduce the wives of plain citizens — was used by other Elizabethan dramatists; but almost always to the discredit of the citizens. Middleton's *Chaste Maid in Cheapside* will serve to illustrate the regular treatment of the situation. In the *Merry Wives of Windsor*, as distinctly as in the *Marriage of Figaro*, the gentleman gets the worst of it. One can hardly believe, however, that this jolly, off-hand play is fundamentally, like that of Beaumarchais, a serious satire.

The most reasonable view of the *Merry Wives of Windsor*, perhaps, is that which groups it with the *Taming of the Shrew*. In substance not artistically serious, not instinct — like the *Midsummer Night's Dream* or the *Merchant of Venice* — with definite artistic motive, it differs from the earliest comedies by being in treatment not experimental but masterly. The man who wrote it thoroughly knew his trade. To all appearances, it belongs, in Shakspere's work, to the period when, by an unparalleled feat of creative imagination, he developed the old chronicle-history into permanently plausible historical fiction. If we regard it as the comparatively thoughtless side-work of a moment when his full energy was busy elsewhere, we shall understand it best.

XI. Henry V.

[*Henry V.*, together with three other plays, was entered in the Stationers' Register on August 4th, 1600, with a note that all four were "to be staied." Quite what this note means nobody has settled. *Henry V.* appeared in a very imperfect form in 1600. There were other imperfect quartos in 1602 and 1608. The full text, as we have it, first appeared in the folio of 1623.

The sources of the play are identical with those of *Henry IV.*

From the fact that Meres, who mentioned *Henry IV.* in 1598, did not mention *Henry V.*, it has been inferred that *Henry V.* is subsequent to 1598. As it was published in 1600, a reasonable date for it seems 1599. This is confirmed by lines 29–34 of the Prologue to Act V., which apparently refer to the expedition of Essex to Ireland, — 15 April–28 September, 1599.]

Identical in origin with *Henry IV.*, and so far as the actually historical scenes go with *Richard II.*, too, *Henry V.* differs from both. It certainly lacks the poetic completeness of *Richard II.*, and just as certainly the inevitable plausibility of *Henry IV.* This may be partly due to the accident that this play deals particularly with the battle of Agincourt, which in Elizabeth's time preserved such pre-eminence of patriotic tradition as in the last century surrounded the name of Blenheim, and in our own time still surrounds the names of Trafalgar and of Waterloo.[1] Whoever should deal with Agincourt in 1599 could not help trying to produce a patriotic effect.

A mere effort to produce a patriotic effect, dramatically conceived, however, would not necessarily have resulted in just such an effect as that of *Henry V.* Somehow, whether one see the play or read it, one is conscious of a strongly hortatory vein throughout. To infer from this that the writer was a deliberate and

[1] See particularly Drayton's ballad : —

" Fair stood the wind for France," etc.

This was the model for Tennyson's " Charge of the Six Hundred."

sincere preacher is not necessary; one can hardly avoid the inference, however, that, as an artist, the writer of *Henry V.* had chiefly in mind some other purpose than a purely dramatic. From beginning to end he seems trying not merely to translate historical material into effective dramatic terms, but also to present that material in such a manner that his audience shall leave the theatre more enthusiastically English than they entered it. As a man he need not therefore have been particularly patriotic; as an artist he seems certainly to have been sensitive to the hortatory nature of his subject.

In that case, we may see at once why the effect of *Henry V.* is often less satisfactory than that of the earlier chronicle-histories. Hortatory purpose is as legitimate for an artist as any other. The most fitting vehicle for such a purpose, however, is certainly the vehicle which involves the least possible suggestion of artificiality or insincerity. Sermons in prose, passionate lyrics in verse, are the normal forms of hortatory literature. The stage, on the other hand, can never free itself from an aspect of artificiality. When you see a play, however much it move you, there is no avoiding knowledge that the actors are pretending to be somebody else than themselves. All this, though perfectly legitimate in their art, is fatal to any lasting personal faith in their hortatory utterances. If the stage be a teacher, it may teach only by parable.

An indication that the trouble with *Henry V.* lies

in this incompatibility of artistic purpose and artistic vehicle may be found in the Chorus:[1] —

> " Pardon, gentles all,
> The flat unraised spirits that have dared
> On this unworthy scaffold to bring forth
> So great an object : can this cockpit hold
> The vasty fields of France ? or may we cram
> Within this wooden O the very casques
> That did affright the air at Agincourt?
> O, pardon ! since a crooked figure may
> Attest in little place a million ;
> And let us, ciphers to this great accompt,
> On your imaginary forces work."

Such lines as these, which fairly typify the senti-ment of all six utterances of the Chorus, really show as acute a sense of the material limitations surrounding an Elizabethan play as is shown by Ben Jonson's well-known prologue to *Every Man in His Humour*.[2] In this Jonson declares that as a dramatic writer he disdains to

> " purchase your delight at such a rate
> As, for it, he himself must justly hate :
> To make a child, now swadled, to proceede
> Man, and then shoote up, in one beard, and weede,
> Past threescore years : or with three rustie swords,
> And helpe of some few foot-and-halfe-foote words,
> Fight over *Yorke*, and *Lancaster's* long jarres :
> And in the tyring-house bring wounds, to scarres.

---

[1] Prologue to Act I. 8 seq.

[2] This play was acted in 1598. The earliest publication of the pro-logue, however, was in 1616. Cf. p. 14.

He rather prayes, you will be pleas'd to see
One such, today as other playes should be;
When neither *Chorus* wafts you ore the seas;
Nor creaking throne comes downe, the boys to please."

The difference between these two comments on
stage-conditions — comments which if the prologue
to *Every Man in His Humour* be as old as the play
are almost exactly contemporary — lies in the fact
that while Jonson condemns the limitations of his
theatre, Shakspere laments them. Generally, with
purely dramatic purpose, Shakspere appears frankly to
accept the conditions under which he must work. In
Henry V., he professes throughout that they bother
him. So far as it goes, this very fact tends to show
that his artistic purpose was not merely dramatic.

The general impression made by the play confirms
this opinion. From beginning to end, Henry himself
is always kept heroically in view; he is presented in
the exasperating way which makes so ineffectual the
efforts of moralizing scribblers, dear to Sunday-school
librarians. Of course he is not such an emasculate,
repulsive ideal as you find in the group headed by Mr.
Barlow, and by Jonas, the hired man of the Hollidays.
Changing what terms must be changed, however, he is
not so foreign to them as he seems; he is rather a moral
hero than a dramatic. For all his humanity, you feel
him rather an ideal than a man; and an ideal, in virtues
and vices alike, rather British than human. He has
sown conventional wild oats; he has reformed; he is
bluff, simple-hearted, not keenly intellectual, coura-

geous, above all a man more of action than of words.
The Shakspere who propounds such an ideal, then,
is limited more profoundly than by mere stage conditions ; throughout his conception he reveals the
peculiar limitation of sympathy which still marks a
typical Englishman.   In the honestly canting moods
which we of America inherit with our British blood
we gravely admire *Henry V.* because we feel sure
that we ought to.   In more normally human moods,
most of us would be forced to confess that, at least
as a play, *Henry V.* is tiresome.

If it be a dull play, however, it is just as surely the
dull play of a great artist; it is full of excellent detail.
In the distinctly historical parts, the excellent detail
is chiefly rhetorical; as such, it is almost beyond
praise.   The eloquence of Henry's great speeches [1]
everybody recognizes.   Perhaps an even more notable
example of Shakspere's now consummate mastery of
style may be found in the Archbishop of Canterbury's
exposition of the Salic law.[2]   The passage — one of
the kind which sometimes makes superficial readers
marvel at the learning of Shakspere — actually states
the law in question, along with many historical details,
about as compactly as any lawyer could have stated it
under Queen Elizabeth.   Besides this, the passage is an
admirable example of that very difficult kind of sonorous declamation which depends for its effect on the

---

[1] I. ii. 259 seq. ; II. ii. 79 seq.; III. i. ; IV. i. 247 seq., 306 seq. ;
IV. iii. 20 seq. ; etc.

[2] I. ii. 33 seq.

skilful use of proper names. A glance at Holinshed [1] will show where all the learning came from, and all the proper names. Compare, for example, these two versions of the historical statement made in lines 69–71. Holinshed writes : —

"Hugh Capet, who usurped the crowne upon Charles duke of Loraine, the sole heir male of the line and stock of Charles the great ; "

and here is Shakspere's rendering of the words : —

> "Hugh Capet also, who usurp'd the crown
> Of Charles the duke of Lorraine, sole heir male
> Of the true line and stock of Charles the Great."

The art by which a dull legal statement is converted into a piece of vigorously sounding rhetoric is all that Shakspere has added. The changes of phrase are incredibly slight, incalculably effective. They mark as clearly as any single passage in Shakspere the moment when his command of style was perhaps most easily masterly ; for they translate the original prose into a blank verse which is free alike from the monotony and the excessive ingenuity of his earlier days, and from the condensation, the lax freedom, and the overwhelming thought of his later.

The excellence of detail in the comic scenes of *Henry V.* is perhaps more notable still. While in substance all the comic characters are what an Elizabethan would have called " humourous," and what we

---

[1] The passage in question is conveniently accessible in Rolfe's edition of *Henry V.*

should now call "eccentric comedy," they are almost all human, too. Comic dialect, to be sure, already proved effective in the *Merry Wives of Windsor*, is repeated in the speeches of Jamy, Macmorris, and Fluellen;[1] repeated, too, is the broad burlesque on the excesses of Elizabethan ranting which pervades the speech of Pistol everywhere. For all this conventional humor, however, one grows to feel of the comic characters in *Henry V.*, as of all the characters in *Henry IV.*, that these are real people.

Perhaps the most subtly artistic touches of all are the repeated ones, each in itself slight, by which the crew of Falstaff are completely removed from any relation with the King himself. To appreciate this we must revert for a moment to *Henry IV.* Commonly one thinks of Falstaff, Prince Hal, and the rowdies of the Eastcheap Tavern, as a constantly intermingled company. A little scrutiny shows that the Prince is actually familiar with only two, — Poins and Falstaff himself. Gadshill, the regular highwayman, appears only in the First Part of *Henry IV.;* Poins disappears with the second scene of the Second Part, — the scene in which we first see Pistol; Pistol and the Prince never meet at all in *Henry IV.;* and Bardolph is throughout a person of lower rank, Falstaff's attendant. The only character with whom a violent break is necessary proves to be Falstaff. However he may morally deserve his fate, one cannot help feeling that the King cruelly kills his heart. Clearly, then,

[1] See III. ii. 79 seq.

to have introduced Falstaff in a play whose artistic object is the apotheosis of Henry would have been a blunder; and to have put his death on the stage, however agreeable to the theatrical custom of the time, could not have been less than shocking. To tell the story of his last hours as Shakspere has told it is to do a thing which no writer ever surpassed. If one were asked to name a single scene where Shakspere shows himself supreme, one would often be disposed to name the third scene of the second act of *Henry V.* Falstaff once removed, the fate of the others comes with no disturbing sense of the King's breach of friendship. How Shakspere managed it, a single example will suggest. In Holinshed we are told that

" a souldiour tooke a pix out of a church, for which he was apprehended, & the king not once remooved till the box was restored, and the offendor strangled."

This incident Shakspere has developed into our last glimpse of Bardolph, involving the quarrel between Pistol and Fluellen,[1] on which turns so much of the comic action towards the end of *Henry V.* And so, by touch after touch, none of which we feel at the moment, the King at last is left alone in his glory.

In the wonderful third scene of the second act there is a famous phrase which illustrates the condition in which Shakspere's text has come down to us.[2]

" For after I saw him fumble with the sheets," says the Hostess, " and play with flowers and smile upon his fingers' ends, I knew there was but one way; for his nose was as sharp as a pen, and a' babbled of green fields."

[1] III. vi. 21–62.   [2] Lines 14–18

In the folio this last phrase appears in a form which for above a century was unintelligible, — " a Table of green fields." Theobald suggested " a' babbled " instead of " a Table." The suggestion was in such harmony with the spirit of the scene that it has been unanimously accepted. Whether Shakspere actually wrote it, however, no one can ever be sure.

What one can be sure of, on the other hand, is that Shakspere never saw a published copy of *Henry V.* which compared either in fulness or in accuracy with the folio of 1623. Such serious discussion of his art and his purposes as we have just emerged from is apt to mislead. To think of Shakspere's plays except as literature is a bit hard ; yet nothing is more certain than that even so serious a work as *Henry V.* could never have appeared to him as anything but a play made for the actual stage. In our study of his artistic development, then, we must finally regard it as a stage play.

Thus it takes its place as chronologically the last of the chronicle-histories, and in the whole scheme of chronicle-history as the link between the series which begins with *Richard II.* and that which ends with *Richard III.* In some details of style superior to any of the others — for nowhere is Shakspere's declamatory verse more simply, fluently sonorous ; and nowhere are his comic scenes more skilfully touched, or much better phrased in terms both of speech and of action — it somehow lacks both the completeness of *Richard II.* and the pervasive plausibility of *Henry*

IV. In other words, while *Henry IV.* showed a development of chronicle-history analogous to that of comedy in the *Midsummer Night's Dream*, or that of tragedy in *Romeo and Juliet*, *Henry V.* shows rather a stagnation than an advance of creative energy. Compared with the plays we have lately considered it lacks spontaneity, it grows conscious. If it stood by itself, we might almost infer that the artistic impulse which has underlain Shakspere's work ever since the *Midsummer Night's Dream* was beginning to flag. To correct this inference we must look at other work attributed to the same time. As more than once before, a comparative weakness in one kind of writing will prove to indicate no more than that Shakspere's best energies were devoted to another.

XII. Much Ado About Nothing.

[*Much Ado About Nothing* was another of the plays entered " to be staied " in the Stationers' Register, on August 4th, 1600. It was again entered, unconditionally, on August 23rd, 1600 ; and was published in a very complete quarto during the same year.

The sources of the serious plot — the loves of Hero and Claudio — are to be found in Ariosto and in Bandello. In the Fourth Canto of the Second Book of the *Faerie Queene*, Spenser tells the story sentimentally. The comic parts of the play, including Benedick, Beatrice, and Dogberry, appear to be of Shakspere's invention.

As the play was not mentioned by Meres in 1598, and existed in 1600, it may, with some confidence, be assigned to 1599. Mr. Fleay, however, eagerly believes it to be a revision of the *Love's Labour's Won*, mentioned by Meres. This view is not generally accepted.]

In the sense that it is a permanently significant work of art, whose maker seems thoroughly to have known both what he wished to do and how to do it, *Much Ado About Nothing* is a masterpiece. Its total effect is as plausible as that of *Henry IV.*; forgetting the means by which characters and incidents are presented, one instinctively thinks of them as real. The plot has definite unity; the characters, all of first-rate individuality, live in a world which seems actual, and constantly express themselves in a style unsurpassed for firmness and decision. All this technical power, too, is used here for a more definite artistic purpose than has generally been perceptible in the earlier work of Shakspere; the mood which underlies *Much Ado About Nothing*, we shall see by and by to be more profound than the moods we have met hitherto. Finally, whether you see the play or read it, you can hardly avoid feeling that it has the inevitable ease of mastery.

Off-hand, such ease and completeness in any work of art seem inborn. Nothing is further from one's instinctive impression than the real truth, that they can be attained only by years of preliminary practice. We have already followed Shakspere's career long enough, however, to assure ourselves that *Much Ado About Nothing* was produced, at least in its final form, only after above ten years of patient stage-craft. During these years he had thoroughly learned two things: first, how to translate into effective dramatic terms the crude material which he found in his narrative sources; and secondly, how to repeat, with just enough variation to make the repetition welcome, characters, scenes, situations, what not, which in previous plays had proved dramatically effective. In *Much Ado About Nothing* he shows both of these traits: the story of Hero and Claudio, which is really the core of the play, he presents far more vividly than anybody else; and by way of contrast and amplification he adds to it, from his own previous stage-work, the story and the characters of Benedick, Beatrice, and Dogberry. The greater vitality of these has perhaps resulted, after all, in a distortion of the effect he first intended, analogous to the possible distortion of *Romeo and Juliet* from the tale of feud promised in the prologue to the tragedy of youthful love known to us all. In each play, your attention ultimately concentrates elsewhere than at first seemed probable. Each alike, however, is masterly, just as each is notable for the firmness with which it sets forth the parts of itself which are peculiarly Shakspere's. In this case, as we have seen, the parts in question include the characters of Benedick, Beatrice, and Dogberry. Under the names of Biron, Rosaline, and Dull, Shakspere had already sketched these in *Love's Labour's Lost*. There have been glimpses of them meanwhile, too; but this fact is enough. If our chronology be anywhere near right, the interval between the first conception of these characters and their final presentation in *Much Ado About Nothing* was something like ten years.

Of course we must remember that *Love's Labour's*

Lost, as we have it, is not the original play of 1589 or
so, but a revision of it for performance at court in
1597.   Whatever alteration of phrase and finish may
then have been made, however, we felt that we might
fairly assume the main outline and the chief traits
of style in *Love's Labour's Lost* to belong to the
beginning of Shakspere's career.   A comparison of
Biron and Rosaline with Benedick and Beatrice will
strengthen that conclusion.   The former pair seem set
forth with no deeper consciousness of their value than
would come from a sense of the undoubted effect their
clever tit for tat must make on an audience.   Benedick and Beatrice, on the other hand, are not independent stage characters ; for all their wit and sparkle,
they have their places in a great, coherent comedy
which, in its entirety, expresses a definite view of
human nature.

In this view of human nature there are two ele-
ments.   The artist who conceived such a work as
Much Ado About Nothing must in the first place have
been keenly sensitive to the inexhaustible power of
deceiving themselves possessed by human beings.
Benedick, Beatrice, Claudio, Dogberry alike are beguiled by intrinsic weaknesses of nature into states of
mind and lines of conduct whose admirable dramatic
effect depends on their incompatibility with obvious
facts in possession of omniscience and the audience.   This fundamental understanding of a human
weakness, however, is not the whole story.   With the
help of a little deliberate rascality, the weakness in

13

question beguiles the wisest and the wittiest of people into a situation which no unaided acts of theirs could prevent from resulting tragically. What does prevent this result is that, by mere chance, the dullest, stupidest creatures imaginable happen to stumble on the real facts. In thus presenting the keenest wit as saved from destruction only by the blundering of boors, Shakspere displays a sense of irony lastingly true to human experience.

Self-deception, the first of these traits, we met in the *Merry Wives of Windsor*. By itself it would distinguish these two comedies from the earlier ones, whose fun is based on the far less plausible and not deeply significant, though perennially amusing, device of mistaken identity. The older comedies are chiefly theatrical ; these become human. When to self-deception is added the sense of irony which pervades *Much Ado About Nothing* we are face to face with another kind of literature than the old. The old was inspired chiefly by observation of the whims of audiences, and by skilful observance of literary and theatrical tradition ; this, for all its technical skill, seems inspired rather by knowledge of human nature.

Technically, at the same time, *Much Ado About Nothing* displays the traits to which we are already accustomed. The vitality of creative imagination which enlivened and even veiled the absurdities of the *Midsummer Night's Dream* and the *Merchant of Venice*, and which brought *Henry IV.* out of chronicle-history into historical fiction, pervades this more profound play.

The constant economy of needless invention, too, which is so marked a trait of Shakspere, appears in various ways. We have already touched on some of the obvious relations of this play to *Love's Labour's Lost* and on the fact that its motive of self-deception was the motive also of the *Merry Wives of Windsor*. Those who know Shakspere well must already have remarked that self-deception is the motive of much work still to come, — of the misadventures of Malvolio, for example, of the jealousy of Othello and of Leontes, of the infatuation of Lear. They must have noticed, too, that Don John comes midway between the Aaron of *Titus Andronicus* and Iago. Not quite so clearly, perhaps, they may have observed that the loss and recovery of Hero have much in common with the situation of Æmilia in the *Comedy of Errors* as well as with that of Juliet; while clearly all these are by and by to be revived in Thaisa and in Hermione. One might thus go on long.

It is better worth our while, however, to consider the trait in which *Much Ado About Nothing* is supreme, — the wit of the chief personages. Of course the humor of Dogberry and Verges, despite its breadth, is lastingly funny ; but certainly it is not unique. Elsewhere in Shakspere, and — to go no further — in Mrs. Malaprop, one finds plenty like it. The equally lasting wit of Benedick and Beatrice, on the other hand, is unsurpassed, and one may almost say unrivalled, in English Literature. For this amazing development of wit, a trait which at first thought seems perhaps the most spontaneous in all human expression, we have already seen causes. From the beginning of Elizabethan Literature whoever had written had been constantly playing on words and with them. Fantastically extravagant as such verbal quibbles generally were, they resulted in unsurpassed mastery of vocabulary. Combine such mastery of vocabulary with an instinctive sense that words are only the symbols of actual thoughts, and your quibbler or punster becomes a wit of the first quality. We have seen that such a sense of the identity of word and thought characterized Shakspere from the beginning. The lasting vitality of his wit, then, as well as of his wisdom, is perhaps traceable to the insatiable appetite for novelty of phrase which pervaded his public. As in his earlier work, so even in *Much Ado About Nothing* one may fairly doubt whether the man himself, accepting his temperament among the normal conditions of life, would generally have distinguished between his own efforts, which resulted in lasting literature, and those of his fellows, which resulted chiefly in ingenious collocations of words. Like the rest, he probably strove merely to put words together in a fresh way. As the years passed, however, he grew less and less able to conceive a word as distinct from a concept; by 1600, then, his peculiar trait had so developed that, by merely trying to make his phrases as fresh as possible, he might unwittingly have set forth the ultimate wit, and the profoundly human characters of Benedick and Beatrice.

For, witty as they are, Benedick and Beatrice are human too. One thinks of them generally together, as an inseparable pair, equally human, equally delightful. To attempt in any way to distinguish between them, then, is perhaps fantastic. On the whole, however, there are touches in the character of Beatrice which seem to mark her as the more sympathetically conceived. When Hero is accused, for example, her conduct is the very ideal of feminine intensity. Her first outbreak,[1] —

"Why, how now, cousin! wherefore sink you down?"

may best be read as an exclamation not of terror but of indignant remonstrance. Her "Kill Claudio!"[2] so much admired by Mr. Swinburne, is more in keeping with that conception. Although these speeches have no gleam of wit, they are better than witty; they express just such impulsive purity of nature as an ideal woman should possess. This heroic trait of Beatrice arouses Benedick to a line of action which in turn makes him heroic. Ultimately one grows to think of *Much Ado About Nothing* as grouping its whole story about the heroine Beatrice.

To guess that such vitality of conception was inspired by a living model is to start on an endless round of conjecture. One may safely say, however, that, even more than Juliet or Portia, Beatrice is a real, living figure. Coming after them, then, she reveals in Shakspere a growing sense of what a fascinat-

[1] IV. i. 111.   [2] IV. i. 291.

ing woman really is, or rather of how a fascinating woman presents herself to a worshipping man. Such a man, enthralled by the outward spell, of look, of action, of speech, instinctively surrounds it with imaginary graces of nature, which make his mistress for the moment divine. What Beatrice expresses is such an ideal of womanhood as this, — womanhood as seen by a man who feels all its charm, who is not yet practised enough to know its vices, who has not yet dreamed of the disenchantment and the satiety of possession.

Whatever the origin of Beatrice, we have fair ground for believing that in 1599 Shakspere was disposed to idealize character. This inclination showed itself in his heroic treatment of *Henry V*. In that play he failed to produce a satisfactory effect, partly because there his ideal was a bit didactic, and partly because, for all its vigor, the play did not seem so alive with creative imagination as those which had just preceded. *Much Ado About Nothing*, almost certainly of the same year, shows us why. In 1599 Shakspere's creative imagination, diverted once more, left chronicle-history where he found it; but turning afresh to comedy, carried comedy to its highest possible point.

XIII. As You Like It.

[*As You Like It* was entered, along with the two preceding plays, "to be staied" in the Stationers' Register, on August 4th, 1600. It was not printed till the folio of 1623.

Its source is a novel by Thomas Lodge, called *Rosalynde, Euphues Golden Legacie,* etc., published in 1590.

From the circumstances of its entry, together with internal evidence, such as the quotation of a line from Marlowe's *Hero and Leander*,[1] published in 1598, its date has generally been conjecturally placed in 1599 or 1600.]

As You Like It, beyond question among the most popular of Shakspere's plays, differs from *Much Ado About Nothing* rather in substance than in manner. Just as masterly, just as far from experimental, it is distinctly less significant. *Much Ado About Nothing*, as we have seen, expresses a mood which, at any period of history, must sometimes possess any thoughtful observer of actual life; *As You Like It*, for all its delicate, half-melancholy sentiment, is in substance purely fantastic.

Its completely fantastic character, to be sure, is somewhat concealed by the art with which the play is composed. Like the *Midsummer Night's Dream* and the *Merchant of Venice*, it begins with the device — very probably suggested by the conventional old inductions — of presenting a scene and a state of things

[1] III. v. 83: and see p. 60.

about mid-way between real life and the impossible fantasies into which it must lead us. In this case the device has proved so generally successful that no comment on *As You Like It* is more frequent than ardent admiration for the open-air quality of the forest-scenes.

To declare so general an opinion mistaken would be stupid ; whoever fails to share it might better lament his own lack of perception. Unquestionably, however, there are moods in which the rhapsodic delight conventionally felt in the forest breezes of Arden sets one to doubting whether those who feel it have ever been much nearer nature than the foot-lights. In such moods, Arden seems as fantastically artificial as the background of any pseudo-classic eclogue or operatic ballet; and wonderful chiefly because everybody does not instantly perceive its trees and stones and running brooks to be paint and pasteboard. What Shakspere has really done in *As You Like It* is to adapt for the stage a kind of story essentially different either from the statements of fact which gave him material for his chronicle-histories, or from the rather bald plots of old Italian novels which generally provided his material for comedy or tragedy. Lodge's *Rosalynde* is a commonplace example of the more elaborate novel of early Elizabethan Literature, the kind of fiction represented in prose by Sidney's *Arcadia* and Lyly's *Euphues*, and in poetry by the aimlessly bewildering plot of the *Faerie Queene*. Such fiction still delights imaginative children ; but to grown folks of our day, who become critical, it generally seems tediously trivial. From this original come the fantastic plot of *As You Like It*, the general atmosphere, and the great tendency to incidental moralizing. Beautifully phrased, this moralizing, even in *As You Like It*, is really almost as commonplace as that of *Euphues* itself. The Duke, and Jaques, and Touchstone alike spout line after line of such graceful platitude as Elizabethans loved, and people of our time generally find tiresome. After all, there is a case for who should say that the open air and the wisdom of *As You Like It* differ less than their admirers would admit from the same traits in the novel of Lodge, where they are palpably make-believe.

This is not to say that *As You Like It* remains no better than the lifeless old story from which it is taken. The fact that, while Lodge's Rosalynde is dead and gone these three centuries, Shakspere's Rosalind survives among the lasting figures of English Literature, would instantly prove the error of any such pert statement as that. What makes the difference, however, is not that Shakspere suddenly becomes a poet of Nature; it is rather the same trait which made the difference between *Romeo and Juliet* and the poem of Arthur Brooke, between the *Merchant of Venice* and the fantastic nursery stories on which it is based, between *Henry IV.* and the lifeless pages of Holinshed. By this time, Shakspere's creative imagination was so easily alert that he could hardly present a character in any play without making it seem human. In *As You Like It*, from beginning to end, and despite an amount of operatic convention which finally brings us unremonstrating to the little Masque of Hymen,[1] the people are real. They are people, too, of a specific romantic kind, who need to keep them alive not the actual breezes of any earthly forest, but an atmosphere where every breath of air feeds a gentle sentiment of romantic love, with melancholy and gayety alike close at hand. When people live for us as Rosalind lives, and Celia, and Orlando, and the Duke, and Jaques, and Touchstone, and Audrey, we accept them as facts; and with them we accept whatever else their existence involves. What makes *As You Like It* live, then, is the spontaneous ease with which Shakspere's creative imagination translated conventional types into living individuals.

There are plenty of traces, at the same time, of the conventional conditions from which and amid which these individuals emerged into the full vitality we recognize. After all, the very open-air atmosphere is only a fresh whiff of what had proved theatrically effective in *Love's Labour's Lost* and the *Midsummer Night's Dream*. The disguise of Rosalind is a fresh and far more elaborate use of the stage device which had proved popular in the *Two Gentlemen of Verona* and the *Merchant of Venice*. The clown, Touchstone, is a curiously individual development from a very old stage type. In the Moralities and the Interludes, the most popular character was the Vice,

---

[1] V. iv. 114 seq.

a personage in many respects analogous to the Clown of pantomime or of the modern circus. In Shakspere's comedies, from Dull, and the Dromios, and Launce, to Dogberry and Verges, there has been a steady line of conventional buffoons. Here, and later, these two conventions seem for a while to merge with the historical tradition of court-jesters — in Shakspere's time still actual facts — in a new convention, different enough from all its sources to seem, for centuries, a thing apart. Touchstone and his fellow-clowns, too, are really more conventional than even this view of them would at first suggest. They are not an essential part of the plays where they appear; without them everything might fall out as it falls. What they provide is only a comic chorus, whose essentially amusing character makes it probably the best theatrical vehicle for such incidental moralizing as is always relished by an English public.

Among the characters in *As You Like It*, if any one emerges from the group as notably sympathetic, it is certainly Rosalind ; if any two, certainly Rosalind and Celia. Perhaps this may be only because they were meant to be charming, and have generally proved so. If we consider, however, that in *Much Ado About Nothing* Beatrice seemed heroine more distinctly than Benedick seemed hero, and if we consider, too, that as far back as the *Merchant of Venice* Portia stood out more conspicuously ideal than anybody else, we have in this constant prominence of idealized women a suggestion that, when these comedies were making, Shakspere was sensitive to feminine fascination, and showed no traces of sensitiveness to the mischief which such fascination involves. To draw from this suggestion any inference as to the circumstances of his private life would certainly be unwarrantable. As a fact in his artistic development, however, as an evidence of the phases of human emotion to which for the moment he was most disposed, the suggestion is worth remembering. For the whole charm of *As You Like It* is based on a sentiment involved in this very prominence of bewitching women. No one could have made such a comedy who was not keenly alive to the delights of virginal, romantic love. Rosalind, in short, is the heroine of such delicately sentimental comedy as expresses the lighter phase of the mood whose tragedy is phrased in *Romeo and Juliet*. The charm of such impressions in real life lies in their half-apprehended evanescence.[1] These are not real women; they are such women as a romantic lover dreams his mistress to be. From all dreams men must wake. From such as these, the wakening is terribly painful. There are men, though, who feel that the memory of the dream is worth all the pain of the waking.

Such romantic sentiments as this, however, perhaps tend to mislead us in our study. *As You Like It* is no impassioned, reckless outburst of romantic enthusiasm. Such an outburst would have been foreign to Shakspere at any time. Over and over again, his work

[1] See p. 126.

expresses moods which none but a passionate nature
could feel. In his expression of such moods, however, he was always a cool, sane artist. All that we
have touched on is in *As You Like It*. To complete
our impression, though, we must remember that in
As You Like It, too, is the well-known expression of
a temper which underlies much of Shakspere's art at
this period : [1] —

> " All the world 's a stage,
> And all the men and women merely players:
> They have their exits and their entrances;
> And one man in his time plays many parts,
> His acts being seven ages," —

which need not be detailed.

XIV. TWELFTH NIGHT.

[In the diary of John Manningham, of the Middle Temple, Barrister-
at-Law, for February 2nd, 1602, occurs this passage : " At our feast
wee had a play called Twelve Night, or what you will, much like the
commedy of errores, or Menechmi in Plautus, but most like and neere
to that in Italian called *Inganni*. A good practise in it to make the
steward beleeve his lady widdowe was in love with him, by counter-
fayting a letter as from his lady, in generall termes, telling him what
shee liked best in him, and prescribing his gesture in smiling, his ap-
paraile, &c., and then when he came to practise making him beleeve
they tooke him to be mad."

The source of the main plot may have been some Italian comedies,
and very probably Barnaby Riche's *Apolonius and Silla*, published in

----

[1] II. vii. 139 seq.

1581. The episode of Malvolio, Sir Toby, etc., seems to be original with Shakspere.

As *Twelfth Night* was not mentioned by Meres, it is confidently assumed to belong somewhere between September, 1598, and February, 1602.]

To many of us nowadays, no play of Shakspere's is more constantly delightful than *Twelfth Night*. Whether you read it or see it, you find it thoroughly amusing; and you are hardly ever bothered by the lurking consciousness, so often fatal to the enjoyment of anything, that you really ought to take this matter more seriously. Rather, if you let yourself go, you feel comfortably assured that here, at any rate, is something which was made only to be wholesomely enjoyed. If you enjoy it, then, you have not only had a good time; you have the added, more subtle satisfaction of having done your duty.

To dwell on *Twelfth Night* in detail, then, would be unusually pleasant. For our purposes, however, which are merely to fix its place, if we can, in the artistic development of Shakspere, we need only glance at it; and in a study which perforce grows so long as this, it were unwise to dwell on anything longer than we need.

The one fact for us to observe, and to keep in mind, is the surprising contrast between the free, rollicking, graceful, poetic *Twelfth Night* which any theatre-goer and any reader of Shakspere knows almost by heart, and the *Twelfth Night* which reveals itself to whoever pursues such a course of study as ours. Taken by itself, the play seems not only admirably complete, but distinctly fresh and new, — spontaneous, vivid, full of fun, of romantic sentiment, and of human nature, and above all individually different from anything else. This Illyria, for example, is a world by itself, whither one might sail from the Messina of Benedick and Beatrice, or perhaps travel from the Verona of Romeo and Juliet, to find it different from these, much as regions in real life differ one from another. For all the romance and the fun of *Twelfth Night*, its plausibility is excellent; and so its individuality seems complete.

As everybody can feel, all this is lastingly true. What is also lastingly true, yet can be appreciated only by those of us who have begun to study Shakspere chronologically, is that, to a degree hitherto unapproached, what is distinct and new in *Twelfth Night* is only the way in which the play is put together. From beginning to end, as we scrutinize it, we find it a tissue of incidents, of characters, of situations which have been proved effective by previous stage experience. Confusion of identity, for example, almost as impossible as that of the *Comedy of Errors*, reappears in Sebastian and Viola. Viola herself, once more the boy-actor playing the heroine unhampered by skirts, revives Julia, and Portia, and Nerissa, and Jessica, and Rosalind — with them foreshadowing Imogen. Like Julia in the *Two Gentlemen of Verona*, Viola, disguised as a page, carries to her rival the messages of her own chosen lover.[1] The tale of shipwreck, again, revives the similar narrative in the *Comedy of*

---

[1] I. v. 178. Cf. *Two Gentlemen of Verona*, IV. iv. 113.

Errors; [1] the friendship of Antonio for Sebastian less certainly revives the analogous friendship of the other Antonio for Bassanio in the *Merchant of Venice*, while from the *Comedy of Errors*, once more, comes the business of the purse.[2] In Malvolio, as we have seen before,[3] self-deception appears as distinctly as ever; while, at least on the stage, the plot of Sir Toby, Sir Andrew, and Maria against Malvolio seems simply a reversal of the plots by which Benedick and Beatrice are united.[4] Sir Toby and Sir Andrew themselves are of the race of Falstaff and Slender, differing from these much as, in any art, idealized figures grow to differ from figures which are taken more directly from life. The Clown is similarly of the race of Touchstone. And so on; the more one looks for familiar things in new guise, the more one finds. What conceals them at first is only that *Twelfth Night* resembles *As You Like It* in being full of a romantic sentiment peculiarly its own, with a less palpable but still sufficient undercurrent of delicate melancholy. Throughout, too, the infusion of this new spirit into these old bodies is made with the quiet ease which we have begun to recognize as the mark of Shakspere's handiwork.

Together with *As You Like It*, then, we may call *Twelfth Night* light, joyous, fantastic, fleeting, — a thing to be enjoyed, to be loved, to be dreamed about;

[1] I. li. Cf. *Comedy of Errors*, I. i. 62 seq.

[2] III. iii. 38 seq.; iv. 368 seq. Cf. *Comedy of Errors*, IV. i. 100 seq.; ii. 29 seq.; iv. 1 seq.

[3] See p. 195.

[4] Cf. II. v. with *Much Ado About Nothing*, II. iii.; III. i.

but never, if one would understand, to be taken with philosophic seriousness. Plays in purpose, poems in fact, these two comedies alike are best appreciated by those who find in them only lasting expressions and sources of unthinking pleasure.

While *As You Like It*, however, differs from Shakspere's other work by translating into permanent dramatic form a dull novel of a kind not before found among the sources of his plays, *Twelfth Night*, far from being essentially different from his former plays, is perhaps the most completely characteristic we have yet considered. Again and again we have already remarked in Shakspere a trait which will appear throughout. For what reason we cannot say — indolence we might guess in one mood, prudence in another — he was exceptionally economical of invention, except in mere language. Scenes, characters, situations, devices which had once proved themselves effective he would constantly prefer to any bold experiment. This very economy of invention, perhaps, contained an element of strength; it left his full energy free for the masterly phrasing, and the spontaneous creation of character, which has made his work lasting. Strong or weak, however, the trait is clearly becoming almost as characteristic as the constant concreteness of his style; and nowhere does it appear more distinctly or to more advantage than when we recognize in *Twelfth Night* — with all its perennial delights — a masterpiece not of invention but of recapitulation.

14

XV. Shakspere from 1593 to 1600.

In the year 1600, we may remember, more works of Shakspere were published than in any other. This alone might have warranted us in considering 1600 as an epoch in his career. The fact that by 1600, however, all the plays considered in this chapter were probably finished gives us a better warrant still ; for clearly we have reached a point where we may conveniently pause to consider the growth and the change in his work since 1593.

To begin with, we may well remind ourselves of at least two inevitable uncertainties. Our chronology, in the first place, is at best conjectural ; in the second place, our texts are almost invariably some years later than the dates to which we have assigned them. In view of the incessant alteration made in dramatic works which hold the stage anywhere, it would be folly to assume the complete integrity of any text in the whole series of Shakspere's plays.

The latter consideration, to be sure, need trouble us less than at first seems probable. While it must surely be of weight in any system of verbal criticism, it does not so seriously affect a study concerned with broad effects. In considering any of the plays before us, however, we must beware of the temptation to assume rigidly that it was finished, just as we have it, at the time to which we conjecturally assign it.

All we can fairly assert in most cases is that on the whole we believe the work, in conception and in general motive, to belong to the period we name.

In the matter of actual chronology, we are more uncertain still. Except in one or two cases — the most definite of which is Henry V. — we are quite unable to specify anything like an indubitable date. What is more, an indubitable date in itself might be misleading. Any single year embraces twelve months; two works properly assigned to it, then, may often be nearer to works of contiguous years than to each other. All we may fairly assert of our chronology, then, is that to a number of critics the order in which we have considered the plays discussed in this chapter has seemed approximately probable; while, with more certainty than is usual in our study, we may feel sure that, in some order or other, and in a condition more or less approaching that in which we possess them, all the plays we have as yet considered existed by 1600.

In 1597 there were quartos of *Romeo and Juliet*, *Richard II.*, and *Richard III.* In 1598, Meres's list mentioned the *Two Gentlemen of Verona*, the *Comedy of Errors, Love's Labour's Lost*, the *Midsummer Night's Dream*, the *Merchant of Venice, Richard II., Richard III., Henry IV., King John, Titus Andronicus*, and *Romeo and Juliet ;* in 1598, too, there were quartos of *Love's Labour's Lost*, and the First Part of *Henry IV.* In 1600 came quartos of *Titus Andronicus*, the *Midsummer Night's Dream*, the *Merchant of Venice*, the

Second Part of *Henry IV.*, *Henry V.*, and *Much Ado About Nothing;* while *As You Like It* was entered in the Stationers' Register. There can be no reasonable doubt that *Henry VI.* is on the whole earlier than any other of the chronicle-histories, nor yet that the *Merry Wives of Windsor* belongs to the period of *Henry IV.* and *Henry V.* This leaves us in doubt only concerning the *Taming of the Shrew*, which is of little weight in our general consideration of Shakspere, and *Twelfth Night*, which was certainly in existence by February, 1602, and with equal certainty contains little which should alter an opinion based on the other plays before us.

Whatever our errors in chronological detail, then, our chronology now warrants the conclusions we may draw about the comparative traits of Shakspere in 1593 and in 1600.

In 1593, we remember, when Marlowe's work was finished, Shakspere, though had he accomplished nothing great, had displayed three marked characteristics, — a natural habit of thought, by means of which he found words and concepts more nearly identical than most men ever find them; restless versatility in trying his hand at every kind of contemporary writing; and finally a touch of originality, in enlivening the characters of romantic comedy by the results of every-day observation.[1] At the age of twenty-nine, after six years of professional life, this seemed the sum of his accomplishment.

[1] See pp. 65, 100–102.

During the seven years which followed, the years
which brought him from twenty-nine to thirty-six, and
in the last of which he had been professionally at work
for thirteen years, all these traits persisted and developed.   While, in view of the intense craving for
verbal novelty which remained so marked a trait of
his public, it would be unsafe to assert that he was
steadily changing his habit of thought from a consideration of mere phrases to one of the concepts for
which in his mind the most trivial phrase would normally stand, it is certain that his style, always pregnant, kept growing more so; and that by 1600 he
was perhaps more perfectly master of concept and
word alike than the growing intensity of his later
thought allowed him to remain.   As for his versatility, we need only remember that when this period
began tragedy remained in the condition of *Titus Andronicus*, comedy at best in that of the *Two Gentlemen of Verona*, chronicle-history in that of *Henry VI.*;
and that by 1600 he had surely produced, to go no
further, *Romeo and Juliet*, *Much Ado About Nothing*,
and *Henry IV*.   As for his observation of life, the first
clear trace of which we found in the *Two Gentlemen of
Verona*, it was the necessary foundation of his characteristic creative imagination, which revealed itself
perhaps most plainly in the development from Oldcastle of Falstaff.

This power of creating character — of making his
personages not only theatrically effective, but so human that posterity has discussed them as gravely

as if they had actually lived — is the most marked trait which appeared in Shakspere during the seven years we are now considering. In 1593 not one of the great Shaksperean characters is known to have existed; by 1600 he had surely created Romeo, and Juliet, and Mercutio, and Richard III., and Shylock, and Portia, and Falstaff, and Hotspur, and Prince Hal, and Benedick, and Beatrice, and Dogberry, and Rosalind, and Jaques, and Touchstone — one might go on for a page or two. A normal result, perhaps, of the traits which he had earlier shown, this creative power had now declared itself with a vigor which makes the result of his work, even had he never done more, sufficient to place him at the head of imaginative English Literature.

A little scrutiny, however, shows that, in spite of its scope and achievement, this power worked and developed very normally. Off-hand one is disposed to think of Shakspere as at any moment able, if he chose, to do anything. Unless our chronology be utterly wrong, however, it proves pretty clearly that when he was busy with one kind of writing he was by no means in condition to do equally well with another. Compare the *Midsummer Night's Dream* with *Richard III.*, for example; *Romeo and Juliet* with *Richard II.;* the *Merchant of Venice* with *King John; Henry IV.* with the *Taming of the Shrew* and the *Merry Wives of Windsor; Much Ado About Nothing* with *Henry V.* Roughly speaking, we may assume each of these groups to be contemporary. Pretty

clearly, for all his power, Shakspere was human
enough to slight one thing when he was giving his
best energies to something else. Along with the old
versatility of effort, then, we find a new trait, or perhaps rather a new development, which we may call
versatility of concentration.

Besides all this, we must emphasize the trait by
which, in the beginning of this chapter, we justified
the separation of the plays here discussed from those
discussed before.[1] Throughout these later plays, sometimes pervading them, sometimes apparent rather in
detail, we are constantly aware of the impulse which
we called artistic. In distinction from the Shakspere
of the old experimental work, the Shakspere who made
the plays now before us must have been so constantly,
spontaneously, profoundly aware of how what he was
dealing with made him feel that he would instinctively
try to express his feeling by every possible means.
In the *Midsummer Night's Dream*, where we considered this trait most carefully, it appeared at once first
and perhaps most purely. Ever since it has appeared
again and again, in constantly varying form.

At the risk of tedious repetition, it is prudent to
warn whoever has not carefully watched the work of
artists that no valid conclusion concerning their actual
lives and characters can be drawn from even their
most sincere artistic achievements. Without other
evidence than is as yet before us, we cannot assert
that Shakspere thought, or believed, or cared for this

[1] See p. 103.

ideal or that; nor yet that to have known in imagination what he has expressed he must personally have experienced certain circumstances, good or evil. We can assert, however, that he could hardly have expressed these things without at least three qualifications : first, a sympathetic understanding of such great historic movement as is finally phrased in *Henry IV.* and *Henry V.;* secondly, a sympathetic sharing of such romantic feeling as underlies both the single tragedy of this period and all the comedies; and thirdly, a sympathetic understanding of how a charming, idealized woman can fascinate and enchain an adoring, romantic lover. All of which, while lastingly true, is not spiritually profound.

We come, then, to what we may call his limitations. In the first place, the only play of this period which involves any profound sense of the evils lurking in human life and human nature, is *Much Ado About Nothing*, where the undercurrent of irony tends slightly toward deeper things. In the second place, as we saw most concretely in *Twelfth Night*, Shakspere throughout this period, though a skilful stage-playwright and easily master of his technical art, was very chary of invention. His mastery is shown not only by his mere verbal style, but by constructive skill. This we saw in *Romeo and Juliet ;* and, better still, in the *Midsummer Night's Dream*, and the *Merchant of Venice*, and *As You Like It*, where he subtly adapted the conventional old Induction, as it appears in the *Taming of the Shrew*, to the form in which, as part of the main action, it removes incredible incidents to plausible distance. His economy, or poverty, of invention, on the other hand, shows itself in his incessant repetition of whatever device — of character, of incident, of situation — had once proved theatrically effective.

In the presence of such work as we have been considering, however, one has small patience with talk of limitations. One's impulse is rather to question whether in seven years any merely human being could possibly have contributed to a stage and a nation which up to that moment had had little permanent literature at all, so wonderful a body of permanent literature as is actually before us. To correct this impression,— to see Shakspere's work in its true relation to its time, — we must glance hastily at the other productions [1] of these seven years.

In 1594 were published, together with *Lucrece*, the first works of Chapman, Hooker, and Southwell, Daniel's *Rosamund*, Drayton's *Idea's Mirror*, and plays by Greene, Lodge, Marlowe, Nash, and Peele. Hooker's work was the most lasting — the first four books of his *Ecclesiastical Polity*. In 1595 came Daniel's *Civil Wars*, Sidney's *Apology for Poetry*, and the *Colin Clout*, the *Astrophel*, the *Amoretti*, and the *Epithalamium* of Spenser. In 1596 came Davies's *Orchestra*, Ralegh's *Discovery of Guiana*, and the last three books of the *Faerie Queene*. In 1597, together with the three first quartos of Shakspere's plays, came

[1] Ryland: *Chronological Outlines*, etc.

the first ten of Bacon's *Essays,* another book of Hooker's *Ecclesiastical Polity,* and the first published works of Dekker and of Middleton. In 1598, together with two new quartos of Shakspere, came the first instalment of Chapman's *Homer,* Drayton's *Heroical Epistles,* Marlowe and Chapman's *Hero and Leander,* and the first published work of Thomas Heywood. In 1599, the year when Spenser died, came Davies's *Nosce Teipsum,* and among other plays Jonson's *Every Man out of his Humour.* In 1600, together with six new quartos of Shakspere, came Dekker's *Fortunatus* and *Shoemaker's Holiday,* Fairfax's *Tasso,* the last volume of Hakluyt's *Voyages,* and Jonson's *Cynthia's Revels.*

This list, a mere hasty culling from Ryland's book, is enough for our purposes. Without pretending to be exact or exhaustive, it shows clearly two facts : at the time when Shakspere was making the plays considered in this chapter, the intellectual life about him was active to a degree unprecedented in English Literature ; and the works contributed to English Literature during this period differed from what had come before almost as distinctly as this second group of Shakspere's plays differs from the first. What came before was archaic ; at least by comparison, what comes now seems modern.

A glance at the mere names of the playwrights will confirm this impression. In Mr. Fleay's *Chronicle History of the London Stage,* he gives in one chapter a list of the authors who wrote between 1586 and 1593,[1]

---

[1] Pages 89–91.

and in the next a list of those who wrote between 1594 and 1603.[1] Shakspere's name appears in both lists. In the first his fellow-playwrights are Peele, Marlowe, Greene, Lodge, Kyd, Nash, and Lyly ; in the second they are Jonson, Dekker, Chapman, Marston, Middleton, and Heywood. The only name besides Shakspere's which the lists contain in common is that of Lyly, an old play of whose was revived after 1597 by the Chapel children of Blackfriars.

These facts are enough. Great as Shakspere's development was during these seven years, it was only a part of the contemporary development which finally modernized both English Literature and the English stage. As was the case with his versatile, experimental beginning, what he accomplished was less extraordinary than it would have been during almost any other equal period of English history. We can hardly wonder that at a moment of such supreme general vigor and activity, he was not remarked as supreme.

For, after all, if one ask how his work and his achievement so far must have presented itself to his own mind, there is no more plausible answer than this : With all his old command of mere language, and with consummate command of theatrical technique, he had been possessed by an amazing power of creative imagination, and by sustained though variable artistic impulse. To these facts the permanence of his achievement during this period is due. In the course of time,

[1] Pages 154–156.

this permanence has obscured the equally true facts that when his energy was concentrated anywhere it weakened somewhere else, and that, in spite of his great power of creating characters and phrases, he was weaker than many of his contemporaries in such ingenious, fresh invention of stage situations as always commands contemporary applause. At the same time, too, he had never used his mastered powers for the serious expression of a profound or solemn purpose. His temper, so far as we may judge it from the work we have considered, was romantic, buoyant, wholesome. To himself, if we had no other evidence, we might guess that he seemed a vigorous, successful playwright, who accomplished tolerable results in spite of obvious limitations and infirmities which he did not allow to bother him. Before completing our notion of him now, however, we must turn to the *Sonnets.*

VIII

SHAKSPERE'S SONNETS

[In 1598, Meres, praising Shakspere, mentioned " his sugred Sonnets
among his private friends." In the *Passionate Pilgrim*, ascribed to
Shakspere though probably in large part spurious, and published in
1599, appeared Sonnets 138 and 144, —

"When my love swears that she is made of truth," etc.,

and

"Two loves I have of comfort and despair," etc.

On May 20th, 1609, "a Booke calles SHAKESPEARES sonnettes"
was entered in the Stationers' Register. In 1609, "Shake-Speares
Sonnets. Never before Imprinted" were published, substantially as we
have them. The book was dedicated by Thomas Thorpe, the publisher, "To the onlie begetter of these insuing sonnets, Mr. W. H."
What the term "begetter" means, and who "Mr. W. H." was, have
never been quite settled.

Concerning the dates of the sonnets we can assert only that some
of them were probably in existence before 1598, that two of the second
series were certainly in existence, substantially as we have them,
in 1599, and that all were finished by 1609. In what order they were
actually written we have no means of determining. For our purposes,
however, we are justified in assuming that, as a whole, the sonnets include work probably done before *Henry IV.*, and also work done during the period covered by the next chapter.]

DURING the last century or so, a considerable literature of comment and interpretation [1] has gathered
about the *Sonnets*. Some of this is instructive, some

---

[1] Conveniently summarized by Tyler: *Shakespeare's Sonnets;* London, 1890, pp. 145–149.

suggestive; much is ingeniously absurd. In general, however, all this criticism alike deals chiefly with the question of whether the *Sonnets* are authentic statements of autobiographic fact, or literary exercises, or perhaps rather allegorical fantasies. A similar unanswerable question exists concerning the first great series of Elizabethan sonnets, — Sidney's *Astrophel and Stella*. About the two other best-known series, there is less doubt: Spenser's *Amoretti* are almost certainly authentic addresses to the lady who became his wife; while Drayton's sonnets to *Idea* are probably mere rhetorical exercises.

If to these names we add that of Daniel, who wrote somewhat analogous verses to one *Delia*, we have completed the list of familiar series of Elizabethan sonnets, as distinguished from stray, independent ones. The names of Sidney, Spenser, Drayton, and Daniel, with whom we here group Shakspere, instantly define one fact about the *Sonnets* which marks them apart from most of Shakspere's work. Sidney and Spenser never wrote for the actual stage ; and, though Drayton seems to have collaborated in a number of plays, and Daniel to have written one or two, both Drayton and Daniel are generally remembered not as dramatists but as poets, the body of whose purely literary work remains considerable. In other words, we group Shakspere now with the masters not of popular, but of polite literature. The *Sonnets*, like almost all the extant work of these other poets, were addressed not to the general taste of their time, but to

the most sensitively critical.   Whatever else, they are
painstaking, conscientious works of art.

Throughout them, too, appears a mood perhaps most
fully expressed in Sonnet 81 : —

> " Or I shall live your epitaph to make,
>   Or you survive when I in earth am rotten;
>   From hence your memory death cannot take,
>   Although in me each part will be forgotten.
>   Your name from hence immortal life shall have,
>   Though I, once gone, to all the world must die:
>   The earth can yield me but a common grave,
>   When you entombed in men's eyes shall lie.
>   Your monument shall be my gentle verse,
>   Which eyes not yet created shall o'er-read,
>   And tongues to be your being shall rehearse,
>   When all the breathers of this world are dead;
>   You still shall live — such virtue hath my pen —
>   Where breath most breathes, even in the mouths of men."

The writer of these sonnets, in short, avows his belief
that they shall be lasting literature.   Not an infallible
sign of serious artistic purpose, this is at least a frequent.   It appears in Spenser's *Amoretti*, and in many
passages of Chapman and of Ben Jonson, like that
superb boast about poetry in the *Poetaster* : —

> "She can so mould Rome and her monuments
>   Within the liquid marble of her lines,
>   That they shall live, fresh and miraculous,
>   Even in the midst of innovating dust."

In small men pathetically comic, such confidence
becomes in great men nobly admirable.   Of Shakspere's *Sonnets*, then, we may fairly assert that they

must have seemed to the writer more important and valuable than his plays.

Such being the case, whoever attempts to define an impression of Shakspere's individuality must take special interest in these most conscientiously artistic of his works. If one could make sure of what they mean, one might confidently feel intimate knowledge of their author. Such confidence, though, has betrayed too many honest critics into absurdity, to prove, nowadays, however tempting, a serious danger. The only impregnable answer to the question of what the *Sonnets* signify is the one lately made by some German writer: " Ignoramus, ignorabimus" (" We do not know, and we never shall").

Keeping carefully in mind, however, the necessary uncertainty of any conclusion, we may fairly incline to one or another of the unproved, unprovable conjectures as to what the *Sonnets* actually mean. The conjecture of Mr. Thomas Tyler, while by no means impregnable, seems perhaps the most plausible.[1] In brief, he believes that the first series of the *Sonnets* — from 1 to 126 — were addressed to William Herbert, Earl of Pembroke, a very fascinating and somewhat erratic young nobleman, whose age fits the known dates; and that the second series — from 127 to 152 — were addressed to a certain Mrs. Mary Fitton, at one time a

---

[1] T. Tyler: *Shakespeare's Sonnets:* London; David Nutt: 1890. Mr. Fleay puts no faith in this Tyler story; and sets forth many reasons for believing the *Sonnets* to have been addressed to Southampton; *Biographical Chronicle of the English Drama:* 208–232.

maid of honor to Queen Elizabeth, and demonstrably a person of considerable fascination and of loose morals. Shakspere, it is assumed, became her lover; and Pembroke, by whom she certainly had a child, is assumed to have taken her from him. The improbability that a woman of her rank should have had to do with theatrical people is met by the fact that in 1600 Will Kempe, the clown of Shakspere's company, dedicated a book to this very lady. The probability that Mrs. Fitton was the woman in question was curiously strengthened by the fact, discovered after Tyler's work was written, that a colored effigy on her family monument shows her to have been of very dark complexion. And so on. The tale is plausible; after all, however, it is only a tissue of past gossip and modern conjecture. The most one can say of it is this: The first series of *Sonnets* expresses a noble fascination; the second, a base one, of which the baseness grows with contemplation. The former is certainly in harmony with what is known of Pembroke, the latter with what is known of Mary Fitton. Had Shakspere actually undergone such an experience of folly and shame as Tyler conjectures, these poems would fitly express it.

Off-hand, of course, one would declare the very frankness of self-revelation thus suggested to be incredible. Sensitiveness, one would say, is essentially reticent; and whoever wrote the *Sonnets* proved thereby the possession of rare sensitiveness. A little consideration, however, proves this objection mistaken.

15

To go no further, Alfred de Musset was sensitive, and
George Sand, and Tennyson, and Mrs. Browning; yet
almost in our own time all four have poured forth
their souls on paper with almost Byronic profusion.
Not long since, an admiring reader of Mrs. Browning
expressed, together with his admiration, deep satisfaction that he never knew her. Had he known her,
he said, he could not have borne the thought that she
had taken the whole world into a confidence which she
could hardly have spoken to her nearest and dearest.
All of which meant that, despite his appreciation, the
reader was not at heart an artist, while Mrs. Browning was. So, very surely, was Shakspere.

Even if the *Sonnets* be self-revealing, however, their
self-revelation takes a very deliberate shape. Nothing
could be much further from a spontaneous outburst
than these Shaksperean stanzas, whose form is among
the most highly studied in our literature. During
the Elizabethan period there were at least three well-
defined varieties of sonnet: the legitimate Italian, or
Petrarchan, generally imitated by Wyatt, Surrey, and
Sidney; the Spenserian, in which the system of rhymes
resembled that of the *Faerie Queene;* and that now
before us, whose most familiar example is in the work
of Shakspere. If not so intricately melodious as the
Spenserian sonnet, nor yet so sonorously sustained
as the Petrarchan, this Shaksperean sonnet is constantly fresh, varied, dignified, and above all idiomatic. Why certain metrical forms seem specially at
home in certain languages, it is hard to say; but as

surely as the hexameter is idiomatically classic, or the
terza rima Italian, or the Alexandrine French, so the
blank verse line of Elizabethan tragedy and the melo-
diously fluent quatrains of the Shaksperean sonnet are
idiomatically English. If one would appreciate at once
their idiomatic quality and the exquisite skill of their
phrasing, one cannot do better than try to alter a
word or a syllable anywhere. In one place Mr. Tyler
has tried. The second line of the 146th sonnet is
corrupt, reading thus : —

> " Poor soul, the centre of my sinful earth,
>   My sinful earth these rebel powers that thee array."

Clearly *my sinful earth* in the second line is a printer's
error. Trying to correct it, Mr. Tyler has suggested
two words which apparently fit the meaning, and has
made the line read

> " [Why feed'st] these rebel powers that thee array ? "

Though one cannot suggest an improvement on this
emendation, one cannot resist a conviction that the
man who wrote the rest of the sonnet could never
have written these two syllables. The example, if
extreme, is typical of the style throughout. Nowhere is Shakspere's art more constantly and elaborately fine.

Whatever else the *Sonnets* reveal, then, they surely
reveal the temperament of an artist, — a temperament,
as we have seen, which is not only exquisitely sensitive to emotional impressions, but is bound to find
the best relief from the suffering of such sensitive-

ness in deliberate, studied expression of it. Whoever, at moments of intense feeling, has felt compelled to scribble doggerel, and consequently — however pitiful his verse — has felt better, must have at least an inkling of what such a temperament is.

Not the least peculiar trait of it is one which, though not generally appreciated, goes far to explain the great emotional relief afforded by even comically inadequate expression. To phrase an emotional mood an artist must, as it were, cut his nature in two. With part of himself he must cling to the mood in question, or at least revive it at will. With another part of himself he must deliberately withdraw from the mood, observe it, criticise it, and carefully seek the vehicle of expression which shall best serve to convey it to other minds than his own. The self who speaks, in short, is not quite the self whom he would discuss. To put the matter otherwise, an artist must sometimes be almost conscious of what modern psychologists would call double personality. To put it differently still, every art of expression involves a fundamental use of the art which is in least repute, — the histrionic. The lyric poet must first experience his emotion, must then abstract himself from it, — thereby relieving himself considerably, — and finally must imaginatively and critically revive it at will. Undoubtedly this process is not always conscious. Beyond question, remarkable artistic effects are sometimes produced by methods which seem to the artist spontaneous. Such effects, however, wonderful though they be, are in a sense

rather accidental than masterly; and whatever else
the art of Shakspere's *Sonnets* may be called, it is
beyond doubt masterly, not accidental.

Granting all this, however, we may still be sure that
even deliberate, conscious, fundamentally histrionic art
can express nothing beyond what the artist has known.
His knowledge may come from his own experience; or
from the experience of others whom he has watched;
or from experiences recorded in history or in literature; or even from the vividly imagined experiences
of creatures whom he himself has invented.   Actually
or sympathetically, however, he must somehow have
known the moods which he expresses.   In the sense,
then, that what any artist expresses must somehow
have formed a part of his mental life, all art may be
called self-revealing, autobiographic.

Shakspere's *Sonnets*, then, may teach us truth
about Shakspere; for what they express, in terms of
emotional moods, cannot be much questioned.   The
real doubt, after all, concerns only what caused these
moods; and that is a question rather of gossip and of
scandal, of impertinent curiosity, than of criticism.
What the *Sonnets* surely express — what no criticism
can take from us — is the eagerness, the restlessness,
the eternally sweet suffering of a lover whose love is
of this world.   Love, sacred or profane, idealizes its
object.   If this object be earthly or human, experience
must finally shatter the ideal.   Religion is a certainty
only because the object of its love is a pure ideal,
which nothing but change of faith can alter.   So long

as any human being cares passionately for anything not purely ideal, so long will he surely find life tragic.

The lasting tragedy of earthly love, then, is what the *Sonnets* phrase; and this they phrase in no impersonal terms, but rather in the language of one whose temperament, as you grow year by year to know it better, stands out as individual as any in literature. To define a temperament thus known, however, is no easy matter. At best one may hope, by specifying a few typical phases and expressions of it, to suggest some inkling of the lasting, strengthening impression of Shakspere's individuality which grows on whoever knows the *Sonnets* well.

Recall, if you will, the 111th Sonnet,[1]

" O, for my sake do you with Fortune chide,"

and compare with it the 29th and the 30th : —

XXIX.

" When, in disgrace with fortune and men's eyes,
I all alone beweep my outcast state
And trouble deaf heaven with my bootless cries
And look upon myself and curse my fate,
Wishing me like to one more rich in hope,
Featured like him, like him with friends possess'd,
Desiring this man's art and that man's scope,
With what I most enjoy contented least;
Yet in these thoughts myself almost despising,
Haply I think on thee, and then my state,
Like to the lark at break of day arising
From sullen earth, sings hymns at heaven's gate;
For thy sweet love remember'd such wealth brings
That then I scorn to change my state with kings.

[1] See p. 46.

XXX.

" When to the sessions of sweet silent thought
  I summon up remembrance of things past,
  I sigh the lack of many a thing I sought,
  And with old woes new wail my dear time's waste:
  Then can I drown an eye, unused to flow,
  For precious friends hid in death's dateless night,
  And weep afresh love's long since cancell'd woe,
  And moan the expense of many a vanish'd sight:
  Then can I grieve at grievances foregone,
  And heavily from woe to woe tell o'er
  The sad account of fore-bemoaned moan,
  Which I new pay as if not paid before.
    But if the while I think on thee, dear friend,
    All losses are restored and sorrows end."

These are more than enough to express a nature of
great natural delicacy, passionately sensitive at once
to the charm of a personal fascination, and to the
inexhaustible pain which must come from surroundings essentially base.[1]

Other sonnets show a temperament equally sensitive
to the spiritual miseries which chasten a passionate
animal nature : —

CXXIX.

" The expense of spirit in a waste of shame
  Is lust in action; and till action, lust
  Is perjured, murderous, bloody, full of blame,
  Savage, extreme, rude, cruel, not to trust,
  Enjoy'd no sooner, but despised straight,
  Past reason hunted, and no sooner had
  Past reason hated, as a swallow'd bait
  On purpose laid to make the taker mad;

[1] See pp. 40–44.

Mad in pursuit and in possession so ;
Had, having, and in quest to have, extreme ;
A bliss in proof, and proved, a very woe ;
Before, a joy proposed ; behind, a dream.
    All this the world well knows ; yet none knows well
    To shun the heaven that leads men to this hell.

CXXX.

" My mistress' eyes are nothing like the sun ;
Coral is far more red than her lips' red ;
If snow be white, why then her breasts are dun ;
If hair be wires, black wires grow on her head.
I have seen roses damask'd, red and white,
But no such roses see I in her cheeks ;
And in some perfumes is there more delight
Than in the breath that from my mistress reeks.
I love to hear her speak, yet well I know
That music hath a far more pleasing sound ;
I grant I never saw a goddess go ;
My mistress, when she walks, treads on the ground :
    And yet, by heaven, I think my love as rare
    As any she belied with false compare."

The bitter irony of that sonnet is not, perhaps, always appreciated.

With all this sensitiveness to actual fact, the man remained profoundly metaphysical. At least he was constantly and instinctively, if not quite consciously, aware of the evanescence of all earthly phenomena, and of the real certainty of analytic idealism. For a plain expression of the first of these traits, the following sonnets will serve : —

LXIV.

" When I have seen by Time's fell hand defaced
　The rich proud cost of outworn buried age;
　When sometime lofty towers I see down-razed
　And brass eternal slave to mortal rage;
　When I have seen the hungry ocean gain
　Advantage on the kingdom of the shore,
　And the firm soil win of the watery main,
　Increasing store with loss, and loss with store;
　When I have seen such interchange of state,
　Or state itself confounded to decay;
　Ruin hath taught me thus to ruminate,
　That Time will come and take my love away.
　　This thought is as a death, which cannot choose
　　But weep to have that which it fears to lose.

LXV.

" Since brass, nor stone, nor earth, nor boundless sea,
　But sad mortality o'er-sways their power,
　How with this rage shall beauty hold a plea,
　Whose action is no stronger than a flower?
　O, how shall summer's honey breath hold out
　Against the wreckful siege of battering days,
　When rocks impregnable are not so stout,
　Nor gates of steel so strong, but Time decays?
　O, fearful meditation! where, alack,
　Shall Time's best jewel from Time's chest lie hid?
　Or what strong hand can hold his swift foot back?
　Or who his spoil of beauty can forbid?
　　O, none, unless this miracle have might,
　　That in black ink my love may still shine bright." [1]

[1] Cf. Sonnet 81, p. 223.

That all the while he knew the consolations of analytic idealism we may be sure from such sonnets as these : —

LXXIII.

" That time of year thou mayst in me behold
When yellow leaves, or none, or few, do hang
Upon those boughs which shake against the cold,
Bare ruin'd choirs, where late the sweet birds sang.
In me thou see'st the twilight of such day,
As after sunset fadeth in the west,
Which by and by black night doth take away,
Death's second self, that seals up all in rest.
In me thou see'st the glowing of such fire
That on the ashes of his youth doth lie,
As the death-bed whereon it must expire
Consumed with that which it was nourish'd by.
   This thou perceivest, which makes thy love more strong,
   To love that well which thou must leave ere long.

LXXIV.

" But be contented : when that fell arrest
Without all bail shall carry me away,
My life hath in this line some interest,
Which for memorial still with thee shall stay.
When thou reviewest this, thou dost review
The very part was consecrate to thee :
The earth can have but earth, which is his due ;
My spirit is thine, the better part of me :
So then thou hast but lost the dregs of life,
The prey of worms, my body being dead,
The coward conquest of a wretch's knife,
Too base of thee to be remembered.
   The worth of that is that which it contains,
   And that is this, and this with thee remains."

All his metaphysics, however, could not make actual life momentarily unreal:

LXVI.

" Tired with all these, for restful death I cry,
 As, to behold desert a beggar born,
 And needy nothing trimm'd in jollity,
 And purest faith unhappily forsworn,
 And gilded honour shamefully misplaced,
 And maiden virtue rudely strumpeted,
 And right perfection wrongfully disgraced,
 And strength by limping sway disabled,
 And art made tongue-tied by authority,
 And folly doctor-like controlling skill,
 And simple truth miscall'd simplicity,
 And captive good attending captain ill :
  Tired with all these, from these would I be gone,
  Save that, to die, I leave my love alone."

XC.

" Then hate me when thou wilt ; if ever, now;
 Now, while the world is bent my deeds to cross,
 Join with the spite of fortune, make me bow,
 And do not drop in for an after-loss :
 Ah, do not, when my heart hath 'scaped this sorrow,
 Come in the rearward of a conquer'd woe ;
 Give not a windy night a rainy morrow,
 To linger out a purposed overthrow.
 If thou wilt leave me, do not leave me last,
 When other petty griefs have done their spite,
 But in the onset come; so shall I taste
 At first the very worst of fortune's might,
  And other strains of woe, which now seem woe,
  Compared with loss of thee will not seem so."

With less direct quotation it would hardly have been possible to define the generalities which attempted to name some of the leading personal traits of Shakspere, as they appear in the *Sonnets*. Nor without much quotation could another of his characteristic traits have been made clear. The deep depression, the acute suffering, the fierce passion which should normally result from what we have seen, Shakspere seems fully to have known. Instead of expressing it, however, in such wild outbursts as one might naturally expect, he displays throughout a power of self-mastery, which gives his every utterance, no matter how passionate, the beauty of restrained and mastered artistic form. A form not in itself beautiful, one grows to feel, must, for its very want of beauty, have been inadequate to phrase the full emotion which such a nature felt.

The *Sonnets*, then, alter any conception of Shakspere's individuality which might spring from the plays we have read. Even though they tell nothing of the facts of his life, the *Sonnets* imply very much concerning the inner truth of it. No one, surely, could have written these poems without a temperament in every sense artistic, and a consciously mastered art. Nor could any one have expressed such emotion and such passion as underlie the *Sonnets* without a knowledge of suffering which no sane poise could lighten, like that of the chronicle-histories ; nor any such cheerful sanity, or such robust irony as the comedies express ; nor any such sentimental sense of tragedy as makes

Romeo and Juliet perennially lovely. Whoever wrote the *Sonnets* must have known the depths of spiritual suffering; nor yet have known how to emerge from them. Such a Shakspere, unlike what we have known hitherto, is not unlike the Shakspere who will reveal himself in the plays to come.

IX

THE PLAYS OF SHAKSPERE, FROM JULIUS CÆSAR TO CORIOLANUS

I.

THE plays to be discussed in this chapter differ from what have preceded somewhat as the plays from the *Midsummer Night's Dream* to *Twelfth Night* differed from the plays discussed before them. This first group, — from *Titus Andronicus* to the *Two Gentlemen of Verona*, — which probably occupied the first six years of Shakspere's professional life, were chiefly experimental. The second group, which probably occupied the next seven years of his professional life, were all more or less alive with the surging forces of artistic impulse and creative imagination; none of them, however, necessarily implied profound spiritual experience. The group to which we now come, which probably occupied the years between 1600 and 1608, mark a distinct development in Shakspere's artistic character.

That the development which we are trying to follow is rather artistic than personal, however, we cannot too strenuously keep in mind. The details of Shakspere's private life, quite undiscoverable nowadays, are, after all, no one's business. For the rest, nobody familiar with the literature and the stage of his time can very seriously believe that in writing his plays he generally meant to be philosophic, ethical, didactic. Like any other playwright, he made plays for audiences. He differed from other playwrights chiefly in the fervid depth of his artistic nature. The circumstances of his life, meanwhile, made the stage his normal vehicle of artistic expression, — the vent for such emotional disturbance as unexpressed would have become intolerable. The subjects which he chose, or which were given him, in short, connecting themselves with the fruit of his actual experience, were bound to throw him into specific emotional moods. These moods he was forced, by the laws of his nature, to infuse into the plays which he was writing, just as Marlowe had more simply and more instantly infused imaginative feeling into his tragedies ten years before. What marks the personal development of Shakspere as an artist, then, is that his emotional motives suggest a deepening knowledge of life. A writer who had never dreamed of such sentiments as underlie the *Sonnets*, might conceivably have written all the plays we have considered hitherto; he could not have written the plays which are to come.

A study of *Julius Cæsar* will serve to define these generalizations.

II. JULIUS CÆSAR.

[*Julius Cæsar* was neither entered in the Stationers' Register nor published until the folio of 1623.

Its source is certainly North's *Plutarch*, which was published in 1579; the general substance of the speech of Antony over Cæsar's body may have been suggested by a translation of Appian's *Chronicle of the Roman Wars*, published in 1578.

Not mentioned by Meres in 1598, *Julius Cæsar* is distinctly alluded to in the following stanza from Weever's *Mirror of Martyrs*, published in 1601 : —

> " The many-headed multitude were drawne
> By *Brutus* speech, that *Cæsar* was ambitious,
> When eloquent *Mark Antonie* had showne
> His vertues, who but *Brutus* then was vicious ?
> Man's memorie, with new, forgets the old,
> One tale is good, untill another's told."

As Mr. Fleay suggests,[1] thereby as usual throwing light on the essentially theatrical nature of even Shakspere's most masterly work, the speech of Polonius,[2] : —

" I did enact Julius Cæsar : I was killed i' the Capitol ; Brutus killed me,"

probably indicates that *Julius Cæsar* had been acted shortly before *Hamlet,* and that the audience would recognize in Polonius the actor who had played Cæsar.

The conjectural date generally assigned to *Julius Cæsar* is from 1600 to 1601.]

At first sight *Julius Cæsar* impresses you as a chronicle-history, differing from what have preceded chiefly in the fact that its subject is not English, but Roman. Even though when the conspirators appear,[3]

> " Their hats are pluck'd about their ears,
> And half their faces buried in their cloaks,"

[1] *Life,* p. 214.
[2] *Hamlet,* III. ii. 108–9.
[3] II. i. 73.

and though in the midst of the ensuing scene the clock strike three,[1] one never thinks of anything in this play as modern. With complete disregard of archæological detail, Shakspere conceived his characters throughout in a manner so true to the spirit of Plutarch that one might almost select *Julius Cæsar* as a model exposition of the temper which tradition assigns to Roman antiquity.

Almost immediately, however, any one familiar with the Elizabethan stage finds in *Julius Cæsar* a marked likeness to another kind of play than chronicle-history. As Mr. Fleay points out,[2] many of the tragedies of blood were in two parts: Marston's *Antonio and Mellida*, Chapman's *Bussy d'Ambois*, Kyd's *Jeronymo*, are familiar examples. In the first part, the hero meets his fate; in the second, he is revenged, with the approving consent of his visible ghost.[3] This is just what happens in *Julius Cæsar*. The first three acts constitute *Cæsar's Tragedy*, the last two, *Cæsar's Revenge*. So marked is this that Mr. Fleay finds reason to believe the play as we have it to be a condensed version of what were originally two.

Without accepting this opinion, we may at least declare it plausible; for surely the effect of *Julius Cæsar* is radically unlike anything else we have met. An interesting view of it is stated in a note by Mr. Young:[4] —

---

[1] Ibid. 192.   [2] *Life*, p. 215.   [3] See p. 252.
[4] Whose kindness is acknowledged in the introductory Note to this book.

"It is a piece of transitional art, a hybrid between the chronicle-histories and the great tragedies. It has neither the lack of artistic or ethical significance characteristic of the former, nor is it, like the latter, dominated by a single great character only. While it has all the unity of interest distinguishing the tragedies, it gets it, not by means of a single informing idea of artistic or ethical significance, but by employing a masterly technique in the service of a chronicle-history motive, to tell just what had happened."

Suggestive as this opinion must be, it does not quite emphasize the full divergence of *Julius Cæsar* from the English chronicle-histories. These are generally obvious dramatic versions of the narratives which they represent. Even though all the substance of *Julius Cæsar*, however, and all its essential unity be traceable to Plutarch, no treatment of Plutarch's material could be much less obvious than Shakspere's. From Plutarch, to be sure, he selects his incidents with the skill in choice of what is dramatically effective, which he has learned by thirteen years of writing for the stage. This is not all, though; he selects not incidents which should tell the recorded story of Cæsar, but incidents which give that story a new and very significant character. To understand *Julius Cæsar*, in short, we must appreciate that when Shakspere read Plutarch, the narrative awakened in him a definite state of feeling; this state of feeling, as well as the facts which awakened it, he was bound as an artist to express.

Easy to appreciate, this feeling is not easy to define. One can point out the technical devices, or situations, or motives which help to compose or to express it. One can show how the motive of self-deception, already so effectively used in comedy, really underlies the conception of Cæsar and of Brutus alike. One can show how the mob, far more seriously treated than the mob in *Henry VI.*,[1] develops and emphasizes the distrust of the rampant, headless, brainless populace to which, at least as an artist, Shakspere was surely sensitive. One can compare the ghost of Cæsar with the bogies of *Richard III.*,[2] and show how these are little better than nursery goblins, while the spirit of Cæsar has a touch of such actuality as in one mood makes one remember the tales of Nemesis, and in another recalls the proceedings of the Society for Psychic Research. Yet all this does not help us far. Unsatisfactory though the phrase be, there is perhaps no more exact term for the underlying mood of *Julius Cæsar* than unpassionately ironical.

In *Julius Cæsar* human affairs have broken loose from human control. Cæsar himself, though to his own mind almost divinely supreme, is only a passing incarnation of the political force everywhere surely, miserably inherent in the folly-stricken populace. The extinction of his person does not so much as trouble this force. Other Cæsars shall come, and others still ; all, like the great Cæsar, to be the sport of fate. Yet those who wish for better things and nobler are just as powerless. Brutus, let him think

---

[1] Compare III. ii. with 2 *Henry VI.*, IV. ii.–viii.
[2] IV. iii. 275 seq. ; cf. *Rich. III.* V. iii. 118 seq.

as he will that he acts freely, is rather passively swept on to the end which now, as then and ever, must await those fervent idealists, born after their moment, who passionately love the traditional virtues of an olden time. What is best in human nature is as powerless as the puppets who deem themselves potent, except, perhaps, that it redeems and ennobles character. Men may still be great; but great or small, they can actually do nothing. Nowhere is the world-old cry of the stricken idealist against the unconquerable progress of vile, overwhelming fact more despairingly uttered than by Brutus:[1]

> "O, Julius Cæsar, thou art mighty yet !
> Thy spirit walks abroad, and turns our swords
> In our own proper entrails."

Such effort as this to expound an artist's mood must always run a double risk of misleading. You may seem, on the one hand, to be stating personal convictions, or, on the other, to assert that the artist criticised was preaching. One cannot repeat too often, then, that a critic's chief business is not to air his own views, but to define those of the artist he discusses; and that so far as the artist is concerned, he need never have abstractly formulated his views at all. The artist, indeed, has done his work if he have but felt his mood and expressed it. From all the foregoing attempt to analyze the mood of *Julius Cæsar*, then, nobody need infer anything more than that

[1] V. iii. 94.

Shakspere's subject made him feel in a specific way. Such analysis of that feeling as we have attempted would probably have been quite foreign to him. For all that, such analysis is helpful to those who nowadays would try to share his feeling.

The mood which underlies *Julius Cæsar* is analogous to the lighter but still serious mood which we found to underlie *Much Ado About Nothing*.[1] Deeper though the mood of *Julius Cæsar* be, however, it never becomes passionate, overmastering. No trait of *Julius Cæsar*, in short, is more characteristic than what, in the broadest sense of the word, may be called its style. This is never overburdened with such a rush of thought and emotion, such a bewildering range of perception, as should overwhelm or confuse it. Nowhere is Shakspere's power more surely poised than here; nowhere is his touch more firm and masterly; nowhere do vivid incidents, individual characters, marvellously plausible background or atmosphere, blend in a verbal style at once stronger and more limpid.

The sense of fate displayed in *Julius Cæsar* warrants, for want of a better word, the term ironical; the cool mastery of style throughout warrants the term unpassionate. Unpassionately ironical, then, we may call the play. As unpassionate, it has much in common with the plays which we have read before. In none of these, for all their beauty, their energy, their power, has there been a surge of thought or feel-

---

[1] See p. 194.

ing which has overwhelmed, overburdened the style.
Rather, Shakspere's style has been constantly freeing
itself from the excessive ingenuity of the older days;
and with all the flexibility which only such ingenuity
could fully have developed, it has been growing more
and more nearly identical with the thought it would
phrase. Here, at last, with full mastery, Shakspere
uses his superb, unpassionate style to express a mood
which allies *Julius Cæsar* to what is coming as surely
as that style allies it to what is past. For, far beyond
any other play we have as yet considered, *Julius Cæsar*
involves a sense of the lasting irony of history, — an
understanding of the blind fate which must always
seem to make men its sport.

III. ALL'S WELL THAT ENDS WELL.

[Like *Julius Cæsar*, *All's Well That Ends Well* was first entered in
1623, and first published in the folio.

Its source is clearly the story of Giletta of Narbona in Paynter's
Palace of Pleasure.

As to its origin and general date there has been much discussion.
From the clearly early character of some passages, as well as from the
general character of the story, many critics have been disposed to think
this play a comparatively late revision of the *Love's Labour's Won*
mentioned by Meres. Mr. Fleay, while admitting the obviously early
passages to be old, is of opinion that if any play is to be recognized as
Love's Labour's Won, it is probably not this one, but rather *Much Ado
About Nothing.*[1] The question can never be definitely settled. From
the general character of the style in the later parts of *All's Well That
Ends Well*, however, critics substantially agree in assigning the play
in its present form to about 1601.]

[1] *Life*, pp. 204, 216.

A short extract from *All's Well That Ends Well*
will illustrate the incongruity of its style. In the
scene where Helena is presented to the King, the dialogue proceeds as follows : [1] —

> " *King.*   I say we must not
> So stain our judgment, or corrupt our hope,
> To prostitute our past-cure malady
> To empirics, or to dissever so
> Our great self and our credit, *to esteem*
> *A senseless help when help past sense we deem.*
>   *Hel.* My duty then shall pay me for my pains:
> I will no more enforce mine office on you;
> Humbly entreating from your royal thoughts
> A modest one, to bear me back again.
>   *King.* I cannot give thee less, to be call'd grateful:
> *Thou thought'st to help me ; and such thanks I give*
> *As one near death to those that wish him live :*
> *But what at full I know, thou know'st no part,*
> *I knowing all my peril, thou no art.*
>   *Hel. What I can do can do no hurt to try,*
> *Since you set up your rest 'gainst remedy.*
> *He that of greatest works is finisher*
> *Oft does them by the weakest minister*," etc.

The lines italicized in this passage are clearly in a
manner quite as early as that of *Love's Labour's Lost*,
which we assigned to 1589. The other lines are in
a manner common with Shakspere twelve years later.
Though the latter predominate in *All's Well That
Ends Well*, there is enough of the former to give the
play unmistakable oddity of effect, and to make its
style in detail a favorite matter of study to those who
love linguistics.

[1] II. i. 122–140.

Distinct in effect from any of the other comedies,
on account of this palpable incongruity of style, *All's
Well That Ends Well* resembles them in its general
economy of invention. The main situation — of a
woman making love to a man — occurs both in the
relations of Phœbe to Rosalind in *As You Like It*,
and in those of Olivia to Viola in *Twelfth Night*. The
device by which Helena finally secures her husband is
clearly repeated in *Measure for Measure*, while the
business of the ring is repeated from the last act of
the *Merchant of Venice*. Parolles is a curious combination of Pistol and Falstaff; his relations to Bertram
being almost a repetition of Falstaff's to the Prince.
Helena's original scheme involves considerable self-
deception; her final stratagem involves mistaken identity. The further we look, in short, the more familiar
matter we find.

Whether *All's Well That Ends Well* be a revision
of *Love's Labour's Won*, or not, then, it is clearly a
play of which part was made early, and part late;
a play, too, where the later part has many traces of
Shakspere's general manner about 1601. We may
fairly guess, accordingly, that if the play were ever
finished in its older form, it may probably have
expressed no more serious view of life than the
Two Gentlemen of Verona, whose motive is remotely
similar. The passages which give it more significance are almost all in the later style.

While its incongruity and consequent lack of finish
make *All's Well That Ends Well* a clearly less serious

work of art than the plays near which we place it,
the mood which it expresses deserves our full attention.   Up to this point when Shakspere has dealt
with love, he has always been romantic.   He has
shown us some rather worthless lovers, to be sure :
Proteus is highly unsympathetic; Romeo, for all his
charm, is neither vigorous nor constant; and Bassanio, when we analyze his conduct, is anything but
heroic.   Throughout Shakspere's love-scenes, in fact,
we have trace after trace of some such fascinating,
volatile youth as seems to have inspired the first series
of sonnets.   Of all the lot, however, none is more volatile and less fascinating, none more pitifully free
from romantic heroism, than Bertram.   What makes
All's Well That Ends Well notable for us, in short,
is that its love passages plainly reveal a sense of the
mysterious mischiefs which must flourish in this world
as long as men are men and women are women.   So
remote is this mood from the old one of romantic
sentiment or romantic happiness that for all the
romantic fidelity of Helena to her worthless husband,
one feels Shakspere to be treating the fact of love
with a cynical irony almost worthy of a modern
Frenchman.

Even though *All's Well That Ends Well* be perhaps,
then, like the *Richards* and the *Merry Wives of Windsor*, the careless work of a moment or of moments
when Shakspere's chief energy was busy elsewhere,
it is significant because it definitely expresses a mood
not hitherto found in his plays.   Restless one feels

this mood, unsettled, unserene, unbeautiful. There is no other work of Shakspere's which in conception and in temper seems quite so corrupt as this, where we are asked to give our full sympathy to Bertram. There are other works of Shakspere which are more painful; there are none less pleasing, none on which one cares less to dwell. No other, however, more clearly reveals a sense which, as distinctly as the sense of irony which we found in *Julius Cæsar*, characterizes the coming work of Shakspere. This sense, abundantly evident in the *Sonnets*, but not shown in the plays we have read before, is a sense of the deplorable, fascinating, distracting mystery which throughout human history is involved in the fact of sexual passion.

The irony of fate underlies the mood of *Julius Cæsar;* under the mood of *All's Well That Ends Well* lies the miserable mystery of earthly love. These motives we shall find henceforth again and again.

IV. HAMLET.

[The *Revenge of Hamlett Prince of Denmark* was entered in the Stationers' Register on July 26th, 1602. In 1603 the *Tragicall Historie of Hamlet Prince of Denmark by William Shake-speare* was published in quarto. This obviously imperfect quarto was probably pirated. Whether it represents an earlier version of the play or is a mutilated version of the whole, remains uncertain. In 1604 appeared a second quarto, which shows the play in substantially its final form. There were subsequent quartos in 1605 and in 1611. Above twenty allusions to *Hamlet* between 1604 and 1616 have been discovered.

There is evidence that a play on this subject, which Mr. Fleay be·
lieves to have been by Kyd, existed as early as 1589. What relation
this old play bore to Shakspere's, and whether he had a hand in it,
remain matters of dispute.

The story, originally told by Saxo Grammaticus, a thirteenth-century
chronicle, was told in French by Belleforest, of whose version an Eng·
lish translation was published in 1608. This translation very probably
existed earlier.

Conjectures as to the date of the finished play range from 1601 to
1603.]

By common verdict — a different thing from fact —
Hamlet is held to be Shakspere's masterpiece. While
thus positively to grade any work of art is uncritical,
we may safely say that *Hamlet* has given rise to more
speculation, to a wider range of thought and comment, than any other single work in English literature. In all modern literature, indeed, its only rival
in this respect is Goethe's *Faust*, a poem not yet old
enough for us to be sure of its permanent character.
Hamlet, then, stands by itself.

In spite of all this comment, *Hamlet* remains a
puzzle, always unsolved, constantly suggestive. Critic
after critic asks what it means ; and each has a new
answer. There are endless minor questions, too : was
Hamlet mad, for example ? was Ophelia chaste ? The
mass of comment grows bewildering, benumbing. In
despair, one puts it aside, turning straight to the text ;
for, after all, the chief thing is not that we should define the play, but that we should know it ; and *Hamlet* is a play which everybody ought to know. It is
surely the work in English Literature to which allusions are most constant and most widely intelligible.

Reading it again and again, you begin to find that you may know it none the less because, for all your reading, it remains inscrutable.

Inscrutable though *Hamlet* remain, however, certain facts about it transpire for whoever considers it coolly. To begin with, in origin and in plot it is clearly a conventional tragedy of blood: the old king has been murdered; Polonius, the Queen, the King, Laertes, and Hamlet, are killed on the stage; and Ophelia, though she dies out of sight, is buried in the presence of the audience. Again, if we did not detect the fact for ourselves, the very title of the entry in the Stationers' Register — the *Revenge of Hamlet*, etc. — would remind us that the play belongs to that class of tragedies of blood, such as we glanced at in discussing *Julius Cæsar*, where a crime is revenged by the intervention of a murdered ghost. Considered as an Elizabethan play, then, *Hamlet* is substantially conventional.

Its effect, on the other hand, is as far from conventional as possible. While retaining traces enough of its origin to remain full of dramatic action, it carries on this action not like the old tragedies of blood and revenge by means of ranting lay figures, but by means of characters as individual as any in literature. The individuality of these characters, however, is always subordinated to the main dramatic motive; one reason why things happen as they do is that these people are temperamentally just what they are. Nor does the subordination of detail to purpose cease here. Sur-

prisingly few speeches in *Hamlet* lack dramatic fitness;
whatever is said generally helps either to advance the
action or to define some character by means of which
the action is advanced. The speeches, then, each
having its proper place in an artistic scheme, are not
essentially salient. Despite their dramatic fitness,
though, these speeches contain so many final phrases,
and such a wealth of aphorism, that the stale joke
is justified which declares the text of Hamlet to consist wholly of familiar quotations. This wonderfully
finished detail of style, an infallible symptom of
thoroughly studied art, is what chiefly gives *Hamlet* the suggestive, mysterious quality which we all
recognize.

How carefully artistic *Hamlet* is, and at the same
time how full of indications that it is only a development from an archaic original of which palpable traces
remain, has been best pointed out, perhaps, in a study
still unpublished, — the Sohier Prize Essay, on the
Elizabethan Hamlet, written in 1893, by Mr. John
Corbin, of Harvard University. How the original
Ghost was wildly ranting; how some of the scenes
which puzzle people most, such as the great scene
between Hamlet and Ophelia,[1] may best be understood when we realize them once to have been conventionally comic; how Hamlet's very madness was
probably intended to make the audience laugh, and so
on, Mr. Corbin has made clear in a way which must
surely be recognized when his essay finally appears.

[1] III. i. 90–157.

Something of the process by which the final form of
Hamlet grew may be guessed by comparing the permanent version with Belleforest and with the quarto
of 1603.

In Belleforest, for example, the lady who at times
answers to Ophelia is a person of easy morals, em-
ployed to ferret out Hamlet's secret in a manner which
reminds one of the gossip concerning the relations of
Fanny Ellsler and the Duc de Reichstadt. In *Hamlet*,
by a refinement of taste peculiar to Shakspere among
Elizabethan dramatists, much of this situation is transferred to Rosencrantz and Guildenstern, while Ophelia
retains hardly any trace of her origin. In the quarto
of 1603, again, Hamlet's soliloquy, and his great scene
with Ophelia occur in what we now call the second act,
before his first interview with Rosencrantz and Guildenstern,[1] instead of in the third act, where their
dramatic effect is probably greater. Such transposi-
tion, however and whenever made, is just the sort of
thing which occurs when any novelist or dramatist is
trying to improve his work. The difference between
the opening speeches in the two versions is more notable still. Here is the version of 1603 : —

> " *Enter two Centinels.*
>
> 1. Stand : who is that ?
> 2. 'T is I.
> 1. O you come most carefully upon your watch.
> 2. And if you meet *Marcellus* and *Horatio*,
>   The partners of my watch, bid them make haste."

[1] Between II. ii. 167, and II. ii. 172.

Similar as this seems to the final version, it is comparatively lifeless. The sentinel on watch, seeing some one approach, challenges him, who declares himself to be the relief-guard. Clearly nothing could be more commonplace. Now turn to the final version : —

> "FRANCISCO *at his post, Enter to him* BERNARDO.
>
> *Ber.* Who's there ?
> *Fran.* Nay, answer me : stand, and unfold yourself.
> *Ber.* Long live the king !
> *Fran.* Bernardo ?
> *Ber.* He.
> *Fran.* You come most carefully upon your hour.
> *Ber.* 'T is now struck twelve ; get thee to bed, Francisco.
> *Fran.* For this relief much thanks : 't is bitter cold,
> And I am sick at heart.
> *Ber.* Have you had quiet guard ?
> *Fran.* Not a mouse stirring.
> *Ber.* Well, good night.
> If you do meet Horatio and Marcellus,
> The rivals of my watch, bid them make haste."

At first this scene looks like the other. On scrutiny, however, you see that the opening challenge is transposed from the mouth of the sentinel on watch, who ought to give it, to that of the relieving sentinel, who ought not to. In a moment, you see why. Bernardo, the relieving sentinel, knows that the ghost is astir ; and seeing a figure in the dark gives the challenge, in a fright which pervades all his speeches. Francisco, the sentinel on watch, knowing nothing of the ghost, only feels cold. Such a change as this, however and whenever made, is the kind of change by which a skilful artist, with a mere touch of the pen, dispels commonplace.

Such evidence as this tends to confirm the opinion that the quarto of 1603 is a mutilated version of Shakspere's own earlier work, and that the final *Hamlet* represents his last revision of it. The differences between the two are generally such as a great imaginative artist, more and more imbued with the artistic significance of his subject, would introduce by way of refinement, finish, adaptation.

Canting as *artistic significance* may sound, the phrase probably contains the clew to *Hamlet*. Every one knows the tragedy to be full of endless, fascinating, suggestive mystery. Critic after critic has tried to solve this mystery, to demonstrate what it signifies. Abandon this effort, and you will see the whole subject in a new and a clearer light. Once for all, there is no need for any solution of *Hamlet;* as it stands, the tragedy finally expresses the mood of an artist who has no answer for the problems which rise before him.

Hamlet, indeed, we may believe to have developed in some such manner as we detected when we considered the character of Falstaff.[1] In him we could faintly trace a conventional old satire on the Puritan hero, Oldcastle. This, we conceived, Shakspere meant to reproduce, much as in *King John* he had reproduced from an old play the Bastard Faulconbridge.

[1] See p. 167–171.

The change from this traditional Oldcastle we conceived to be spontaneous. The conventionally burlesqued Puritan we conceived, of its own accord, to grow into something so remote from its origin that the epilogue could truly say, " Oldcastle died a martyr, and this is not the man." [1] Imagine the same process here. The old tragedy of blood possesses the imagination of the poet, perhaps for years. What it means, what it signifies, he, as an artist, neither knows nor cares. To an artist, thus possessed, the vital question is not what his conceptions mean, but what they are. They grow within him, they will not let him rest; he must speak them out, must tell what they are. That very process for the moment exhausts him ; it is all he cares about ; for himself it is enough.

For critical students, like us, however, the case is otherwise. Not knowing the artistic mood spontaneously, we must perforce ask ourselves not only what it is but what it means. Without such guidance as should come from answers to this question, which very probably involves matters of which the artist never was aware, we may fail to understand him.

In *Hamlet*, then, one notable trait appears for the first time. Whatever else we find in the tragedy, we surely find an activity of intellect which at first seems superhuman. Putting wonder aside, however, and asking whether, in real life, we have met anything like it, we discover a startling answer close at hand. Any of us must have known people whose tremendous

[1] See p. 172.

mental activity makes them, in comparison with every-day mortals, seem divinely gifted; and most of us must have become aware that such a trait indicates, in the stock which breeds it, a marked tendency to insanity.   In other words, there are always people about us whose minds have the diseased activity, without the aberration, of mania.   Such a mind wrote *Hamlet*.

At the same time, as distinguished from men who display the vagaries of genius, Shakspere was always exceptionally sane.   The trait which balanced his abnormal activity of intellectual perception was an equally active and pervasive power of reflection. Whatever he perceived, he could consider, could comment on.   Besides, as we have seen before, he was by this time a consummate artist; and artistic expression, involving a deliberate severance of personality within the artist himself,[1] is often what saves men of genius from Bedlam.   With one part of their being they may yield to all the ecstasy of divine madness; with another, they must contemplate and phrase the maddening thoughts and feelings which surge within them, preserving, in spite of all, the cool cunning which masters technical obstructions.

Such tremendous activity, mastered and controlled by equally tremendous power, infuses every line of *Hamlet;* yet in *Hamlet* it always subserves a constant emotional purpose.   The resulting state of the poet's mind is best indicated perhaps by the words of a critic

[1] See p. 228.

who, having known the tragedy for thirty years, and having loved it passionately, declared that from the beginning he had never once been able to think of it without a faint, lurking consciousness of some unphrased musical cadence beneath it all. Beneath it, then, he for one could perceive some fundamental emotion which no language can express, — something so ethereally beyond the range of what all men realize that it cannot be couched in any vehicle so definite as words. Words, he found, could help him no farther than when he called this emotion a quivering sense of the eternal mystery of tragic fate.

A sense of tragic fate, then, in all its horror — not the balanced, judicial fate of the Greeks, but the passionate, stormy, Christianized fate of Romantic Europe — underlies the mood which *Hamlet* would express. Men are the sport of such fate : thought, emotion, conduct, life in all its aspects, are alike at the mercy of this unspeakable, inexorable force. Yet, all the while, these very men, whirled onward though they be toward and through the portals of eternity, must think, must feel, must act, must live ; to others and even to themselves they must seem, even though they may never truly be, the responsible masters of themselves. This is the fact which the maker of *Hamlet* contemplated. The reaction which stirred within him from this contemplation was a passionate, restless acknowledgment of endless, unfathomable mystery. No words can quite phrase it ; perhaps none can phrase it better than some fragmentary lines

from Hamlet's great soliloquy, — all the truer to our
elusive meaning if we leave them subjectless : —

> " Puzzles the will,
> And makes us rather bear those ills we have
> Than fly to others that we know not of." [1]

The ills we have, all the while, we know with an
intensity of suffering hardly to be borne. Chief
among them are those which spring from the fact
that men are men and women are women. It is no
intentional evil-doing which has led the King and the
Queen to their grim career of incest and murder ; it
is rather that, being the mortals they are, they have
lived and done their deeds in a world where damning
sin held them in its toils. And Ophelia is a woman,
and Hamlet is a man, and therein lies the seed of
the ills we have, and the ills to come. A knowledge of these ills, perceived with the keenness of an
intellect alive to the very utmost limits of human ken,
underlies the mood of *Hamlet*. Were not the master-
mind, too, artistically alert to the utmost limits of
human power, it could not have phrased, with an art
at once ultimately dramatic and ultimately poetic, and
with a philosophic insight which seems illimitable, this
mood whose depth of mystery is best proved by the
truth that throughout the centuries it remains mysterious. Fateful, passionate, inscrutable, — such is
the life which *Hamlet* sets forth.

Was Hamlet mad ? critic after critic has asked.
In all human probability, Shakspere himself could

---

[1] III. i. 80.

have answered the question no better than we. Artists know less of what they do not tell us than inartistic critics give them credit for ; Thackeray, they say, was never quite sure how far Becky Sharp had gone with Lord Steyne. How Hamlet may have presented himself to Shakspere, is aptly suggested in a note by Mr. Greene [1] : —

"Perhaps Shakspere hardly recognized that *Hamlet* was essentially not a chronicle-history. He applied his realistic, his 'objective' method persistently; and with his own pessimistic temper at the time he produced what had been only hinted at in *Julius Cæsar,* — a psychologic tragedy. There is little formal analysis; only aspects are depicted; but our interest centres on the mental states which cause those aspects. The fact that Shakespere has kept to the 'objective' method accounts for the puzzling character of the work. A real man lives in Shakspere's brain, and speaks, and acts. Why he so speaks and acts we can only guess — and Shakspere can only guess. Therefore the question as to the true nature of Hamlet's character is essentially insoluble."

Of only one thing concerning Hamlet, indeed, may we feel sure. So unfathomable is his range of thought and emotion that actor after actor can play the part with masterly intelligence, and each can be different from any other Poetic Booth, for example, sad Lawrence Barrett, demoniacally witty Henry Irving, romantic Mounet-Sully are as unlike as any four human beings

[1] Whose kindness is acknowledged in the introductory Note to this book.

can be ; yet in none can you find a trait unauthorized by the text. Fateful, passionate, inscrutable, — such seems Hamlet to himself, such to his impersonators ; and such, we may believe, he seemed to his creator.

Slight as this treatment of *Hamlet* is, and surely neglectful though it be of endless facts and theories which even superficial students of the subject are bound to know and to consider, it should serve our purpose. Our business, after all, is not to fathom the depths of *Hamlet*, but only to assure ourselves of *Hamlet's* relation to Shakspere's development as an artist. In it we have found many traces of his old methods of thought and work. In it, too, we have found again both the profound sense of irony so unpassionately set forth in *Julius Cæsar*, and the knowledge of what evil comes from the fact of sex so cynically set forth in *All 's Well that Ends Well*. In it, furthermore, we have found a terrible activity of roused intellect which in a less balanced nature might have led to madness. In it, finally, we have found a Shakspere different, in his whole artistic nature, from the Shakspere whom we have known hitherto ; for here at last we find him, in the full ripeness of his power, passionately facing the everlasting mysteries, and, for all his greatness, as little able as the least of us to phrase an answer to their eternal enigma.

V. MEASURE FOR MEASURE.

[*Measure for Measure* was first entered in 1623, and first published in the folio; but according to Mr. Fleay,[1] it was acted at court in December, 1604.

The main outline of the story — without the episode of Mariana, whom Shakspere substitutes at a crucial moment for the original heroine, — exists in Whetstone's *Promus and Cassandra*, published in 1578, and in his *Pentameron*, published in 1582. It is based on the Italian of Cinthio's *Hecatommithi*.

From internal evidence — allusions and style combined, — *Measure for Measure* has been conjecturally assigned to 1603 or 1604.]

At first sight, *Measure for Measure*, like so many other of Shakspere's plays, seems strongly individual. Its general effect, certainly, — the mood into which it throws you, — is unique : a little consideration, however, reveals, in both its motive and its method, the economy of invention so characteristic of Shakspere.

In *Julius Cæsar*, as we have seen, he expressed very plainly the sense of irony which now for a while so pervades his artistic feeling. In *All's Well that Ends Well*, he expressed his equally persistent sense that while men remain men and women remain women, there will surely be trouble. In *Hamlet* he expressed a fiercely passionate sense of the mystery which hangs over life, wherein the two preceding motives remain constant. In *Measure for Measure* all these motives

[1] *Life*, 235.

reappear : the slightest consideration of the story of
Angelo will reveal the two first; the prison scene,[1]
particularly when Claudio shudders in the face of
death,[2] will reveal something of the last. So, too,
more subtly but just as surely, we find in *Measure for
Measure* the motives which underlie both series of the
Sonnets : Claudio is another example of such fascinating youth and weakness as may have inspired the
first series ; and, though in the serious parts we have no
actively evil woman, the stories of Isabella, of Mariana,
and of Juliet, constantly suggest the evils which arise
from the fascinating fact of sex. What makes *Measure
for Measure* seem individual, then, is not that its motives are new, but that they are newly combined ; they
differ from the old not in kind, but in proportion.
Here, for example, the irony, while far more passionate
than that of *Julius Cæsar*, lacks the overwhelming intensity which marks it in *Hamlet*. Here, too, the sense
of sexual evil is at once more profound than that of
All 's Well that Ends Well, and so firmly set forth that
you feel its greater depth to imply more certain insight. Here, finally, while there is no direct self-
revelation, the frequent analogies to the moods
expressed in the *Sonnets* go far to make you feel that
the mood of *Measure for Measure* is unstudied, spontaneous, sincere.

In the matter of dramatic detail, even to many of
the speeches, *Measure for Measure* is almost recapitulatory. The old stage situations and devices of

[1] III. i.   [2] 118 seq.

the comedies — mistaken identity and self-deception —
are persistently used.   Their effect, however, is no
longer comic.   The disguised Duke is a very different
figure from a girlish heroine in a page's hose and
doublet.   Still more, Angelo is a very different figure
from Malvolio, or Benedick, or Falstaff.   By almost
any other Elizabethan dramatist, indeed, he might
have been made ribaldly amusing.   Imagine him, and
his situation on the modern French stage, and you will
see for yourself what a chance for loose fun they afford.
That this chance is neglected, that Angelo is rather a
tragic figure than a comic, is deeply characteristic both
of Shakspere and of this moment in his career.
Recapitulation, with due variation, however, does
not end with such general matters as these.   The
career and the fate of Lucio are closely akin to those
of Parolles and of Falstaff, just as his ribald chat has
something in common with Mercutio's.   Clearly, too,
Mariana simply revives the Diana of *All's Well that
Ends Well ;* and Claudio, at least in his weakness, has
much in common with Bertram.   The last acts of
these two plays, furthermore, are so much alike that
this portion of *All's Well that Ends Well* might almost
be regarded as a study for this portion of *Measure for
Measure.*

Even more notable, however, is the reminiscent, if
not exactly recapitulatory, flavor of many actual
speeches.   This is so marked that we may to advantage compare two passages from *Measure for Measure*
with similar ones from earlier works.

The first of these passages is that where Isabella pleads for mercy on Claudio; it instantly suggests Portia's more familiar plea for mercy with Shylock. Here is Portia's:[1] —

> " The quality of mercy is not strain'd,
>   It droppeth as the gentle rain from heaven
>   Upon the place beneath : it is twice blest :
>   It blesseth him that gives and him that takes :
>   'T is mightiest in the mightiest : it becomes
>   The throned monarch better than his crown ;
>   His sceptre shows the force of temporal power,
>   The attribute to awe and majesty,
>   Wherein doth sit the dread and fear of kings ;
>   But mercy is above this sceptred sway ;
>   It is enthroned in the hearts of kings,
>   It is an attribute to God himself ;
>   And earthly power doth then show likest God's
>   When mercy seasons justice."

Here is Isabella's plea with Angelo :[2] —

> " No ceremony that to great ones 'longs,
>   Not the king's crown, nor the deputed sword,
>   The marshal's truncheon, nor the judge's robe,
>   Become them with one half so good a grace
>   As mercy does.
>   If he had been as you and you as he,
>   You would have slipt like him ; but he, like you,
>   Would not have been so stern.
>
>   .   .   .   .
>
>   Alas, alas !
>   Why, all the souls that were were forfeit once ;
>   And He that might the vantage best have took
>   Found out the remedy.   How would you be,

---

[1] *Merchant of Venice*, IV. i. 184 seq.
[2] II. ii. 59 seq.

> If He, which is the top of judgement, should
> But judge you as you are? O, think on that;
> And mercy then will breathe within your lips,
> Like man new made."

The second passage from *Measure for Measure* which here deserves attention is Claudio's speech on death, which resembles Hamlet's great soliloquy,[1] —

> "To be or not to be," etc.

A few lines should serve to remind every one of that: —

> "To die: to sleep;
> No more; and by a sleep to say we end
> The heart-ache and the thousand natural shocks
> That flesh is heir to, 't is a consummation
> Devoutly to be wish'd. To die, to sleep;
> To sleep: perchance to dream: ay, there 's the rub;
> For in that sleep of death what dreams may come
> When we have shuffled off this mortal coil,
> Must give us pause: there 's the respect
> That makes calamity of so long life.
> . . . . . .
>   Who would fardels bear,
> To grunt and sweat under a weary life,
> But that the dread of something after death,
> The undiscover'd country from whose bourn
> No traveller returns, puzzles the will
> And makes us rather bear those ills we have
> Than fly to others that we know not of."

Compare with this Claudio's speech:[2] —

> " Ay, but to die, and go we know not where;
> To lie in cold obstruction and to rot;

[1] *Hamlet*, III. i. 56 seq.   [2] III. i. 118 seq.

> This sensible warm motion to become
> A kneaded clod ; and the delighted spirit
> To bathe in fiery floods, or to reside
> In thrilling region of thick-ribbed ice ; [1]
> To be imprison'd in the viewless winds,
> And blown with restless violence round about
> The pendent world ; or to be worse than worst
> Of those that lawless and incertain thought,
> Imagine howling : [2] 't is too horrible !
> The weariest and most loathed worldly life
> That age, ache, penury and imprisonment
> Can lay on nature is a paradise
> To what we fear of death."

With less direct quotation, it would have been hard to make clear a distinct difference, in something more tangible than mood or temper, between *Measure for Measure* and the plays we have considered before. The passages we have just read are enough alike to demonstrate that the very style of *Measure for Measure* has a certain heaviness which we have not met hitherto. The comparison also suggests that the change is due to increased activity of thought. Unimpulsively, but intensely and constantly, reflective, the mind which wrote *Measure for Measure* was actually overburdened with things to say. Here, then, we have a fresh symptom of the abnormal mental activity which pervades *Hamlet*. It reveals itself now in a compactness of style hitherto strange to Shakspere. The passages

---

[1] Compare these five lines, too, with the Ghost's speech, — *Hamlet*, I. v. 9-20.

[2] Cf. *Hamlet*, V. i. 265.

just quoted are by no means the most compact of *Measure for Measure*, which often becomes positively obscure. One feels at last as if Shakspere's abnormal activity of mind, prevented by his lack of inventive power from dashing into regions foreign to his older experience, were writhing about every concept he had, striving with the linear vehicle of language to enwrap elusive solidity of thought. While not constant hereafter, this trait is henceforth characteristic of Shakspere's style.

Taking all these considerations together, we find in the mood of *Measure for Measure* a normal reaction from the passionate sense of mystery so wonderfully phrased in *Hamlet*. Tacitly assuming, as usual, the conventional ideals of virtue and of life still instinctive to the normal English mind, Shakspere faces the fact of sexual passion. Like the fate which Hamlet faces, the thing is at once mysterious and evil. In *Hamlet* Shakspere expressed his sense of the mystery; in *Measure for Measure* he expresses his sense of the evil. Here his dominant mood is grimly contemplative, almost consciously philosophic. No more than in *Hamlet* can he offer any solution of the dreadful mystery; but he can state fact, and can comment on it inexhaustibly. The mood is a mood of reaction, — of slumbering passion, but of enormous, sombre latent feeling.

Strangely enough, this mood has much in common with a potent contemporary mood which has left a widely different record, — the Calvinistic philosophy of the Puritans. As with them, life is a positively evil thing, made up of sin, of weakness, of whatever else should deserve damnation. Fate is overpowering; pure ideals are bent and broken in conflict with fact; and, above all, sexual love is a vast, evil mystery. Even though, here and there, a gleam of persistent purity suggest the possibility of rare, capricious election, most men are bound by the very law of their being to whirl headlong toward merited damnation. In *Measure for Measure* — so strangely named a comedy — one may constantly find this unwitting exposition of Calvinism, with no gleam of hopeful solution. This evil fact is the real world; see it, hate it, grimly laugh at it if you can and will; God knows what it means; all we know is that it can surely mean no good. Meanwhile, however, it can afford us endless material for comment; and comment is essentially anæsthetic.

So this mood, after all not peculiar to Shakspere, but a mood very potent throughout his time, takes its place between the moods which his work has already expressed and the moods which are to come. Deeper and deeper insight they show into the depths of human experience; but not a spiritual insight which pierces higher and higher.

VI. Troilus and Cressida.

[On February 7th, 1603, *Troilus and Cressida*, "as it is acted by my
Lord Chamberlain's men," was entered in the Stationers' Register, to
be published by one James Roberts, "when he hath gotten sufficient
authority for it." This authority seems never to have been gotten, for
no further mention of *Troilus and Cressida* occurs until January 28th,
1609, when it was again entered in the Stationers' Register. During
the same year it was twice published in quarto, as "*Written by* William
Shakespeare;" in the first of these quartos is an apparently mendacious
preface, suppressed in the second, stating that the play was "never
stal'd with the stage, never clapper-clawed with the palmes of the
vulger." In the folio of 1623, *Troilus and Cressida* is printed between
the histories and the tragedies, and it does not appear at all in the
general list of plays. Apparently the editors could not decide how to
classify it.

Its sources are evidently the mediæval versions of the story of Troy,
of which the most notable in English is Chaucer's *Troilus and Creseide*.
Possibly it may have some connection with Chapman's *Homer*.

Conjectures as to the date of the play vary widely. From the evidence stated, as well as on other grounds, many are now disposed to
think that the plan of the play is very early, that an acting version of
it, similar to the final one, was produced about 1602, and that the
whole thing was revived about 1609. In the squabbles of the Grecian
heroes Mr. Fleay [1] believes that we may detect allusions to theatrical
squabbles prevalent in London about 1602.]

Just when, or how, or why *Troilus and Cressida* was
written nobody knows ; yet clearly, we must put it
somewhere. For one thing, then, the very fact that
in so many aspects it is puzzling might incline us
fantastically to group it with plays whose chief trait

[1] *Life*, 220–224.

is that they express a puzzled, indeterminate mood. Besides, whatever doubts may exist about *Troilus and Cressida*, there can be no doubt that it deals with both of the motives just now so palpable in Shakspere's work, — the irony of fate and the mischief which women make. Again, while it displays nothing which may fairly be called exhaustion, it has throughout such a quality of creative inertia as we have seen to characterize work done by Shakspere when his best energy was concentrated elsewhere. Finally, while the character of Cressida has an obvious likeness to that of Cleopatra, which might warrant us in placing this play near that of which Cleopatra is heroine, it has an equal and less generally recognized likeness to the character of Desdemona. Taken together, these considerations — none of them very cogent — perhaps warrant us in considering *Troilus and Cressida* before *Othello*.

Palpable in the very construction of *Troilus and Cressida*, the least dramatic of Shakspere's plays, the puzzling quality pervades it everywhere. Of late certain critics have wondered whether it be not deliberately satirical ; certainly, they say, Shakspere, dealing with a heroic subject, carefully refrains from making anybody in the least heroic. However agreeable to modern ways of thinking, such a view is hardly consonant with Elizabethan temper. It were more rational to say that in this case Shakspere has really done afresh what he has done all along : he has translated into dramatic form material which he found in narrative ;

and so doing he has, as usual, made his characters considerably more human than he found them. By the very process of humanizing them, however, he has permeated them with the view of human nature which possessed him at about the time to which we venture to assign the play.   Essentially, then, these personages become bad and inexplicable, — such figures as in actual life furnished the data of Calvinism.   Human beings, thus regarded, are puzzling facts; hence the puzzle of *Troilus and Cressida*.

The persistence in *Troilus and Cressida* of the two motives so characteristic of this period goes far to confirm this impression.   Clearly neither the Greeks nor the Trojans here are really free agents.   As Cassius played on Brutus, to be sure, so Ulysses plays on whoever comes near him, and so to a certain degree Pandarus plays on the lovers.   Beneath them all, however, an overmastering, blind fate — in this case by no means passionately recognized — drives every one together nowhither.   The means it takes to drive them, too, is more palpable than before ; what breeds the trouble is the wantonness of woman.   Though we see little of Helen, we rarely lose the sense of her damning presence ; and in Cressida we have a full-length portrait of a fascinating wanton, all the more fatal because of her momentary, volatile sincerity. The more one studies the character of Cressida, the more one feels its truth.   Of Cressida, however, we shall see more a little later.

With all its puzzling humanity, and all its persist-

ence of motive, *Troilus and Cressida* must always have
been a dull play. This is partly a question of actual
construction. The real action here is very slight; the
background, against which it is played, is very heavy.
When Troilus, or Cressida, or Pandarus are on the
scene, to be sure, something happens; but they are
not on the scene often enough or long enough to distract our attention from the endless harangues and the
pointless squabbles of Greeks and Trojans. Of course
these Greeks and Trojans live; compared with any
of the sources from which Shakspere may have drawn
them, they are remarkable for vitality. In no case,
however, do they live nobly or heroically ; nor yet do
they display themselves in phases of life or conduct
which even Elizabethans could have found dramatically interesting. Elizabethan audiences could relish
things which nowadays would put audiences to sleep;
in sonorous rant and prolonged soliloquy they could
find such delight as modern audiences seek in the
music of grand opera ; in fantastic plays on words and
turns of phrase they could find such pleasure as nowadays audiences feel in catching tunes ; and if a text
were really comic they could enjoy it heartily without
the aid of action. Even an Elizabethan audience,
however, could hardly have stomached the prolonged
philosophizing which fills pages of *Troilus and Cressida*. In the first scene at the Grecian camp,[1] for
example, no human being could ever have spouted the
lines of Agamemnon, and Nestor, and Ulysses, so that

[1] I. iii.

any considerable body of human listeners, wishing to be amused, could patiently have borne them. A good deal of this philosophizing, to be sure, is admirable; for a reader with a taste for aphorism, *Troilus and Cressida* is an agreeably pregnant piece of literature. No appetite for aphorism, however, could stand such philosophizing at the theatre. Few ardent church-goers even would relish quite such compactly serious matter in sermons. Yet the philosophizing, commentative mood expressed in these long speeches and pregnant phrases is the mood which seems uppermost in *Troilus and Cressida;* and *Troilus and Cressida* was meant for acting. The creative inertia thus indicated goes far to justify our placing of the play between *Hamlet* and *Othello.*

We had another reason, however, for placing it near *Othello.* At first thought, no two personages seem much less similar than the gentle Desdemona and the wanton heroine who emerges as the most vividly individualized character in *Troilus and Cressida.* Nowadays we know them both chiefly from the printed page, a vehicle which defines all their divergence. To the dramatic writer, however, who conceived them as they should present themselves to an audience, they were not disembodied personalities; they were rather visible women, who acted and looked in a definite way. Now compare the first scene between Troilus and Cressida [1] with Othello's familiar account of the wooing of Desdemona,[2] —

[1] III. ii. 41-220.   [2] *Othello,* I. iii. 158 seq.

> " My story being done,
> She gave me for my pains a world of sighs :
> She swore, in faith, 't was strange, 't was passing strange,
> 'T was pitiful, 't was wondrous pitiful :
> She wished she had not heard it, yet she wish'd
> That heaven had made her such a man : she thank'd me,
> And bade me, if I had a friend that loved her,
> I should but teach him how to tell my story,
> And that would woo her."

This simple, conscious, girlish coquetry, in Desdemona
compatible with such exquisite delicacy of nature as
she finally shows,[1] must have looked almost exactly
like the behavior of Cressida in the orchard of
Pandarus. Again, compare the civilities which pass
between Desdemona and Cassio on their first landing
in Cyprus,[2] with the proceedings of Cressida on her
arrival in the Grecian camp.[3] The actual conduct in
each case is agreeable to polite Elizabethan manners;
but while in Desdemona it means no more than a
waltz means to-day, in Cressida it means, at best, a
fatal weakness of nature. The more one considers
these two characters together, in short, the more plausible becomes the surmise that they might have been
studied from the same model. The wide divergence
of view which they express concerning the same visible
lines of conduct is certainly characteristic of Shakspere. In *Love's Labour's Lost*, we remember, he
constantly burlesqued the very affectations he was
perpetrating. In *Pyramus and Thisbe*, he gave a

---

[1] *Othello*, IV. iii.   [2] *Othello*, II. i. 97–103, 168–179.
[3] IV. v. 17–63.

comic version of his own first tragedy. We have lately seen such variations on the same theme as the speeches of Portia and of Isabella on mercy, or, better still, the speeches on death of Hamlet and of Claudio. Another similar variation on a given theme we may reasonably guess to occur in the characters of Cressida and of Desdemona.

For all this, we must never forget that *Troilus and Cressida* is a play concerning which, in such a study as ours, we may never speak with certainty. All we may surely say is that, wherever it belong, it is a reflective, and so a bad play, which expresses very definitely Shakspere's artistic sense both of the irony of fate, and of the evil inherent in the fact that women are women. Here, for the first time, indeed,— apart from such figures as Doll Tearsheet and Mistress Overdone, — we find bad women. In all this there are analogies to the plays which certainly belong hereabouts. *Troilus and Cressida*, too, reveals the sort of inertia which generally marks the minor work of a period when Shakspere's greater work was doing. A puzzle we found *Troilus and Cressida*, though, and a puzzle we must leave it; our best comment must be guess-work.

VII. OTHELLO.

[*Othello* was entered in the Stationers' Register on October 6th, 1621 ; and appeared in an abridged quarto in 1622. It is the only play of Shakspere's first published between 1609 and the folio of 1623. In the diary of the Secretary to Prince Louis Frederick of Würtemberg, it was thus mentioned on April 30th, 1610 : "Lundi . . . S. E. alla au Globe, lieu ordinaire au l'on joue les Commedies, y fut representé l'histoire du More de Venise." It is also recorded among fourteen plays given at court shortly before May 20th, 1613. According to Mr. Fleay,[1] it was acted at court on November 1st, 1604.

Its source is evidently a novel in Cinthio's *Hecatommithi*, of which no early English translation is known.

Critics are generally agreed in conjecturally assigning it to 1604.]

If *Troilus and Cressida* be a puzzle, nothing in Shakspere is less like it than *Othello*, which is perhaps the most modern of Shakspere's plays. On our own stage no other is so absorbing, so free from traces of archaic origin, which we must overcome before we can surrender ourselves to the performance.

A suggestive reason for this peculiar effect of *Othello* has been proposed by Mr. Greene : —

"The most obvious characteristic of *Othello* seems to be an attempted return to convention. Shakspere has here taken a tale of blood, and has set to work to produce a sensational play. His almost involuntary truth turns Othello from its possibilities of mere blood-tragedy to what it is, — a broadly handled tragedy of character."

[1] *Life*, p. 235.

Such *Othello* certainly is; just as surely it is also what commonplaces call it, — the supreme tragedy of jealousy. Everything in the play tends to set forth this lasting fact of human nature. There is no under plot; hardly any scenes do not bear directly on the story; there is less discursive matter than we find almost anywhere else. Naturally, then, we think of this broadly handled tragedy of character, dealing so consummately with an absorbing human passion, as a thing apart in the work of Shakspere; or at least as related to his other work by little else than its passionate conception and its masterly handling.

Only after we are free from the spell which, whether we read or see *Othello*, the play must cast upon us, can we trace its relations to other works. After a while, the similarity of its general motive to the story of Claudio and Hero and Don John, in *Much. Ado About Nothing*, begins to appear; and we find Shakspere once more presenting old matter in a new light. The new light, however, makes the matter seem new. What this light is has been suggestively stated by Mr. Young: —

"The mood [of *Othello*] seems to me something more than jealousy and the agony of it, — it seems a sense of the power of sexual love as a motive force in life. The subject-matter of many of the preceding plays, it may be recalled, was chiefly concerned with this passion in its darker aspects. Shakspere's mind, it may be said safely enough, had dwelt on this subject. The result was a pretty clear perception of the nature of this passion, of its different manifestations in persons of different character, and of its influence upon personal conduct and upon the general surface aspect of life. The perception of these facts Shakspere seems to have recorded in the artistic terms of the plot, the characterization, and the atmosphere or background of *Othello.* . . . The plot shows first that the fortuitous meeting of Othello and Desdemona, and the existence of sexual love in its purer, nobler form between them, warped the life of each from that normal line of development which their environment would naturally have determined. These lives were brought to a tragic end by the machinations of a villain actuated, to be sure, not essentially by lust, but by ambition; the special direction of which, however, was given by a desire to revenge himself upon two men — Cassio and Othello — whom he suspected of intrigue with his wife. . . . The characterization is even more significant than the plot of Shakspere's perception of the power of sexual love as a motive force in life. Not a character of any importance but is subject to this passion in some form. In Desdemona it was of course beautifully pure and ideal; in Othello not so much of the beast had been worked out; . . . in Iago there was just enough of this passion to keep him from being a mere flame of villany — in which respect he is singularly like Goneril and Regan; in Roderigo was the mere gross sensuality, of which [a comparison of *Othello* with its sources shows that] Shakspere deliberately relieved Iago; in Emilia, the vulgar half-virtue could become, for reason enough, something worse; in Cassio and Bianca the passion . . . was manifest in its mercenary aspect. In no case, except that of Bianca, did this passion operate, as a motive force, in the form of *mere* jealousy."

Mere jealousy, however, without subtle analysis, would have been enough finally to remind us that the concentrated passion and power of *Othello* only intensify the old motive of the mystery inherent in the fact that men are men and women are women. Jealousy, after all, is but a new phase of this, and a more absorbing. Again, the fact that Othello's jealousy is really groundless revives the old motive of self-deception, now become fiercely tragic. The way, furthermore, in which every one is juggled with by Iago, to an end ultimately abortive, is a fresh, more limited expression of the ironical motive. Here, indeed, we have such a tragedy as but for the blundering of clowns might have happened in Leonato's city of Messina.

Considering *Othello* as a technical work of art, one first notices the surprising theatrical skill of its construction. One thinks of it generally as a series of sustained, crescent scenes and situations, still admirable on the stage, which lead the story straight from its romantic beginning to its tragic end. So constantly are the characters subordinated to their dramatic purpose — saying, doing, thinking, being little else than what the plot demands — that only when we consider them apart do we begin to appreciate how thoroughly each, from greatest to smallest, is individual.

Most individual of all, perhaps, is Iago. Concerning Iago, Mr. Greene's notes are suggestive. Referring to his belief that in *Othello* Shakspere meant to return to convention, he declares Iago to be

" the most striking illustration of this attempted reaction. Iago is undoubtedly built up from the conventional villain. The traces of the original are still evident in his essential devilishness. Crime is pleasant to him. I will not assert that such a man cannot exist; but I know that he is improbable. Shakspere, however, started out with him, and having done so imagined him so really . . . that he is plausible. Shakspere gives him motives not strong enough for a healthy mind ; they are not enough to make him real. His cynical worldly wisdom, though, added to his apparent blunt honesty, makes him alive as a thinker, in spite of his conventional origin . . . and of the frequently conventional method by which Shakspere treats him. Iago is made to go into direct self-revelation by monologue to an exaggerated extent ; . . . and yet Iago is alive. This life comes from the things which Iago says and does that astound you by the absolute certainty that he, not Shakspere, did or said them. For instance, when the fiend kneels with Othello [1] we are astonished, while we know that he did it. Shakspere's insight is what saves the play, and, indeed, keeps the careless reader from guessing how nearly it is a conventional gore-piece."

This criticism touches on a phase of Iago which is not generally noticed. His motives, it says, are not strong enough for a healthy mind. As Mr. Young's criticism suggested, indeed, the Iago of Shakspere has distinctly less motive than the character in Cinthio's novel from which he is developed ; that personage was possessed by the passion for his general's wife which Shakspere has transferred to the witless

[1] III. iii. 461.

Roderigo. Yet in this drama of which the chief trait is concentration, Iago, for all his lack of motive, seems concentration personified. Diabolical, one feels like calling him, — diabolical both in the inhuman activity of his intelligence and in the inhuman concentration of his almost motiveless evil purpose. Yet Iago is not a devil; though horribly abnormal, he remains comprehensibly human. Not diabolical, then, but abnormal, we find him. It is only a step further to feel that his abnormal activity and abnormal concentration of mind are almost maniacal. Then look at his last speech : [1] —

> " Demand me nothing : what you know, you know :
> From this time forth I never will speak word."

Without being an expert in lunacy, one knows of the silent, glaring madmen. It is with figures like these that Iago ranges himself at last.

The notion that Iago was mad would probably have been new to Shakspere. To Shakspere, Iago would probably have seemed, like Hamlet and Falstaff and all the rest before him, only one of those mysterious creatures of imagination who somehow grow into independent existence. Hamlet, to be sure, might seem mad to some, who were welcome to think him so if they chose ; even Othello might seem swept by self-deluding passion beyond the verge of reason ; but Iago — cool, cunning, shrewd — could never seem anything but an incarnation of diabolical

[1] V. ii. 303.

intelligence.   This very fact throws startling light
on the state of Shakspere's mind.   The Shakspere of
Othello is quite as sane and as masterly as the Shakspere of *Hamlet;* but, like the Shakspere who created
Hamlet, the Shakspere who created Iago sympathetically understood, while at the same time he utterly
controlled, a specific phase of madness.

Here, then, is an analogy, both to *Hamlet* and to
King Lear, which has not been generally remarked.
Throughout the period of his great tragedies, Shakspere gave evidence, partly unwitting, that he understood madness.   Such an analogy as this is probably
too subtle to have been known to the man whose
mental state it illustrates.   An analogy of which, on
the other hand, he might probably have been aware
is that which has already been pointed out between
Cressida and Desdemona.[1]   In character, as well as
aspect, Desdemona and Cressida have one common
trait: both are untruthful.   In Cressida the fact is
constantly palpable; in Desdemona one feels it less.
Look at the indirectness of her coquetry, though, in
half wooing Othello;[2] look at Brabantio's last speech
to her,[3] true enough to contain the seed of final evil;
look at her prevarication about the handkerchief.[4]
For all her tenderness and purity, Desdemona's word
is not always to be trusted.   There is something in
her nature, as well as in her aspect, which groups her
with the Trojan wanton, giving color to the slanders

[1] See p. 275.   [2] I. iii. 145–170.
[3] Ibid. 293.   [4] III. iv. 23–29, 52–102.

of Iago. The more one studies these characters together, the more alike they seem.

Desdemona, however, is in no sense a repetition of
Cressida. Like every other character in *Othello* she
is completely individual. This thorough individualization of character gives *Othello* its specific atmosphere. The presence of so many real people involves
a real world for them to live and move in. One asks
no questions as to what or where this world is; one
accepts it; and finally one grows aware that it is not
only real, but actually foreign to England. Here we
touch on one of the most marked traits of *Othello*.
Exactly how one cannot say, the play is consummately
Italian, — a more veracious piece of creative fiction
than was ever made by all the scribblers of pedanti-
cally accurate detail. In origin, of course, the plot is
Italian; the characters fit the plot so perfectly, that
they and their background alike become Italian, too.
See *Othello* played by an Italian company, and you
will feel this more and more. For all that you lose the
wonderful poetry of the lines, you often seem nearer
the truth than any English actors can bring you.

To lose the poetry of *Othello*, however, to lose any
detail of its style, is to lose much. This style is very
different from that of *Measure for Measure*, of *Troilus
and Cressida*, and of other plays, still to come, where
the lines are overcharged with meaning. Almost
every line of *Othello* is so adapted to its purpose that
we accept speech after speech as actual utterances.
On consideration, however, we find that nobody has

been speaking the plain dialect of daily life; one and all the personages have sustained throughout the lasting elevation of poetry. The delight the style has given us, then, proves different from what we first thought it — or, better, more profound. Not only is every word in character, but every word also adds to the beauty of a noble tragic poem. No style could be theoretically better.

The superficial simplicity of *Othello* strengthens the general impression which the play makes. By this time we have seen enough of Shakspere to understand that some of his works seem more consciously self-revealing than others. In some, at least, one feels that he must have been aware of the underlying motive: as an artist, for example, whatever his private convictions, Shakspere must have realized the beauty of the *Midsummer Night's Dream*, the patriotic didacticism of *Henry V.*, the passionate art of the *Sonnets*, the irony of *Julius Cæsar*, the mystery of *Hamlet*, the grim philosophy of *Measure for Measure*. In other works, one feels that to Shakspere himself the effects detected by modern criticism would have been surprises; his effort, one feels, was simply, with full control of his power, to express a mood or a fact which seemed wholly foreign to himself: such, for example, would be the sentimental tragedy of *Romeo and Juliet*, the romantic comedy of the *Merchant of Venice*, the uncontrollable vitality of Falstaff. It is among these works, which to the artist we may suppose to have seemed thoroughly objective, that we may most reasonably class *Othello.*

Objective and concentrated, then, we may believe Shakspere to have deemed this tremendous study of an isolated passion; purely artistic in motive, beyond the plays lately considered. Modern analysis, however, can discover in *Othello* unsuspected analogies to the work about it. One of these is its irony; its constant dwelling on the mysteries of sex is another; others still are the maniacal activity and concentration of Iago, the Cressid-like surface of Desdemona, the fatal self-deception of Othello. Whatever be the truth of our chronology, in short, *Othello* is surely such a work as one might expect after *Hamlet* and *Measure for Measure* and *Troilus and Cressida.*

VIII. — KING LEAR.

["Master William Shakespeare his historye of Kinge Lear, as yt was played before the Kinges Majestie at Whitehall uppon Sainct Stephens night at Christmas last" was entered in the Stationers' Register on November 26th, 1607. The play thus entered was twice published in quarto during 1608. In each case the titlepage is peculiar, reading as follows : —

"M. WILLIAM SHAKE-SPEARE,
HIS
True Chronicle History of the life
and death of King Lear, and his
three Daughters

With the unfortunate life of EDGAR
sonne and heire to the Earle of *Glocester*, and
his sullen and assumed humour of TOM
of Bedlam.

At the head of the text is a similarly peculiar title : —

"M. WILLIAM SHAKE-SPEARE

HIS

History, of King Lear."

This unique emphasis on the name of Shakspere is probably due to the publication in 1605 of an old play, entered in the Stationers' Register on May 8, 1605, as "The Tragical History of King Leir and his three daughters, as it was lately acted ;" but really rather a comic than a tragic chronicle-history. This publication is believed to have been an attempt to avail of the popularity of Shakspere's play.

The probable sources of Shakspere's *King Lear* are this old play and the chronicle of Holinshed ; and, for the story of Gloster, the tale of the blind king of Paphlagonia in Sidney's *Arcadia*. The story of Lear, however, was familiar, existing in many early versions, of which the most familiar is Spenser's.[1]

From various internal evidence, together with the publication of the rival play, *King Lear* is generally assigned to 1605.]

One is apt to forget that a play which seems so modern as *Othello* was made for the Elizabethan theatre. After *Othello*, then, we need some sharp reminder that this Shakspere whom we are studying could never have dreamt of such a stage or such a world as ours. We could have none sharper than we find in *King Lear*.

Whether you read this great tragedy, or see it on the stage, the effect produced by any single and swift consideration of it must nowadays be one of murky, passionate, despairing confusion. The common answer to any consequent complaint, is that to appreciate *King Lear* you should study it. This is perfectly true. Equally true, however, is a fact not so often

[1] *Faerie Queene*, II. x. 27–32.

emphasized : *King Lear* was certainly meant to be acted ; and when a play is acting neither players nor audience are at liberty to stop for reflective comment. Far more than a novel, or a poem, or any piece of pure literature, a play, which is made to be played straight through, must be conceived by both its maker and its audiences as a unit. In criticising any stage-play, this fact should never be forgotten. Whoever remembers it will probably continue to find *King Lear*, read or seen at a single sitting, magnificently confused.

For this there are several obvious reasons. In the first place, the style of the play is overpacked with meaning; in the second place, the situations are so often rather intellectually than visibly dramatic that to see them helps little toward their interpretation ; in the third place, the technical traits which probably made *King Lear* popular with Elizabethan audiences belong, far more than is usual in Shakspere's later work, to the obsolete conditions of Shakspere's time.

Two or three examples may serve to emphasize the excessive compactness of *King Lear*. Perhaps none are more to our purpose than may be found in the trial by battle.[1] This clearly revives a situation previously used with effect, — perhaps in the combat between Hector and Ajax,[2] and certainly in the trial at arms between Hamlet and Laertes, and in the final struggle between Richard III. and Richmond. Dis-

---

[1] V. iii. 107–150.
[2] *Troilus and Cressida*, IV. v. 65-117.

tinctly the most elaborate previous use of it, however, and the use most similar to what we find here, occurred in *Richard II.* There the first 122 lines of the third scene are given to the trial by battle between Bolingbroke and Norfolk. Every one of these lines is a sonorous piece of half-operatic verse ; though they do not mean much, they sound splendidly ; and no matter how fast the actors should rattle them off, there is no serious danger of obscurity. The first challenge [1] is a fair example of the whole scene : —

> "*Mar.* In God's name and the king's, say who thou art
> And why thou comest thus knightly clad in arms,
> Against what man thou comest, and what thy quarrel :
> Speak truly, on thy knighthood and thy oath ;
> As so defend thee heaven and thy valour !
>   *Mow.* My name is Thomas Mowbray, Duke of Norfolk ;
> Who hither come engaged by my oath —
> Which God defend a knight should violate ! —
> Both to defend my loyalty and truth
> To God, my king and my succeeding issue,
> Against the Duke of Hereford that appeals me ;
> And, by the grace of God and this mine arm,
> To prove him, in defending of myself,
> A traitor to my God, my king, and me :
> And as I truly fight, defend me heaven !"

Compare with this the challenge in *King Lear :* [2] —

> "*Her.*   What are you ?
> Your name, your quality ? and why you answer
> This present summons ?
>   *Edg.*   Know, my name is lost ;
> By treason's tooth bare-gnawn and canker-bit :
> Yet am I noble as the adversary
> I come to cope."

[1] *Rich. II.* I. iii. 11–25.   [2] V. iii. 119–124

A little later in the scene Edmund thus returns the lie to Edgar : [1] —

> " Back do I toss these treasons to thy head;
> With the hell-hated lie o'erwhelm thy heart;
> Which, for they yet glance by and scarcely bruise,
> This sword of mine shall give them instant way,
> Where they shall rest for ever.   Trumpets, speak ! "

Read these last two speeches as fast as an actor, duly counterfeiting the excitement of the moment, must give them, and you will find that they puzzle any hearer who does not know them by heart.   The contrast shown by these quotations persists throughout the scenes in question.   In *Richard II.* the trial by battle fills 122 lines, and even then only begins ; in 44 lines of *King Lear,* which involve vastly more dramatic expression of character than is found in the older scene, the trial by battle is carried to an end.

Actual compactness, then, is one reason why the style of *King Lear* is at first glance obscure.   Philosophizing thrown in with no dramatic purpose often deepens the obscurity.   In the first scene of the fourth act, for example, Edgar enters and soliloquizes thus : —

> " Yet better thus, and known to be contemn'd,
> Than still contemn'd and flatter'd.   To be worst,
> The lowest and most dejected thing of fortune,
> Stands still in esperance, lives not in fear :
> The lamentable change is from the best;

[1] Ibid. 146–150.

> The worst returns to laughter. Welcome, then,
> Thou unsubstantial air that I embrace!
> The wretch that thou hast blown unto the worst
> Owes nothing to thy blasts. But who comes here ?"

In response to this cue, Gloster enters, blind, and led by an old man, to whom within a few lines he remarks : [1] —

> " I have no way, and therefore want no eyes;
> I stumbled when I saw : full oft 't is seen,
> Our means secure us, and our mere defects
> Prove our commodities."

Though any one can study out what these generalizations mean, no human being could ever have guessed from a single hasty hearing ; yet, apart from their actual meaning, they have no dramatic use. The truth is that such detailed illustration of the obscurity which pervades *King Lear* was probably needless. Open the play anywhere, read a dozen lines, and you will find yourself either amazed by their concentrated significance, or puzzled by their excessive compactness. On the stage such a style could never have been effective.

Ineffective on the stage, too, for all the intellectually dramatic strength of their conception, are many notable situations in *King Lear*. A single example will serve our purpose : take the great sixth scene of the third act, where mad King Lear, and his mournful Fool, and Edgar, who feigns madness, sit together, like a court in bank, to judge

[1] Lines 20–23.

an imaginary Goneril and Regan. However skilfully this be played, the grotesqueness of the three mad figures is bound to distract any modern mind from the tragic significance of the situation Yet, to any modern mind, the thought of regarding such a scene as grotesque is repellent.

So we come to the third reason why *King Lear* is nowadays puzzling. The superficial grotesqueness of that very scene clearly suggests this reason.

Glance at the titlepage of the quarto. *King Lear* was evidently set forth as a chronicle-history; and indeed it differs from what we still recognize as chronicle-history more in substance than in manner. Nowadays we make a sharp distinction between Plantagenets and the legendary sovereigns of prehistoric Britain. Holinshed makes little; no Elizabethan audience would have made much; and *King Lear* is translated straight from Holinshed to the Elizabethan stage. A playwright who should make a popular chronicle-history, however, was bound to translate his material into popular terms. In the case of *King Lear*, the rival quarto of 1605 and the emphasis on Shakspere's name in the two quartos of 1608 go far to prove that, at least when new, Shakspere's chronicle-history of *King Lear* was popular. Clearly this must have been in spite of the undue compactness of style which gives us fresh evidence of Shakspere's abnormal mental activity. At first sight, too, this popularity would seem to have existed in spite of the essentially unactable quality of such scenes as that where the mad court sits.

Glance again, though, at the titlepage. Remember that on the titlepage of the quarto of *Henry IV.* Falstaff had as much room as the King; and that on the titlepage of the quarto of *Henry V.* there was almost as much space given to Ancient Pistol. Clearly enough, these were the brands of comic sauce which added relish to the serious portions of the older chronicle-histories. On the titlepage of *King Lear* we find the same prominence given to " Edgar, sonne and heire to the Earle of Glocester, and his sullen and assumed humour of Tom of Bedlam." Startling as the obvious conclusion may seem, it is unavoidable: the character of Edgar, at least so far as his feigned madness went, was intended to be broadly comic. In this respect, too, it was not peculiar but conventional. To go no further, consider the comic scenes of Middleton's *Changeling;* and that dance of madmen in Webster's *Duchess of Malfi*, which nowadays seems so inexplicable. Once for all, the ravings of actual madness were conventionally accepted as comic by an Elizabethan audience, just as drunkenness is so accepted to-day.

Grasp this fact, and you will find the strangest of transformations in King Lear himself. Shakspere never conceived a character with deeper sympathetic insight. Nowadays, that is what we think of, just as nowadays we think of Shylock's profound human nature.[1] To go no further than the scene of the mad court, however, Lear is shown to us as a raving madman, and as such still looks grotesque. When Shaks-

[1] See p. 151 seq.

pere wrote, this grotesqueness, to-day so repellent, was a thing in which audiences were accustomed to delight. Only when we understand that King Lear, for all his marvellous pathos, was meant, in scene after scene, to impress an audience as comic, can we begin to understand the theatrical intention of Shakspere's tragedy.

Conventionally comic in this aspect, the part of King Lear appealed also to another Elizabethan taste of which little trace remains. As any of the old tragedies of blood or chronicle-histories will show, Elizabethan audiences delighted in sonorous rant. If no traces of the older plays were left, Hamlet's advice to the players[1] would suggest this, as well as the existence of a ripening taste which deprecated undue bombast. At the same time, this ripening taste, according to Ben Jonson,[2] had not prevailed even in 1614, when there were still men left to " sweare *Jeronimo* or *Andronicus* are the best playes." How to gratify this taste for rant without violating propriety, then, was a fine artistic problem. Shakspere solved it in the tremendously ranting speeches which fitly express the madness of Lear. At once ranting and grotesque, the madness of Lear, to-day so supremely and solely tragic, was probably the trait which chiefly made the Elizabethan public relish this play.

To dwell on these obsolete, archaic traits of *King Lear* has been doubly worth our while. They should

[1] *Hamlet,* III. ii.
[2] Induction to *Bartholomew Fair.* See p. 66.

serve, in the first place, to remind us of what we have lately inclined to forget, — that, with all their lasting greatness, Shakspere's tragedies were made for conditions so remote from ours that any student who should neglect their history runs constant risk of misunderstanding. In the second place, more notably still, such obsolete Elizabethan traits as probably secured the early popularity of *King Lear* are traits which the author must deliberately have introduced. Without meaning to, an artist may imply endless truth; when his art adapts his work to a popular demand, however, he can hardly be unaware of it.

The traits which make *King Lear* permanently great, on the other hand, are very different from what we have considered. No popular audience could ever much have relished them. They are the traits of thought, of imagination, of diction alike, which are generally characteristic of Shakspere. Nowhere do they appear, on study, more distinctly. No play of Shakspere's more surely rewards elaborate consideration. A single example will suffice us, — the excellent reasons which Goneril and Regan have to justify what is commonly held to be their gross ingratitude.

In the first place, these women have inherited from their father an impetuous, overbearing temper, of the kind which is especially sensitive to the exhibition of its own weaknesses by other people. Constitutionally, then, they would be specially liable to provocation by a man so like them as their father. In the second place, their elaborate professions of filial devotion are not essentially insincere; they are simply elaborate manifestations of such formal etiquette as still appears in the formulæ of correspondence. Cordelia's sincerity is an excess of not too mannerly virtue; Goneril's and Regan's protestations of love are only what court manners conventionally require. Lear, quartered with Goneril, behaves outrageously,[1] and she is justifiably angry; her anger manifests itself, characteristically, not by a direct outburst, but by orders, quite in accordance with court etiquette, that Lear and his rowdies be treated with abruptness. Just at this moment, Lear engages as a servant the disguised Earl of Kent, a very loyal, but a very hot-tempered nobleman.[2] When Goneril's steward is rude to Lear, Kent — believed to be an ordinary serving man — trips the steward up, thereby giving full color to the worst tales of Lear's rowdyism. Goneril thereupon, in fierce temper, remonstrates. Whereupon, amid the noisy chatter of his Fool, Lear, instead of listening to reason, proceeds to curse her, to rave, and to rush off to Regan. Naturally incensed, Goneril sends to Regan an unvarnished statement of what has occurred. Her messenger is the very steward whom Kent has thrashed. Kent meets him at Gloster's castle;[3] and addresses him in a way which, while perhaps tolerable from a nobleman to a servant, is quite intolerable between men of equal rank, which the disguise of Kent makes them appear. Another quarrel ensues. Regan and her husband come

[1] I. iii.   [2] I. iv.   [3] II. ii.

on the scene, to receive from Kent, Lear's messenger, no more explanation of his violent behavior than that he does not like the countenance of Goneril's steward. Cornwall, Regan's husband, suggests that his own personal appearance, or Regan's, might perhaps be equally distasteful. To which Kent answers,[1] —

> "Sir, 't is my occupation to be plain :
> I have seen better faces in my time
> Than stands on any shoulder that I see
> Before me at this instant."

Such conduct in a man whom nobody dreams to be anything but a common servant, merits the stocks. The worst stories of Goneril are confirmed, before Regan hears them, by this scandalous conduct of Lear's insolent follower. When Lear arrives,[2] Regan, once for all, will no more harbor rowdyism than will Goneril. Lear's behavior is in no way conciliatory. Finally, before he plunges off into the storm, both of his daughters have been worked up into such a rage that if they had acted as modern moralists command they would certainly have been too good for human nature. Given their temperaments, the conduct of Lear, and the misunderstanding involved in the clash between the character and the disguise of Kent, and nothing could be more humanly justifiable than their behavior. Yet so carefully is the intention of the plot preserved that to this day these passionate, human women are considered to be what Lear and the

---

[1] Lines 98–101.   [2] II. iv.

audience were expected to find them, — monsters of ingratitude.

To a student such not obvious but clearly discoverable traits as this, make any work of art fascinating; and *King Lear* constantly rewards minute criticism. Some have made a pathologic study of Lear's madness; others have delighted in æsthetic study of the means by which so painful a tragedy has been made to produce an effect of lasting beauty. Any study of *King Lear* reaps rich results. The intensity, the concentration of the play makes many critics speak of it as Shakspere's masterpiece.

This criticism is surely not final. Vastly though *King Lear* reward study, it surely demands study; and a masterpiece should possess not only the complexity but also the simplicity of greatness. Simplicity *King Lear* lacks, from the constant intensity of its concentration. Almost every other trait of greatness, however, it possesses; among them the trait that, whether we understand it or not, it produces an emotional effect peculiarly its own. The mood which underlies it is hard to phrase; murky, one may call it, passionate, despairing, terrible, transitory — and never be much nearer the truth than one began.

In this mood, however, there is clearly irony. Men are the sport of fate, as surely as were Iago and Hamlet and Brutus. The irony of *King Lear*, however, differs from the irony we have known before; it is accompanied by a rush of emotion which at first seems

to overpower thought. What need of thought? seems
the impulse here: thought cannot help us anywhither.
To the winds with it! Yet yield to emotion — as
Lear yields — and fate is just as pitiless; fate is even
more horrible still, for that way lies madness. Clearly
enough, in this conscious presentation of madness
there is trace of the overwrought state of mind which
revealed itself in the insane concentration of Iago, in
the maniacal intellectual activity of Hamlet.

Again, in the villainy of Goneril and of Regan, in
the story of Edmund, in the bitter obscenities of Lear's
ravings and of the Fool, we have fresh evidence of the
sexual mystery so constantly touched on in *Othello*,
in *Troilus and Cressida*, in *Measure for Measure*, in
Hamlet, in *All's Well that Ends Well*, and in the
Sonnets.

Throughout *King Lear*, too, passionate emotion
sweeps on with a surge hitherto unfelt. It tran-
scends all human power. It must needs be set in
the most passionate of natural backgrounds, — the
fiercest of actual tempests. Such critics as might
feel beneath the mood of *Hamlet* a lurking musical
cadence could find no hidden music here, but rather
would dream of the roll of thunder in the night.

In *King Lear*, however, there is something even
more profound than this storm of passion. *Othello*
contained wonderful touches of concentrated pathos;
every one must find them, for example, in the last
hours of Desdemona.[1] In *King Lear* one feels pathos

---

[1] *Othello*, IV. iii.

throughout. Fate-ridden, passionate man is pitiful, pitiful. Finally comes a deeper emotion still. The storm lulls ; death reveals itself, no longer a mystery, but a despairing solution of the problem of human agony. Such timid dreams as Hamlet's and Claudio's have no place in such misery as Lear's. There is no need to vex ourselves with fancies of what may lie beyond. No world, no life could be more evil than this of ours. Kent's farewell to the old King[1] speaks the final word of *King Lear :* —

> "Vex not his ghost : O, let him pass ! he hates him
> That would upon the rack of this tough world
> Stretch him out longer."

This overpowering mood which underlies *King Lear* seems, like the mood of *Hamlet,* emotionally sincere — self-revealing — to a degree unusual with Shakspere. To know such a mood, one grows to believe, he must have penetrated, really or sympathetically, deeper than we have yet guessed into the depths of spiritual suffering. For whoever wrote *King Lear* must have been intellectually alert to the verge of madness ; passionately sensitive the while to all the misery he perceived ; ironical yet pitiful ; kept within the bounds of sanity mostly by the blessed accident that he had mastered and controlled a great art of expression ; and yet despite his art, able to find no better comfort for all this misery than the certainty that, at all events as we know life, life mercifully ends.

[1] V. iii. 313.

IX. MACBETH.

[The first record of *Macbeth* is in the note-book of one Dr. Simon Forman, who saw it at the Globe on April 20th, 1610. His note which is too long for quotation here, begins thus : "There was to be observed, first how Macbeth and Banquo, two noblemen of Scotland, riding through a wood, there stood before them three women Fairies, or Nymphs, and saluted Macbeth, saying three times unto him, Hail, King of Coder, for thou shalt be a King, but shalt beget no Kings, etc." No other indubitable mention of *Macbeth* has been discovered until its entry in 1623, and its publication in the folio.

Its source, like that of *King Lear* and the chronicle-histories, is Holinshed. There seems to have been an earlier play on the subject.

Macbeth, in its present condition, is evidently incomplete, — either an unfinished sketch, or an abridgment of a finished play. There has been much discussion as to whether much of the witch-scenes was not probably added by Middleton. On various internal grounds, however, including the fact that so-called light and weak endings to lines here first appear to any considerable degree, *Macbeth* has generally been assigned to about 1606.]

At a glance one can see that *Macbeth* differs conspicuously from any other play of Shakspere's. It is comparatively very short,[1] very monotonous, and very firm. There is hardly any underplot, hardly any comic matter. One scene, to be sure, — that of the bleeding sergeant,[2] — is so archaic as to suggest that it may possibly be a fragment of some older play ;

---

[1] In the *Globe Shakespeare* it occupies 22 pages, while *Hamlet* occupies 35, and *King Lear* and *Othello* each occupy about 32. The Leopold Shakspere, p. cxxiii., gives Hamlet 3931 lines, *King Lear* 3332, *Othello* 3317, and *Macbeth* 2108.

[2] I. ii.

another, — that where Macduff and Ross meet Malcolm in England,[1] — while taken straight from Holinshed, is so highly finished as to suggest either that it is the single remaining fragment of a more elaborate play than now remains, or else that it was either written in a momentary lapse of mood, or inserted later, when the emotional impulse which pervades *Macbeth* had subsided. Apart from these scenes, hardly anything but the Witches and the Porter interrupts the swift, steady progress of the action.

Similar concentration of purpose we found in *Othello*. While every detail of *Othello*, however, is developed with masterly care, *Macbeth* is only blocked out with masterly firmness of hand; it is nowhere elaborated. Not long ago, an Elizabethan play — the *Maid's Tragedy*, of Beaumont and Fletcher — was adapted for a private performance by the simple process of striking out the underplot, and whatever else did not concern the principal story. The result was a short, admirably dramatic play, remarkable for swift firmness of action and development, but somehow — while essentially complete — subtly unfinished. In other words, after due allowance for the difference between Shakspere and Beaumont and Fletcher, the effect produced by thus isolating the main plot of the *Maid's Tragedy* was closely analogous to the effect of *Macbeth*.

Macbeth, in short, is just what we should expect from a collaborator who had agreed to furnish the serious part of a chronicle-history, or a tragedy, to be

[1] IV. iii.

completed by comic scenes from somebody else. Better still, perhaps, it is what we should expect from an Elizabethan playwright who, carried away by one aspect of his subject, had finished one part independently, leaving the rest for some future moment which never came. Equally, of course, it is what you may make of any complete Elizabethan tragedy by cutting out everything but the main action. If it were ever finished, this is probably what has happened to it; if not, the play gives two or three indications of why further finish may have seemed needless. One of these is its dramatic effectiveness; it still acts admirably. Another is that, while too long to admit a fully developed underplot within the limits of a single performance, it is too compact to be abridged without injury.

As to whether *Macbeth* be a sketch or an abridgment there is no direct evidence. Mr. Fleay [1] and many other competent critics believe it an abridgment. The analogies between the witch-scenes and Middleton's *Witch* [2] might be held to point the other way. Conceivably they might indicate that the witch-scenes in the original play were so slight as to need augmentation; if so, there would be a little reason to believe *Macbeth* not an abridgment but a sketch. The general effect of the style, too, points slightly towards the same conclusion; throughout the play there is such

---

[1] *Life*, 238–242.

[2] Discussed in Furness, *Variorum Shakespeare: Macbeth*, pp. 388–405.

swift precision of touch as one would expect in a hasty, consecutive piece of master-work. What *Macbeth* lacks, too, apart from comic passages and under-plot, is chiefly that elaboration of minor characters and of subtle phrase which careful finish would supply, and which a sketch would probably lack.

To say that *Macbeth* lacks anything, however, seems stupid; it lacks nothing essential; in total effect no play could be more definitely complete. Until one count the lines, indeed, it is hard to realize how few the strokes are by which this effect is produced. Elaboration could add nothing but detail and occasional relief.

In certain moods, one may fairly feel that *Macbeth* needs relief. Its temper is certainly monotonous, with a terrible monotony of despair. Macbeth himself is a wonderful study of fate-ridden, irresponsible, yet damning crime. Meaningless in one aspect such a figure seems; yet its appalling, unmeaning mystery is everlastingly true. This view of human nature is again like that formulated by Calvinism.[1] Forced to sin by an incarnate power beyond himself, man, eternally unregenerate, is nevertheless held to account for every act of a will perverted by the sin and the curse of ancestral humanity. He is the sport of external powers; and so far as these powers deal with him they are all evil, malicious, wreaking ill without end. Life, then, is a horrible mystery; it is a " fitful fever," [2] after which perhaps the chosen few may sleep well; it

---

[1] See pp. 269, 273.   [2] III. ii. 23.

is " a tale told by an idiot, full of sound and fury, signifying nothing." [1] Consciousness, indeed, is a delirium,
a raving imbecility; yet when the end comes he who
first cries " Hold, enough ! " [2] is damned for the deeds
of his delirious raving. The hackneyed rhyme of
Macbeth's last speech makes us forget, for an instant,
the full horror of its triumphantly Calvinistic meaning. As we ponder, the horror grows; there are
moods in which we cry out a protest.

In other moods, more subtly æsthetic, we may find
in *Macbeth* as it stands all the relief we need. Its
amazing precision of style is so stimulating that one
may constantly delight in the lines, quite apart from
their significance. [3] In *King Lear*, as we saw, a tremendous access of thought deprives the style of simplicity. In *Macbeth* the superficial simplicity of style
is remarkable; one is rarely puzzled by overpacked
meaning. Somehow, though, for all its superhuman
power, the style of Macbeth has not the final quality
which marks the difference between a masterly sketch
and a finished work of art. Yet no one would alter it.

Quite apart from style, too, the ultimate truth to
life of both characters and situations throughout gives
one a pleasure which goes far to obviate the horror
of the motive. This truth to life is nowhere more
remarkable than in the supernatural passages. Fantastically weird as these seem, they actually fall in
with some of the results approached by modern inves-

---

[1] V. v. 26.   [2] V. viii. 34.
[3] A random example will illustrate this: e. g. II. ii. 9–21.

tigators who are scientifically observing occult phenomena. The Witches stand for such introducers to the hidden realms as in our unromantic world are called mediums. Macbeth's fancy once enthralled by these, he becomes something of a medium himself: he sees a phantom dagger, he hears warning voices, he is visited by the spectre of Banquo, he witnesses the mysteries of the Witches' cavern. Meanwhile, from beginning to end, he is undergoing that subtle, intangible, inevitable process of intellectual and moral degradation which is bound to ruin whoever, without holiest motive, ventures into occult mysteries.[1] The truth of these supernatural scenes, indeed, seems to indicate that Shakspere's knowledge of occult phenomena was growing. In *Richard III.*, his ghosts were mere nursery goblins; in *Julius Cæsar*, the spirit of the murdered Cæsar had become a sort of incarnate fate; in *Hamlet*, the ghost was the individual disembodied spirit of tradition; in *Macbeth*, the dagger, the weird voices, and the ghastly shape of Banquo are such visions, or delusions, as throughout human history constantly occur to unhappy men.

In connection with this matter, a note by Mr. Greene is suggestive : —

"Semi-insanity begins to seem almost subjective in Shakspere, especially in this case where it takes an aspect not uncommon in literary men. The beings whom they create first begin to act independently of the writer's

[1] Cf. a paper on the Salem Witches, in *Stelligeri and Other Essays Concerning America.*

volition, then to appear as hallucinations unsummoned. Very likely this happened to Shakspere not merely when he dreamt, but when he was awake; and this is just what happens to Macbeth: First he sees a dagger which he recognizes as unreal but cannot dismiss. Then a voice says to him 'Sleep no more.' Finally he thinks the ghost real whom only he sees. Perhaps this is complete insanity; but probably Shakspere did not think so."

The means by which the characters of Macbeth and his Lady are expressed, indeed, would suggest doubt as to whether Shakspere could have deliberately thought of them at all, except as concepts which he was bound to embody in phrase. The amazing compactness of their lines surprises whoever counts the words. In the first act, where both of these great psychological conceptions are thoroughly set forth, Lady Macbeth has fourteen speeches, comprising 864 words, and Macbeth has twenty-six speeches, comprising 878 words. In all, the speeches of Lady Macbeth number less than 60, many of them very short; and those of Macbeth, some of them equally short, number less than 150. The art with which in so little space Shakspere has created and defined two of the most vital characters of all literature is a matter for constant admiration.

So constant is one's admiration for *Macbeth* that one is apt to forget the archaism which really pervades all the work of Shakspere. In this case, Dr. Forman's note of the play should bring us to ourselves. On April 20, 1610, " there was to be observed," he writes,

" how Macbeth and Banquo, two noblemen of Scotland, *riding through a wood*, there stood before them three women, etc." The fact that these personages were riding through a wood was presented to the eyes of Dr. Forman by the stage arrangements of the Globe Theatre. The methods by which it was probably presented would now seem incredible. Instead of a painted scene illuminated by green foot-lights, the wood probably consisted either of one or two Christmas trees, lugged in by attendants, or else of a placard posted at the back of the stage, at the sides of which Dr. Forman and his friends would sit, chatting and eating fruit, in plain sight of the audience. As to the riding, Macbeth and Banquo probably made their first entry with wicker-work hobby-horses about their waists, with false human legs, of half the natural length, dangling from the saddles, and with sweeping skirts to hide the actors' feet. Monstrous as such a proceeding seems, it might still occur in serious tragedy on the Chinese stage ; and the Chinese stage is very like the Elizabethan. A fact in *Macbeth* which slightly tends to prove this conjecture is that just before Banquo is killed he dismisses his horses behind the scenes,[1] and enters on foot. To die with a hobby-horse about one's waist would have been too much for even Elizabethan conventions.

The peculiar effect of *Macbeth*, then, we have traced to the facts that while its stage conventions are ultimately archaic and its general treatment is remarkably

[1] III. iii. 8-14.

sketchy, its conception and style are profoundly true to human nature. In a subtle way, too, *Macbeth*, as one grows to know it, impresses one like *Othello* as strongly objective. The moods which underlie *Hamlet* and *King Lear* seem moods of which the poet might sometimes have been conscious as his own. The moods of *Othello* and *Macbeth* seem rather moods which the poet, if conscious of them at all, would probably have thought that he was inventing by sheer force of sympathetic imagination.

As we have seen before, however, even work which is not primarily self-revealing can never express anything but what in some form or other its maker has known.[1] *Macbeth*, accordingly, once more displays the traits which pervade the other tragedies. To begin with, as Mr. Greene's note suggested, it shows fresh traces of an overwrought state of mind. The restless activity of Hamlet, the concentration of Iago, the passion of Othello, the raving of Lear, the ghost-seeing of Macbeth, the sleep-walking of Lady Macbeth, all show the same morbid tendency. It is not for a moment to be guessed that Shakspere was insane; his constant judgment, his artistic sanity were enough to preserve him from any such fate. Beyond reasonable doubt, however, his mind was at this period abnormally active; and, perhaps in consequence, his imagination centred on morbid mental conditions. Again, in *Macbeth*, woman plays the devil's part. Compare the second series of the *Sonnets*, the relation of

---

[1] See p. 229.

the Queen and Ophelia in *Hamlet* to the men whom
they half-innocently destroy, the wantonness of Cressida, the effect on Othello of the self-destructive gentle-
ness of Desdemona, the cruelty and lust of Goneril and
Regan, the active mischief of the Witches and of Lady
Macbeth. All alike reveal a mind keenly alive to
the manifold harm, wittingly or unwittingly, done by
women. Finally, in *Macbeth*, the mood which we
have called Calvinistic expresses, with unprecedented
abandonment to artistic passion, an ultimately ironical
view of human life. At least to human beings, life is
an unrelieved misery — a tale told by an idiot, full of
sound and fury, signifying nothing. Taken for all
in all, *Macbeth* reveals deeper knowledge of spiritual
misery than we have fathomed before.

To appreciate this, we may best glance back at the
four serious tragedies which have preceded. In each
there are a few lines broadly suggestive of the temper which pervades it. Take Juliet's last speech to
her nurse : [1] —

> " Farewell!   God knows when we shall meet again;"

or Romeo's final words : [2] —

> " Here 's to my love !   O true apothecary !
> Thy drugs are quick.   Thus, with a kiss I die."

Somehow these lines recall the sentimental pathos of
Romeo and Juliet, that romantic poem which beside
the great tragedies seems hardly tragic at all.

---

[1] *Romeo and Juliet*, IV. iii. 14.   [2] Ibid. V. iii. 119.

Take Hamlet's dying speech to Horatio : [1] —

> " If thou didst ever hold me in thine heart,
> Absent thee from felicity awhile,
> And in this harsh world draw thy breath in pain,
> To tell my story ; "

and Horatio's farewell words : [2] —

> " Now cracks a noble heart.   Good-night, sweet prince,
> And flights of angels sing thee to thy rest !"

These words somehow imply the mood of one who should dream of death as after all an end to the bewilderment of human existence.

Take Othello's savagely conscious death-cry : [3] —

> " Set you down this ;
> And say besides, that in Aleppo once,
> Where a malignant and a turban'd Turk
> Beat a Venetian and traduced the state,
> I took by the throat the circumcised dog,
> And smote him, thus ! "

Somehow death comes as a splendid climax of passion. In *Othello*, as in *Hamlet*, life is a mystery ; death is a mystery, too ; but there may be dreams of compensation.

Then take Kent's speech of farewell to the dying Lear : [4] —

> " Vex not his ghost: O, let him pass ! he hates him
> That would upon the rack of this tough world
> Stretch him out longer."

Life here is unmixed agony.   Only in death can there be even a dream of peace.

---

[1] *Hamlet,* V. ii. 357.

[2] Ibid. 370.

[3] *Othello,* V. ii. 351.

[4] *King Lear,* V. iii. 313.

Then take the words we have already cited from *Macbeth* : —

> " Duncan is in his grave ;
> After life's fitful fever he sleeps well." [1]

> " Life's but a walking shadow, a poor player
> That struts and frets his hour upon the stage
> And then is heard no more : it is a tale
> Told by an idiot, full of sound and fury,
> Signifying nothing." [2]

Finally, take Macbeth's last shout : [3] —

> " Lay on, Macduff,
> And damn'd be he that first cries ' Hold, enough!' "

One feels in *Macbeth* the climax of all, — a knowledge of the last word of soul-sick despair.

X. ANTONY AND CLEOPATRA.

[*Antony and Cleopatra* was entered in the Stationers' Register on May 20th, 1608. It was not published until the folio of 1623.

Its source is North's Plutarch.

On internal evidence, it is generally assigned conjecturally to 1607.]

Composed throughout according to the conventions of chronicle-history, *Antony and Cleopatra* is at first sight bewildering. Whoever would appreciate it must deliberately revive the mood of an Elizabethan public, abandon himself to this mood, accept as normal what is really archaic. The effort is worth all the

[1] III. ii. 22.   [2] V. v. 24.   [3] V. vii. 33.

pains it may cost; for while very close to its narrative source, *Antony and Cleopatra* displays at once masterly discretion in the selection of dramatic material, masterly power of creating both character and atmosphere, and unsurpassed mastery of language. The old conventions once accepted, indeed, the play may without extravagance be called the masterpiece of the kind of literature which began with *Henry IV.*, — of historical fiction.

To appreciate its full power, we may best compare passages from it with other treatments of the same or similar subjects. As a matter of mere description, for example, take the account in North's Plutarch of how Antony first sees Cleopatra, and compare with it the version of the story in Dryden's *All for Love*, and finally Shakspere's.

Here is North's version:[1] —

"She disdained to set forward otherwise, but to take her barge in the river of Cydnus; the poop whereof was of gold, the sails of purple, and the oars of silver, which kept stroke in rowing after the sound of the music of flutes, howboys, cithernes, viols, and such other instruments as they played upon in the barge. And now for the person of her self, she was laid under a pavilion of cloth of gold of tissue, apparelled and attired like the goddess Venus, commonly drawn in picture: and hard by her, on either hand of her, pretty fair boys apparelled as painters do set forth god Cupid, with little fans in their hands, with the which they fanned wind upon her. Her ladies and gentlewomen also, the fairest of them, were apparelled like the nymphs

[1] Rolfe: *Antony and Cleopatra*, 151.

Nereids (which are the mermaids of the waters) and like the Graces; some steering the helm, others tending the tackle and ropes of the barge, out of the which there came a wonderful passing sweet savour of perfumes, that perfumed the wharf's side, pestered with innumerable multitudes of people."

Dryden's *All for Love*, published in 1678, as a matter of avowed rivalry with Shakspere, puts this passage into the mouth of Antony, who rehearses it to Dolabella,[1] as follows : —

" Her galley down the silver Cydnos rowed,
  The tackling silk, the streamers waved with gold;
  The gentle winds were lodged in purple sails :
  Her nymphs, like Nereids, round her couch were placed ;
  Where she, another sea-born Venus, lay.

   .   .   .   .

  She lay, and leant her cheek upon her hand ;
  And cast a look so languishingly sweet,
  As if, secure of all beholders' hearts,
  Neglecting, she could take them : boys, like Cupids,
  Stood fanning, with their painted wings, the winds
  That played about her face : but if she smiled,
  A darting glory seemed to blaze abroad,
  That men's desiring eyes were never wearied,
  But hung upon the object : to soft flutes
  The silver oars kept time ; and while they played,
  The hearing gave new pleasure to the sight ;
  And both to thought.   'T was heaven or somewhat more;
  For she so charmed all hearts, that gazing crowds
  Stood panting on the shore, and wanted breath
  To give their welcome voice."

Compare with these the version which Shakspere puts into the mouth of cool, shrewd Enobarbus : [2] —

[1] III. i.   [2] II. ii. 196–223.

The barge she sat in, like a burnish'd throne,
Burned on the water : the poop was beaten gold ;
Purple the sails, and so perfumed that
The winds were love-sick with them; the oars were silver,
Which to the tune of flutes kept stroke, and made
The water which they beat to follow faster,
As amorous of their strokes.   For her own person,
It beggar'd all description : she did lie
In her pavilion — cloth-of-gold of tissue —
O'erpicturing that Venus where we see
The fancy outwork nature : on each side her
Stood pretty dimpled boys, like smiling Cupids,
With divers-coloured fans, whose wind did seem
To glow the delicate cheeks which they did cool,
And what they undid did.   .   .   .   .
Her gentlewomen, like the Nereides,
So many mermaids, tended her i' the eyes,
And made their bends adornings : at the helm
A seeming mermaid steers : the silken tackle
Swell with the touches of those flower-soft hands
That yarely frame the office.   From the barge
A strange invisible perfume hits the sense
Of the adjacent wharfs.   The city cast
Her people out upon her; and Antony,
Enthron'd i' the market-place, did sit alone,
Whistling to the air; which, but for vacancy,
Had gone to gaze on Cleopatra too,
And made a gap in nature."

At once far closer to the original than Dryden, and
less ingeniously laborious in his variations, Shakspere
is at the same time more poetic and more plausible.

Now for the character of Cleopatra.   In *All for
Love,* Dryden brings her face to face with Octavia,[1]
and here is what passes : —

[1] III. i.

"*Octav.* I need not ask if you are Cleopatra;
Your haughty carriage —
   Cleo.   Shows I am a queen:
Nor need I ask you, who you are.
   Octav.   A Roman;
A name that makes and can unmake a queen.
   Cleo. Your lord, the man who serves me, is a Roman.
   Octav. He was a Roman, till he lost that name,
To be a slave in Egypt; but I come
To free him thence.
   Cleo.   Peace, peace, my lover's Juno.
When he grew weary of that household clog,
He chose my easier bonds."

Admirably theatrical though that dialogue be, compare it with the passage from Shakspere, where Cleopatra believes that Antony has received a stirring message from his wife:[1]

"*Cleo.*   I am sick and sullen.
   Ant. I am sorry to give breathing to my purpose, —
   Cleo. Help me away, dear Charmian; I shall fall:
It cannot be thus long, the sides of nature
Will not sustain it.
   Ant.   Now, my dearest queen, —
   Cleo. Pray you, stand farther from me.
   Ant.   What's the matter?
   Cleo. I know, by that same eye, there's some good news.
What says the married woman?" etc.

Just as theatrical, and far more colloquial, Shakspere's scene seems comparatively like a fragment of real life. So any treatment of Cleopatra by Shakspere seems when we put it beside any of Corneille's, — as, for example, when she declares to Cæsar:[2]

---

[1] I. iii. 13.   [2] Corneille, *Pompée*, IV. iii.

"Je scais ce que je dois au souverain bonheur
Dont me comble et m'accable un tel excés d'honneur.
Je ne vous tiendray plus mes passions secrettes ;
Je scais ce que je suis, je scais ce que vous étes;
Vous daignastes m'aimer dès mes plus jeunes ans ;
Le sceptre que je porte est un de vos presens;
Vous n'avez par deux fois rendu le diadème:
J'avouë après cela, Seigneur, que je vous aime," etc.

John Fletcher, too, treated the loves of Cleopatra
and Julius Cæsar ; and here is how he made her
coquet with the great Roman:[1]

> "*Cleo.* (*giving a jewel*). Take this,
> And carry it to that lordly Cæsar sent thee ;
> There's a new love, a handsome one, a rich one,
> One that will hug his mind: bid him make love to it;
> Tell the ambitious broker, this will suffer —
>   *Apol.* He enters.
>   *Enter* Cæsar.
> *Cleo.*   How!
> *Cæs.*   I do not use to wait, lady;
> Where I am, all the doors are free and open.
>   *Cleo.*   I guess so by your rudeness;"

And so on.

The very end of *Antony and Cleopatra*, however, is
perhaps more typical than any other passage. Here
is North's version of Cleopatra's death:[2] —

"When they had opened the doors, they found Cleopatra stark-dead, laid upon a bed of gold, attired and
arrayed in her royal robes, and one of her two women,
which was called Iras, dead at her feet: and the other
woman (called Charmion) half dead, and trembling, trim-
ming the diadem which Cleopatra wore upon her head.

[1] *The False One*, IV. ii.   [2] Rolfe, 167.

One of the soldiers seeing her, angrily said unto her: 'Is that well done, Charmion?' 'Very well,' she said again, 'and meet for a princess descended from the race of so many noble kings:' she said no more, but fell down dead hard by the bed.''

In *All for Love*, Dryden makes Cleopatra greet the asp thus:

> " Welcome, thou kind deceiver!
> Thou best of thieves ; who with an easy key
> Dost open life, and, unperceived by us,
> Even steal us from ourselves," and so on.

The guard at that moment clamor for admission; whereupon, in the presence of both Iras and Charmian, Cleopatra thus applies the asp:

> " Haste, bare my arm, and rouse the serpent's fury.
> Coward flesh,
> Wouldst thou conspire with Cæsar to betray me
> As thou wert none of mine ?   I 'll force thee to it,
> And not be sent by him,
> But bring myself, my soul, to Antony.
> Take hence; the work is done.''

The women then apply asps to themselves. Iras instantly dies. The guard break in, and one exclaims:

> " 'T was what I feared, —
> Charmion, is this well done ?
> *Char.* Yes, 't is well done, and like a queen, the last
> Of her great race: I follow her.   [*Dies.*]''

In *Antony and Cleopatra*, Iras dies before Cleopatra applies the asp. Then come these marvellous speeches:[1]

[1] V. ii. 303 seq.

> " *Cleo.*   This proves me base ;
> If she first meet the curled Antony,
> He 'll make demand of her, and spend that kiss
> Which is my heaven to have.   Come, thou mortal wretch,
> With thy sharp teeth this knot intrinsicate
> Of life at once untie: poor venomous fool,
> Be angry, and dispatch.   O, couldst thou speak,
> That I might hear thee call great Cæsar ass
> Unpolicied !
>   *Char.*   O eastern star !
>   *Cleo.*   Peace, peace !
> Dost thou not see my baby at my breast,
> That sucks the nurse asleep ? "

Finally, when the queen is dead, and the guard break
in, a soldier speaks : —

> " What work is here !   Charmian, is this well done ?
>   *Char.*   It is well done, and fitting for a princess
> Descended of so many royal kings.
> Ah, soldier !   [*Dies.*]"

This prolonged quotation was probably the shortest
as well as the most definite means of showing how,
amid a considerable group of skilful historical fictions,
Shakspere's *Antony and Cleopatra* emerges as a masterpiece of history.   While the other treatments of
Cleopatra are theatrically effective, Shakspere's not
only creates a miraculously human woman, but actually revives the death throes of the ancient world.
Of course *Antony and Cleopatra* is a great poem.
For all its light and weak endings, all the growing freedom of style which marks the beginning of
metrical decay, its phrasing throughout is far above

the indignity of actual life. No human being, for example, would ever have uttered many of the phrases we have considered already; nor yet such words as the more famous ones with which the play teems:

> " Age cannot wither her, nor custom stale
>   Her infinite variety;"[1]

>   " She looks like sleep,
>   As she would catch another Antony
>   In her strong toil of grace;"[2]

and more. All its veracity of detail does not make *Antony and Cleopatra* realistic in style. The difference between this great poem, however, and the most literally phrased of modern histories is only a difference of method. Essentially each brings us face to face with an actual historic past; each leaves us in a mood which we might have felt, had we known that past in the flesh.

In the flesh whoever knew it must have known it best. The life here brought back from the dust was nowise spiritual. The world which *Antony and Cleopatra* revives was dying. What had made Rome Roman, Greece Greek, Egypt Egyptian, was passing. Ruin was everywhere impending, not instant, but none the less fatal. The old ideals were gone; nor was there yet any gleam of the new ideals to come. This falling world, though, once great and noble, retained even in its fall the aspect of its past grandeur; and like all great moments of decadence it afforded to whoever would plunge into its vortex such splendor of

---

[1] II. ii. 240.   [2] V. ii. 349.

sensuous, earthly delight that in certain moods one still envies the animal ecstasies of those who fell, disdaining all nobler sense. Nor is such sympathy with the intoxication of evil a thing in which even the purest of heart need feel shame. No one can know the real grandeur of moral conquest who does not also realize the alluring delights of moral degradation over which such conquest must triumph.

We wander from Shakespere, however. Such matters as we have just touched on are not specifically set forth in *Antony and Cleopatra*. What Shakspere there does, as we have seen, is simply to present the facts of Plutarch's narrative in a grandly objective way. In these facts themselves were inherent all this sympathetic knowledge of fleshly delight, and all these splendid gleams of what made noble classic antiquity. In the facts, too, was inherent the great solemnity of world ruin. All this the very facts make us feel. Nowhere in literature is the atmosphere of an historic past more marvellously or more faithfully revived.

In this atmosphere live men and women whose individuality, like that of men and women in the flesh, while complete, is not instantly salient. What one first feels in *Antony and Cleopatra* is the world-movement which whirls all these people on, the local and temporal atmosphere which enshrouds them. By and by, however, as one grows to know them better, each personage begins to stand out as distinct as any living individual whom one grows really to know.

Take, for example, the scene on Pompey's galley.[1] In
Plutarch there is the merest hint for this scene:[2]

"So he cast anchors enow into the sea, to make his galley
fast, from the head of Mount Misena: and there he wel-
comed them, and made them great cheer. Now in the
midst of the feast, when they fell to be merry with Anto-
nius' love unto Cleopatra, Menas the pirate came to Pompey, and whispering in his ear, said unto him : 'Shall I
cut the cables of the anchors, and make thee lord not only
of Sicily and Sardinia, but of the whole empire of Rome
besides ? ' Pompey, having paused awhile upon it, at
length answered him: 'Thou shouldest have done it, and
never have told it me ; but now we must content us with
that we have ; as for myself, I was never taught to break
my faith, nor to be counted a traitor ! ' "

From this plain statement of fact Shakspere developed one of the most consummately dramatic scenes in
literature. The triple head of imperial Rome is drunk,
each in his own way: Antony boisterous, Octavius
gravely silent, Lepidus silly. All are utterly in the
power of an unscrupulous enemy ; all are saved from
a fate which might have altered the course of history
by the single surviving scruple of a man who usually
had none. Then the drunken Lepidus is bundled over
the side ; and the empire is safe. This whole story is
told in seventy-five lines, which not only set forth the
intensely dramatic situation, but preserve meanwhile a
constant sense of how funny men are when the worse
for drink. Every syllable of this astonishing scene
has a specific office.

[1] II. vii.   [2] Rolfe, 154.

This scene, then, clearly displays the trait which distinguishes *Antony and Cleopatra* from the plays which precede. As we have already seen again and again, Shakspere's power of creating individual character, and thereby of creating an atmosphere, remains unsurpassed. The tremendous activity of mind which has been palpable from *Hamlet* onward remains constant, too; every syllable is packed with meaning. On the other hand, however, the profound emotional impulse which has surged beneath the great tragedies seems here to slacken. *Antony and Cleopatra* has passion enough and to spare; but it is passion presented in a coolly dramatic, dispassionate way. The effect is perhaps of more supreme mastery than any we have met before. More than before, however, the sense that this is mastery obtrudes itself. What makes *Antony and Cleopatra* so peculiarly great, indeed, is probably a slight relaxation of that intense artistic impulse which made so great in a different way *Hamlet*, and *Othello*, and *King Lear*, and *Macbeth*.

Creative power, however, even though it lack a little of the spontaneous intensity which one felt in Hamlet, in Iago, in Lear, in Macbeth, is as great as ever. To pass from the lesser characters, each of whom is thoroughly individual, there are in all literature no two personages more consummately alive than Antony and Cleopatra themselves. So living do they seem, indeed, that to analyze them is as grave a task as to analyze real human beings. Each is not only true to fact, but more. Antony is not only the Antony, and

Cleopatra the Cleopatra of recorded history; each broadly typifies eternal phases of human nature. Antony is the lasting type of that profound infatuation which is the most insidious snare of passionate middle-life; Cleopatra is the supreme type of all that in womanhood is fatal.

In this view of woman as fatal to man, whoever has pursued our course of study must find the culmination of a series of moods concerning sexual relations, for whose origin we must look far back. From the Rosaline of *Love's Labour's Lost* through Portia to Beatrice, and Rosalind, and Viola, we had a series of figures which expressed the mood of innocent, adoring fascination. In *All's Well that Ends Well*, in *Hamlet*, in *Measure for Measure*, we had expressions, in varying terms, of the troubles which spring from such beginnings, when without relaxing its hold fascination is invaded by doubt. In *Troilus and Cressida* and in *Othello* we had doubt more definitely and more passionately stated, with all its bewildering uncertainty. In *King Lear* we had cruelty incarnate in woman; in *Macbeth* woman embodied all the evil influences and the evil counsel which may ruin man. Here in Cleopatra we have the whole story summed up, in a masterly psychologic recapitulation, which reminds one of the masterly dramatic recapitulation so characteristic of Shakspere, and most evident in *Twelfth Night*. It is idle to deny, too, that the moods thus recapitulated are very like what we may believe to underlie the second series of *Sonnets*.

The unanswerable question which that last suggestion raises, however, — as to whether Beatrice and
Cleopatra be different portraits of the same living
woman who inspired the *Sonnets*, — is impertinent.
The Shakspere with whom we may legitimately deal
is not the man, who has left no record of his actual
life, but the artist, who has left the fullest record of
his emotional experience. To search for the actual
man is at once unbecoming and futile. What we can
fairly assert of this great *Antony and Cleopatra* is
enough for our purpose: If we once accept the conventions of chronicle-history, this play reveals an artist,
objective in temper and consummate master of his art,
who has told a historic story with supreme artistic
truth; and the story, impregnated at once with the
sense of irony which we have learned to know and with
a more profound sense than ever of the evil which woman may wreak, is a story which supremely, dispassionately expresses the tragedy of world-decadence.

XI. Coriolanus.

[*Coriolanus* was first entered in 1623 and published in the folio. No
earlier allusion to it is known.

Its source, like that of *Antony and Cleopatra*, is North's *Plutarch*.

Verse-tests[1] place it near *Antony and Cleopatra*. For examples of
"light" endings, see II. i. 238, 241, 243, 245; for "weak" endings, see
V. vi. 75, 76. The number of weak endings in *Coriolanus* is exceeded
only in *Cymbeline*. Shakspere's verse is clearly breaking down. On
this ground chiefly, common conjecture now assigns *Coriolanus* to
about 1608.]

[1] See Dowden's *Primer*, 39-44, and Mr. Ingram's paper in the New
Shakspere Society's Transactions for 1874, p. 442.

Like *Antony and Cleopatra* and *Julius Cæsar,* *Coriolanus* at first appears to be a chronicle-history based on Plutarch instead of on Holinshed, not English but Roman. Whatever its relations to *Julius Cæsar,* however, it proves in total effect very unlike *Antony and Cleopatra.* That masterpiece of historical fiction impresses whoever will accept its conventions as actual history. *Coriolanus,* on the other hand, impresses one neither as actual history nor yet exactly as historical fiction. It seems rather a presentation, in dramatic form, of a historical story the conception of which is affected throughout by a definite philosophical bias.

This does not mean, of course, that *Coriolanus* any more than *Henry V.* may rationally be deemed a philosophical treatise. Throughout this study we cannot too often remind ourselves that Shakspere was an artist, — a man who finding that experience, actual or recorded, excited in him specific moods, gave his conscious energy to the expression of those moods with little care for their ultimate meaning. What moods mean is a question for philosophers and critics, not for artists; even in Genesis, the Creator does not pronounce his work good until it is finished. An artist's moods, however, may be very various; now and again their relation to actual life and conduct may be far closer than usual. That seemed the case with *Henry V.;* in a different way it seems again the case with *Coriolanus.*

The technical factor of *Coriolanus* in which this

change of mood most distinctly appears is the characterization. The personages remain individual, of course; by this time Shakspere's hand was too practised to leave any figure indefinite. Compared with the personages in the plays we have considered from *Romeo and Juliet* forward, however, those in *Coriolanus* seem not so conspicuously individual, as typical. Volumnia, for example, is not only the mother of Coriolanus; she is the sort of figure which moralizers have in mind when they expound the virtues of " the Roman mother " in general. So Virgilia is the devoted wife; so Menenius Agrippa is the wise old friend; so, more notably still, the tribunes, Sicinius and Brutus, are twin types of the demagogue. This typical quality of the characters in *Coriolanus* is so marked, indeed, that in the Elizabethan sense of the word we may almost call the characterization throughout this play " humourous." Such " humourous " treatment of character prevails throughout didactic fiction. So *Coriolanus* seems didactic.

The trait is most palpable in the twin demagogues. We have seen forerunners of them in Jack Cade and in the tribune whose incendiary eloquence during the first scene of *Julius Cæsar* is so hackneyed at school.[1] Neither of these, however, is anything like so strongly emphasized or so fully developed as Sicinius and Brutus. Nor in *Henry VI.* or *Julius Cæsar* is there anything like so fully developed a presentation of the populace whom tribunes or demagogues lead.

[1] See pp. 80, 243.

The people, in fact, — that great underlying mass of humanity in which must reside the physical power of any nation, — is presented in *Coriolanus* with ultimate precision. In *Henry VI.* the vivid sketch of Jack Cade's rebellion shows a turbulently unreasonable mob which quickly comes to grief. In *Julius Cæsar*, the mob is actually the seat of power, which it transfers, at unreasoning impulse, from one great leader to another; but the great leaders, no unequal rivals, stand ready each in turn to personify imperial sovereignty. In *Coriolanus*, the mob, unreasoning, turbulent, capricious as ever, becomes a devouring monster. It no longer contents itself with transferring power; it seizes power for itself, and once possessed of power behaves with suicidal unreason. The climax from *Henry VI.*, the experimental chronicle-history, through *Julius Cæsar*, the last play in which we feel serene artistic poise, to *Coriolanus*, which concludes the period of fiercest passion, may be described as from comic, through dramatic, to tragic.

For what the mob attacks throughout, and in *Coriolanus* what the mob devours, is literally aristocracy, — the rule of those who are best. This, with instinctive democratic distrust of excellence or superiority, the mob is bound to overthrow. In Shakspere's earlier work we have had pictures of aristocracy, strong and weak. In *Henry V.*, like *Coriolanus* a play whose mood is didactic, we saw aristocracy wholesomely, sympathetically, worthily dominant. In *Antony and Cleopatra*, a play which, with all its chances for an

Alexandrian mob, is notable for neglect of the common people, we saw aristocracy toppling on the verge of ruin, decadent through the inherent corruption of human nature. In Coriolanus himself we have aristocracy as nobly worthy of dominance as in Henry V., and yet as inexorably doomed as in Antony. The fate of Coriolanus, more cruelly tragic than Antony's, comes from no decadence, no corruption, no vicious weakness, but rather from a passionate excess of inherently noble traits, whose very nobility unfits them for survival in the ignoble world about them.

These traits are palpable in the scene of Coriolanus' candidacy.[1] There, too, palpably appears the pride which commonplaces declare to be his fatal vice. Perhaps it is. Clearly, however, he takes pride in nothing but worthily conscious merit; nor does he despise anything not essentially contemptible; his mood is phrased in the lines,[2] —

> " Better it is to die, better to starve,
>   Than crave the hire which first we do deserve."

In the whole play Coriolanus only once despises anything not really mean; this is when, in a moment of victory, he begs that a poor man shall be spared, and then does not take the trouble to remember his name.[3] The hastiness thus indicated is of course a second fault of Coriolanus, whose temper is passionately infirm. Much as he rages, however, his indignation is almost always righteous, excited chiefly by what is

---

[1] II. iii.   [2] 120–121.   [3] I. ix. 79–92.

really ignoble in humanity. The weakness of his
temperament is not that his anger is unreasonably
aroused, but that, once aroused, it is excessive.

In view of this, the manner in which the character
of Coriolanus is set forth becomes extraordinary.
Passionate as the man is, the presentation of his story,
at least compared with that of all the stories we have
lately considered, seems cold. Like the other characters in this play, Coriolanus himself seems, by comparison, almost "humourous." Certainly the temper
in which Shakspere presents him is almost unsympathetic; it is surprisingly free from such suggestion of
deep personal feeling as has now and again seemed
like self-revelation.

The plays we have lately considered contain three
phases of such self-revelation. From *Much Ado
About Nothing* forward there has been a palpable
sense of irony, at first comic, later becoming a deep
tragic recognition of destiny. From even earlier —
from the *Merchant of Venice* itself — to *Antony and
Cleopatra*, there was a constant, crescent sense of what
delights and mischiefs come from the loves of men
and women. From *Hamlet* to *Macbeth*, there were
traces of such over-excitement of mind as frequently
suggested madness. This last trait disappeared with
Macbeth, unless we detect some relic of it in the tremendously pregnant style both of *Antony and Cleopatra* and of *Coriolanus* itself. With *Antony and
Cleopatra* disappeared the second trait, — the haunting sense of what mischief women can work. In

Coriolanus, then, we have left of this unwitting self-revelation only an intensified irony, strangely divorced from passionate feeling. Here, in short, we have a cold abstract contrast between ideally noble traits and ideally vile. They clash; and vileness conquers.

So far does vileness conquer, indeed, that the real climax of *Coriolanus*, obviously intended for a triumph of virtue, seems comparatively weak. When Volumnia appeals to the magnanimity of her son, stirring it to conquer his revengeful pride,[1] her speeches hardly justify her success. Instead of such supreme eloquence as the moment demands, we find admirable rhetoric, versifying and giving sonorous dignity to the harangues of Plutarch; but not wakening them into the inevitable vitality which is the master-sign of Shakspere's great work. To the end Volumnia remains " the Roman mother."

To this weakness of climax, which apparently comes from weakness of emotional sympathy with a situation intellectually understood, may be traced part of the artistic dissatisfaction sometimes caused by *Coriolanus*. The play, however, has other tiresome traits. While by no means short, it is very monotonous; it lacks the relief of such underplot and comedy as enliven the great English chronicle-histories. It lacks, too, the beauty of style which might make delightful a less significant story. As verse-tests indicate,[2] the style of *Coriolanus* has neither the lucidity nor the grace of Shakspere's best writing; it is pregnant, even over-

[1] V. iii. 131–182.   [2] See p. 326.

packed with meaning, but it suggests no underlying music. Shakspere is nowhere less lyrical, nowhere the writer of words which, as distinguished from the terms of poetry, produce an effect more like that of masterly prose.

The prose of *Coriolanus*, to be sure, is masterly; the play remains Shakspereanly great. Its greatness, however, is not ultimate; its style lacks simplicity and beauty, its conception lacks poise, sympathetic serenity, artistic purity. For Shakspere, indeed, as we have seen, the mood which underlies it is strangely akin to one of political or social philosophy; and a philosophy, too, of a grim, repellent kind. Nowhere can we feel more distinctly why to some modern philanthropic dreamers Shakspere, for all his art, presents himself as a colossal enemy, as a tradition which advancing Humanity ought ruthlessly to overthrow. For, very surely, no work in literature more truly and unflinchingly expounds the inherent danger and evil of democracy; nor does any show less recognition of the numerous benefits which our century believes to counterbalance them.

When we remember that verse-tests, and little else, place *Coriolanus* where we consider it, the relation of its mood to those which precede becomes very striking. Æsthetic conviction confirms a classification which at first seems blindly inappreciative. From the unpassionate irony of *Julius Cæsar* we have followed Shakspere through the series of plays which remain emotionally his greatest. These, we found, artistically expressed a mental activity and an intensity of passion which uncontrolled might have threatened reason itself. These, too, we found, constantly expressed, in varied terms, a sense of the troubles involved in the relations of the sexes. From this storm of passion we emerged through the sternly objective study of decadent virtue so ultimately made in *Antony and Cleopatra*. Here, in *Coriolanus*, we finally find Shakspere, with almost cynical coldness, artistically expounding the inherent weakness of moral nobility, the inherent strength and power of all that is intellectually and morally vile.

This mood of cold depression involves a fundamental lack of enthusiasm, unlike anything we have met before. The tremendous creative impulse which has pervaded everything since the *Midsummer Night's Dream* seems somehow weakened. The same impression results finally from the " humourous " treatment of character in *Coriolanus ;* the same from the philosophical, as distinguished from dramatic, temper which pervades it ; the same, too, from the inadequacy of Volumnia's appeal, which ought properly to stir one to the depths. *Coriolanus* is a great tragedy ; but, for all its greatness, one finds in it symptom after symptom of weakening creative energy.

XII. SHAKSPERE FROM 1600 TO 1608.

In this chapter we have considered the work of Shakspere between 1600 and 1608. These years took him from the age of thirty-six to that of forty-four, and from the thirteenth year of his professional life to the twenty-first. They were years, too, when various records show him to have been pretty steadily improving in worldly fortune.[1] It is worth while now to pause for a moment, and review our impression of this period.

Once for all, again, we must admit our chronology to be uncertain. With the exception of *All's Well that Ends Well*, however, — which may be the *Love's Labour's Won* mentioned by Meres in 1598, — none of the plays considered in this chapter are known to have been alluded to before 1600. The inference is that none of them existed earlier. In 1601 there was a distinct allusion to *Julius Cæsar;* in 1603 and 1604 there were quarto editions of *Hamlet;* in 1608, *Antony and Cleopatra* was entered in the Stationers' Register, and *King Lear* was published; in 1609, *Troilus and Cressida* was published; in 1610, *Othello* and *Macbeth* were acted. Within two years of 1608, then, we have evidence that all but three of the plays considered in this chapter existed. These three are *All's Well that Ends Well,* which after all makes little dif-

[1] See p. 18.

ference in our total impression; *Measure for Measure;* and *Coriolanus.* For the dates of the last two we must rely wholly on internal evidence, — allusions and verse-tests. This evidence, however, places them near other plays so like them in mood that we are warranted in accepting the result with considerable confidence. On the whole, then, we may fairly assume that, with the exception of a few stray passages, none of the work considered in this chapter existed in 1600; and that all of it was substantially finished by 1608. Our business now is to define afresh our impression of Shakspere.

Already we have similarly defined our impression of him three times. First, we found that in 1593, at the age of twenty-nine, and after six years of professional life, he had displayed a habit of mind by which words and concepts seemed almost identical; he had shown unusual versatility in trying his hand at all kinds of contemporary writing; and, finally, by enlivening characters with the results of actual observation, he had made some of his personages more human than any others on the English stage. Apart from this, the work of these six experimental years amounted to little.

Our next summary revealed a very different state of things. In 1600, at the age of thirty-six, and after thirteen years of professional life, Shakspere had produced not only his best comedies and histories, but *Romeo and Juliet*, and a constant series of characters which, in themselves, suffice to place him at the head of imagi-

native English Literature. After his prolonged period
of experiment his creative imagination had at last begun to work spontaneously, with generally increasing
precision and power. Pretty clearly, however, it did
not always work with equal strength in every direction;
and the old trait of versatility displayed itself under the
new aspect of versatile concentration. His imagination, too, revealed its creative strength, not by inventing new things, but by developing old ones. His
characters certainly began to live like actual people.
His phrases began so to simplify and to strengthen
that one instinctively tended to believe him more and
more conscious of thought, as distinguished from word.
At least in the matter of stage-business, however, and
a little less palpably in other matters too, he showed
so marked a disposition to repeat, with subtle variation, whatever he had once found effective, that we
saw reason to wonder whether he might not have felt
hampered by a conscious sluggishness of invention.
No depressing sense, though, of limitation or of anything else, affected his work, which was animated
throughout by a robust, buoyant vigor of artistic
imagination.   In the chronicle-histories, too, there
was a grand sense of historic movement; in *Romeo
and Juliet*, and in all the comedies, there was a delightful romantic feeling; in the substitution of self-
deception for mistaken identity as the chief device
of comedy, there was at least increasing maturity;
and in the idealized heroines, from Portia to Viola,
there was clear understanding of how a charming

woman can fascinate a romantic lover. Apart from the touch of irony in *Much Ado About Nothing*, however, we could detect hardly any deep knowledge of spiritual experience.

The *Sonnets*, which we considered next, indicated something more. Whatever their origin and their history, they not only expressed, in distinctly personal terms, the profoundly artistic temperament and the consciously mastered literary art already impersonally evident in the plays. They revealed, besides, a sympathetic understanding of spiritual suffering; and the terms by which they revealed it involved equal knowledge of the tragic misery which comes from passionate human love.

Through the *Sonnets* we approached the plays considered in this chapter. In these we have found deeper traits still. While, like all the plays of Shakspere, even the great tragedies are distinctly intended for the stage, — and, what is more, despite thoroughly changed conditions, are still theatrically effective, — they involve on the part of their writer something deeper than mere mastery of his art, and vigorous, spontaneous creative imagination. Unlike the earlier work, these later plays reveal an unswerving artistic impulse. Versa tility of experiment and of concentration gives place to sustained intensity of feeling. Over and over again, in endless variety of substance and of detail, of conception and of phrase alike, these plays show themselves the work of one who at least sympathetically has sounded the depths of human suffering; and has

sounded them, too, in a manner like that already suggested by the *Sonnets*. The temperament revealed
by these plays, meanwhile, confirming our impression
from the *Sonnets*, is distinctly individual. Individual,
too, is the mood which, taken together, the plays
reveal. Throughout is a profound, fatalistic sense of
the impotence of man in the midst of his environment; now dispassionate, now fierce with passion,
this sense — which we called a sense of irony — pervades every play from *Julius Cæsar* to *Coriolanus*.
In the second place, from *All's Well that Ends Well*
to *Antony and Cleopatra*, there is a sense of something
in the relations between men and women at once
widely different from the ideal, romantic fascination
expressed by the comedies, and yet just what should
normally follow from such a beginning. Trouble first,
then vacillating doubt, then the certainty that woman
may be damningly evil, succeed one another in the
growth of this mood which so inextricably mingles
with the ironical. Finally, from *Hamlet* to *Macbeth*,
along with the constant irony and the constant trouble
which surrounds the fact of woman, we found equally
constant traces of deep sympathy with such abnormal,
overwrought states of mind as, uncontrolled by tremendous power both of will and of artistic expression,
might easily have lapsed into madness.

These three traits together reached their climax in
Macbeth. In *Macbeth*, too, persisted that increasing
precision and compactness of style which leads one
constantly to feel that Shakspere, who surely began

his conscious artistic career as a maker of phrases, tended almost steadily to consider phrases less, and concepts more. The trait of style which first appears in *Macbeth* — the weak ending — points to this conclusion. Conceivably, of course, only a fresh metrical experiment by a writer who had always been eager for verbal novelty, this undoubted symptom of a weakening verse seems rather evidence that at last the writer cared less for how his verse sounded than for what it meant. From the very beginning, Shakspere's lines have tended to mean more and more; and this tendency — involving his tremendous activity of thought — never weakens to the very end.

With *Macbeth*, however, disappeared the essentially overwrought mood which appeared with *Hamlet; Antony and Cleopatra*, in some respects the most masterly of Shakspere's plays, contained no suggestion of this fiercest tendency of the great tragedies — the tendency toward something like madness. With consummate command of conception and of style alike, it presented the greatest picture in English Literature of decadent virtue; and in Cleopatra herself it presented such a summary of evil womanhood as we have found Shakspere prone to make of matters from which he was passing. In the Falstaff scenes of *Henry IV.*, for example, he gave a final picture of the actual condition of life from which he had emerged. In *Twelfth Night*, he recapitulated the whole joyous mood of his early comedy. So in Cleopatra he finally summed up, with retrospective completeness, his sense of all the harm

which woman can do; and with Cleopatra damning
fascination disappeared.

Not so the irony, however. In *Coriolanus*, irony —
unrelieved, dully passionate — was fiercer, more savage,
than ever. Somehow, though, it had become the inspiring force no longer of emotion, but of solid thought.
The contrast between good and evil had become so
abstract that it phrased itself, for the first time in
Shakspere's serious work, rather deliberately than
imaginatively. For the first time since the *Midsummer Night's Dream*, if not indeed for the first time
of all, the characters set forth by Shakspere seemed
rather "humourous" than human; after the traditional English fashion, they seemed made to embody
traits; they were not, like the great creations of
Shakspere, beings which had grown of themselves into
all the inevitable complexity of human individuality.
In *Coriolanus*, for the first time since the experimental
work of so many years before, we missed the spontaneity of imagination which had pervaded both the
merely artistic work of Shakspere's second period,
and this passionate work of his third.

Exhaustion seems a strange word to use about
Coriolanus; yet this weakening of creative energy is
surely a symptom of such exhaustion as should normally follow the unprecedented, unequalled activity
of creative power which had gone before. If exhaustion it be, however, which this cold, bitter tragedy
reveals, it is surely an exhaustion which the artist to
whom it came would hardly recognize as such. For

eight years, we have seen, — from thirty-six to forty-
four, — he had been constantly producing great tragic
poems, unsurpassed for range and power, and at
their height full of overwrought spontaneous intensity.
All along this intensity had been accompanied by a
growing power both of philosophic thought and of
verbal expression. Intellectually, Shakspere had never
been more powerfully active than he shows himself
in *Coriolanus*. As the intensity of emotional impulse weakened, then, while the full power of vigorous thought remained, we may imagine Shakspere
himself to have felt conscious rather of increasing
self-mastery than of any loss. *Coriolanus*, indeed, is
such work as an artist, with what seems perversity,
is apt to deem his best. The very weakening of spontaneous power which puts an end to merits of which
an artist is normally unconscious, emphasizes the
more deliberate merits of which, above any spectator
or reader, an artist is aware.

In these eight years, from 1600 to 1608, then, the
years when Shakspere surely did the work which
makes him supremely great, we may believe him at
last to have been actuated by a really profound series
of emotional impulses which forced him to express
them with every engine of his art. At the height of
this tremendous artistic experience came an overwrought intensity of mind which carried the inherent
misery of tragic conception almost to the verge of
madness. Then, slowly, came growing self-control,
increasing vigor of concentrated thought, finally

what should seem fresh certainty of mastery. Unwittingly to the master, however, this very self-mastery meant that his great power of spontaneous imagination, which for thirteen years, from the *Midsummer Night's Dream* to *Antony and Cleopatra*, had been constant, was at last deserting him.

In view of this, we may now well turn to the other records of English Literature during these eight years.[1] In 1601 were published Bacon's account of the *Treasons of the Earl of Essex*, and Jonson's *Poetaster ;* in 1602 came Campion's *Art of English Poetry*, Davidson's *Poetical Rhapsody*, Dekker's *Satiromastix*, Marston's *Antonio and Mellida* and *Antonio's Revenge*, and Middleton's *Randall, Earl of Chester*, and *Blurt, Master Constable ;* in 1603 came Bacon's *Apology concerning the late Earl of Essex*, Florio's *Montaigne*, Heywood's *Woman Killed with Kindness*, and Jonson's *Sejanus*. This, we remember, was the year when Queen Elizabeth died and King James came to the throne. In 1604 were published King James's *Counterblast to Tobacco*, and Marston's *Malcontent ;* in 1605, came Bacon's *Advancement of Learning*, Camden's *Remains*, Chapman's *All Fools*, and plays by Jonson and Marston, — Jonson's *Volpone*, too, was acted ; in 1606 were published plays by Chapman and by Marston, and Stowe's *Chronicle ;* in 1607, the *Woman Hater* — the first play of Beaumont and Fletcher — was acted, and among the publications were Chapman's *Bussy d'Am-*

[1] As before, we may conveniently rely on Ryland's *Chronological Outlines*, which suggests enough for our purpose

bois, Dekker and Webster's *Westward Ho*, Marston's *What You Will*, and Tourneur's *Revenger's Tragedy*. In 1608 — the year when Clarendon, Fuller, and Milton were born — Beaumont and Fletcher's *Philaster* was perhaps acted ; and among the publications were Hall's *Characters of Virtues and Vices*, and plays by Chapman and by Middleton.

Hasty and incomplete though the list be, it is enough for our purpose. A mere glance at it will show that, in comparison with either of the earlier periods of publication which we considered,[1] the preponderance of dramatic work is marked ; and what is more, that this work includes not such archaic plays as those which Shakspere found on the stage in 1587, but the ripest work of Dekker, Heywood, Jonson, Marston, and Middleton ; and good work by Beaumont and Fletcher, Tourneur, and Webster. It was during the period of Shakspere's great tragic plays, in short, that what we now think of as the Elizabethan drama came into existence ; and in 1608, when at last Shakspere's creative energy showed symptoms of exhaustion, he was surrounded on every side by rival dramatists, of great inventive as well as poetic power, whose work was so good that no contemporary criticism could surely have ranked it below his own.

[1] See pp. 97, 210.

X

TIMON OF ATHENS, AND PERICLES, PRINCE OF TYRE

[*Timon of Athens* was first entered in 1623 and published in the folio.

Its sources are Paynter's *Palace of Pleasure* and a passage from the Life of Antony in North's *Plutarch*.

On internal evidence it has been conjecturally assigned to the period we have now reached, about 1607.

Pericles was published in quarto, with Shakspere's name, in 1609. It was republished in 1611 and in 1619, but was not included in the folio of 1623. It was not added to Shakspere's collected works until the third folio, — 1663–4. Among the seven plays then added to the old collection this is the only one not generally thought spurious.

Its sources are Lawrence Twine's *Patterne of Painefull Adventures*, and Gower's *Confessio Amantis*. Parts of the story may be traced back to the fifth or sixth century.

On internal evidence, *Pericles* has been conjecturally assigned to 1608 or thereabouts.

In both *Timon* and *Pericles* there is much matter believed not to be by Shakspere. In the Transactions of the New Shakspere Society for 1874 [1] appear conjectural selections of what passages in these plays are believed to be genuine. Just what part Shakspere had in these plays, — whether he planned, or retouched, or collaborated, — nobody has determined.]

BEFORE this we have seen work by Shakspere which is comparatively weak. Even after his experimental period, at the time when his imagination was beginning to display its utmost vigor, we found that when

[1] Pages 130, 253.

his attention was concentrated on anything, something else was apt to suffer. Since *Titus Andronicus* itself, though, we have found nothing so palpably weak as the two plays which we here consider together. In total effect, neither of them seems anywhere near worthy of Shakspere.

This weakness, of course, is partly due to the generally admitted fact that considerable portions of these plays are by other hands. This does not cover the matter, however. The *Taming of the Shrew* is said to be largely by other hands ; yet the *Taming of the Shrew* never seems, like *Timon* and *Pericles*, essentially unworthy of a place in Shakspere's work. To appreciate why these plays are given such a place, we must for the moment abandon our habit of considering plays as complete works, and attend only to details. Take, for example, Timon's speech to Apemantus : [1] —

> " Thou art a slave, whom Fortune's tender arm
> With favour never clasp'd ; but bred a dog.
> Hadst thou, like us from our first swath, proceeded
> The sweet degrees that this brief world affords
> To such as may the passive drugs of it
> Freely command, thou wouldst have plunged thyself
> In general riot," etc.

Or again, take Timon's better-known last speech : [2]

> " Come not to me again : but say to Athens,
> Timon hath made his everlasting mansion
> Upon the beached verge of the salt flood ;
> Who once a day with his embossed froth
> The turbulent surge shall cover."

[1] IV. iii. 250.   [2] V. i. 217.

Without knowing why, any one who knows Shakspere's style, must feel sure that Shakspere wrote these lines. They are typical of many in *Timon of Athens;* weak though the play must remain as a whole, it contains passages good enough for any one.

With *Pericles* the case is similar. Here, to be sure, Shakspere's work is supposed to begin only with the third act, where the shipwreck scene has such obvious likeness to the better shipwreck scene of the *Tempest.* From thence on we may find many traces of Shakspere. The scene between Marina and Leonine, in the fourth act,[1] for example, while none too powerful, is distinctly in his manner. So is the last scene, particularly where Pericles and Marina meet;[2] the situation, which in any other hands than Shakspere's might have become intolerably monstrous, is treated with a delicacy distinctly his own.

These occasional passages, amid so much that is worthless, give these plays their place among those generally ascribed to Shakspere; and so far as verse-tests can guide us under such uncertain conditions, both plays seem to belong nearly where we place them, — a conclusion which in the case of *Pericles* is supported by the fact of its publication in 1609. Thus placed, these plays, so uninteresting in themselves, become unexpectedly notable.

They belong, we assume, at the end of the passion-ate period which produced the great tragedies; they precede, as we shall see, three plays, *Cymbeline*, the

[1] IV. i. 51–91.   [2] V. i. 64 seq.

Tempest, and the *Winter's Tale*, of which the temper is not gloomy or passionate, but serenely romantic. Between this group and the tragic group there is a very marked contrast; the groups express totally different artistic moods.

Such sudden contrasts are common in artistic careers. From time to time an artist will find himself possessed of an imaginative impulse which seems final. In the mood which that impulse involves — grand or petty, solemn or gay — the whole truth of life, so far as he can express it, will seem compressed. He will go on, expressing himself in phrase after phrase concerning this elusive, inspiring impulse. All of a sudden his power will lapse. He can do no more; he can only caricature his old self, or blunder vaguely in search of some new, equally or freshly potent motive. The experience is as frequent in tyros and scribblers as in the great artists whose manners change. At one moment, for example, a youth can write sentimental verse; the vein runs dry; he flutters about searching for rhymes and melodies that will not come; and by and by proves to have a vein of light satire, instead, or of serious critical thought, and so on. Between these two periods of production there will almost always come an interval of transitional stagnation, comically or painfully like the calm between two adverse breezes.

Between the general mood of *Timon* and that of *Pericles* there is just such a contrast as marks an

artistic transition from one dominating mood to another; and throughout both plays, even in the parts
which seem genuinely Shakspere's, there is just such
weakness of imaginative impulse as normally belongs
to such transition. All this matter, of course, is
hypothetical. How much of these plays is Shakspere's, and when he wrote his part of them, can
never be determined. That modern verse-tests place
these plays here, though, quite apart from their
substance, becomes notable when we consider their
artistic character; for, if our chronology be true,
we have met hardly any fact which goes further
than the weakness of these transitional plays to prove
that, vast as Shakspere's genius was, it worked by
the same laws which govern the æsthetic experience
of any honest modern artist.

To consider these plays in more detail, *Timon* is
the last work of Shakspere's where the predominating
mood is gloomy. Broadly, if monotonously planned,
it is throughout exasperatingly undramatic. The plot
is not only capable of dramatic treatment, but essentially probable. What happens might happen anywhere: a man, born rich, wastes his substance, and
when he is poor finds his swans all geese — wherefore
misanthropy. Yet, for all this inherent plausibility,
Shakspere is never less plausible. The first scene,
to be sure, is broad, firm, and not without action;
even here, however, the characters are presented so
externally, so "humourously," that the scene seems
more like Ben Jonson's work than Shakspere's. At

times, indeed, it reminds one rather of the classic French comedy than of English. After this first scene, one never feels as if anything in *Timon* were so. Except very faintly in Timon himself there is never a trace of real, as distinguished from conventionally "humourous," character; there is nowhere a whiff of real atmosphere, either, — what happens, takes place only on the stage. In this respect *Timon* is at the opposite pole from the *Merchant of Venice*: there the vigor of Shakspere's creative imagination made characters and atmosphere so real that we never stop to think what absurd things are going on [1]; in *Timon* there is such weakness of creative imagination that we can hardly realize how what goes on might really occur anywhere. The merit of *Timon*, in short, so far as it has any, lies wholly in isolated passages, notable for firmness of phrase. It is just such merit as we should expect to survive, no matter how fully imaginative impulse should desert a poet like Shakspere. After above twenty years of faithful work, his masterly style was bound to have become a fixed habit of expression. Had he failed now and again to phrase single thoughts with ultimate felicity, he would almost have been writing in a new language. Apart from this mere survival of style, *Timon* throughout indicates exhaustion of creative energy. Its impotently " humourous " treatment of character reminds one, rather painfully, of the first symptoms of creative weakness in *Corio-*

[1] See p. 148.

lanus. Its general mood, too, is colder, more cynical,
darker even than that. The misanthropy which underlies *Timon*, indeed, is savage enough to suggest
the more masterly misanthropy of Swift. If *Timon*
be the darkest of all the plays, though, it is likewise
the most impotent as yet.

In impotence, however, *Pericles* perhaps outstrips
it.   *Pericles*, too, has other symptoms of decline.
Among Shakspere's plays it is unique for monstrosity
of motive; and even though its most monstrous passages occur in the first act, which is thought to be by
another hand, Shakspere probably accepted them as
part of the scheme into which his own work should fit.
Such monstrosity of motive is a frequent symptom of
artistic transition.   Aware that creative energy is exhausted, an artist is apt to grow reckless ; and, if he
be addressing a popular audience, he is tempted to
supply his lack of imagination by shocking or monstrous devices. Some such phenomenon marks the
decay of many schools of art, and of none more
distinctly than the Elizabethan drama.   In motive,
then, even more than in impotence, *Pericles* is a play
of the Elizabethan decadence.

The impotence shown in *Pericles*, however, differs
essentially from that of *Timon*.   Here the weakness
is not so much of exhaustion as of experiment.   The
word "experiment," to be sure, recalls Shakspere's
earliest plays, which are very unlike this.   There is
nothing in *Pericles* to remind one of *Titus Andronicus*,
or of *Henry VI.*, or of *Love's Labour's Lost*, or of the

Comedy of Errors, or of the *Two Gentlemen of Verona*.
Like them, however, *Pericles* may fairly be regarded
as preliminary to what shall follow. The difference
between this experiment and the old ones is that while
those were formal, this, which now and again reveals
disdainful mastery of mere form, tries to express a kind
of motive whose substance is new to Shakspere.

Unlike *Timon*, and all the plays we have considered since *Twelfth Night*, *Pericles* is in no sense
a tragedy; it is a romance, which carries its story
through a period of dismay and confusion to a serene
close. In this respect, to be sure, we might group it
with many of the earlier plays, — with the *Merchant
of Venice*, for example, and *Much Ado About Nothing*,
and *As You Like It*, and *Twelfth Night*; or even in
some degree with *All's Well that Ends Well*, and
Measure for Measure. From all of these, however,
it may be distinguished by at least two traits which
group it with the three great romances still to come,
—*Cymbeline*, the *Tempest*, and the *Winter's Tale*: in
the first place, it attempts within the limits of a single
performance to deal with the events of a whole lifetime,
in much such manner as Sidney's *Defence of Poesy*
ridiculed. In the second place, the ultimate serenity
comes not after a short, concentrated period of dis-
aster, but only after a long and seemingly tragic
experience of the rudest buffets of life. Underlying
such a conception as this is a new artistic mood: the
world still seems evil, to be sure; but wait long enough,
and even in this world the evil shall pass.

In this aspect, which some critics, deeming Shakspere more moralist than artist, take to involve a
deliberate preaching of reconciliation, *Pericles* fore-
shadows the three romances to come. In more than
one detail, too, it suggests them. The shipwreck, for
example, reminds one a little of *Twelfth Night* and
the *Comedy of Errors*, but far more of the *Tempest*.[1]
The story of Marina has something in common with
that of Miranda, and more with that of Perdita. The
recovery of the priestess Thaisa, recalling that of
Æmilia in the *Comedy of Errors*, is still more like
that of Hermione in the *Winter's Tale*. Clearly
enough, *Pericles* bears to the coming romances a
relation very like that borne to the great comedies
by the experimental. Just as this second period of
experiment is shorter, and its fruit less ripe than
was the case before, however, so the foreshadowing of
what is to come is less complete. In reviving, after
eight years of passionate gloom, a fresh gleam of
romantic feeling, *Pericles* is perhaps most noteworthy.

In *Timon*, then, we have the definite close of the
period of passionate gloom, — a mood of which in
Coriolanus we observed traces of exhaustion. In
Timon, too, we have such paralysis of creative power
as normally belongs to a period of artistic transition.
In *Pericles*, we have the feeble, experimental beginning of Shakspere's final period. During this period,
though it is short and its production less ideally finished than that of either the artistic period or the

---

[1] Cf. *C. of E.* I. i. 63 seq.; *T. N.* I. ii.; *Per.* III, i.; *Temp.* I. i.

passionate, we shall find something like a fusion, in lifelong romances, of all the moods which have preceded, — of the darkness of tragedy, the gayety of comedy, the serenity of romance. Though of little intrinsic worth, then, *Timon* and *Pericles*, considered in relation to Shakspere's development, may be regarded as deeply significant.

XI

THE PLAYS OF SHAKSPERE FROM CYMBELINE TO HENRY VIII

I.

WHILE by common consent, *Cymbeline*, the *Tempest*, and the *Winter's Tale* are thought to have been written after the plays we have already considered, and before *Henry VIII.*, there is nothing but verse-tests to fix their order. The order in which we shall consider them, then, is little better than arbitrary. Any line of development which we may be tempted to trace within the series must be even more conjectural than usual. Keeping this in mind, however, we may suggestively compare these plays with each other; and, with fair confidence in our chronology, we may compare them with anything which we have considered hitherto.

II. CYMBELINE.

[*Cymbeline* is first mentioned in the note-book of Dr. Forman. His note about it is undated, but as his note of *Macbeth* is dated April 20th, 1610, and that of the *Winter's Tale* is dated May 15th, 1611, it probably belongs to about the same period. As Forman died in September, 1611, that year is the latest possible for his note. *Cymbeline* was entered in 1623, and published in the folio.

The historical parts of *Cymbeline* are based on Holinshed; the story of Imogen, including both the trunk-scene and the disguise, is based on a story in the *Decameron*, of which no English version is known to have existed before 1620; the death-like sleep of Imogen, so obviously like Juliet's, is also like a familiar German story. In general, perhaps, the resemblance of incidents in *Cymb.li.e* to incidents in Shakspere's earlier plays is more noteworthy than the relation of either to their actual sources.

By verse-tests *Cymbeline* is placed between *Coriolanus* and the *Tempest*. It is generally assigned to 1609 or 1610; but Mr. Fleay thinks that certain parts of it were written as early as 1606, when Shakspere was engaged in extracting from Holinshed material for *King Lear* and *Macbeth*.]

A hasty critic lately said that *Cymbeline* sounds as if Browning had written it. Though crude, the remark is suggestive. The style of *Cymbeline* has at least two traits really like Browning's: the rhythm of the lines is often hard to catch; and the thought often becomes so intricate that, without real obscurity, it is hard to follow. Take, for example, the opening of the third scene of the first act, a conversation between Imogen and Pisanio: —

> "*Imo.* I would thou grew'st unto the shores o' the haven,
> And question'dst every sail : if he should write
> And I not have it, 't were a paper lost
> As offer'd mercy is.   What was the last
> That he spake to thee ?
>   *Pis.*   It was his queen, his queen!
>   *Imo.* Then waved his handkerchief ?
>   *Pis.*   And kiss'd it, madam.
>   *Imo.* Senseless linen! happier therein than I!
> And that was all ?
>   *Pis.*   No, madam; for so long
> As he could make me with this eye or ear
> Distinguish him from others, he did keep
> The deck, with glove, or hat, or handkerchief,

Still waving, as the fits and stirs of 's mind
Could best express how slow his soul sail'd on,
How swift his ship.
 Imo. Thou shouldst have made him
As little as a crow, or less, ere left
To after-eye him.
 Pis. Madam, so I did."

This passage is enough to illustrate the peculiar
metrical structure of *Cymbeline*. Endstopped lines
are so deliberately avoided that one feels a sense of
relief when a speech and a line end together. Such a
phrase as

 " How slow his soul sail'd on, how swift his ship "

is deliberately made, not a single line, but two half-
lines. Several times, in the broken dialogue, one has
literally to count the syllables before the metrical
regularity of the verse appears. The meaning, too,
is often so compactly expressed that to catch it one
must pause and study. Clearly this puzzling style is
decadent; the distinction between verse and prose is
breaking down. Again, take this passage from the
scene when Imogen receives the letter of Posthumus
bidding her meet him at Milford:[1] —

    " Then, true Pisanio, —
Who long'st, like me, to see thy lord; who long'st, —
O, let me bate, — but not like me — yet long'st,
But in a fainter kind: — O, not like me;
For mine 's beyond beyond — say, and speak thick;
Love's counsellor should fill the bores of hearing
To the smothering of the sense — how far it is
To this same blessed Milford."

   [1] III. ii. 53–61.

Here the actual sentence is only " Pisanio . . . say . . . how far it is to . . . Milford." Nothing but the most skilful elocution, however, could possibly make clear to a casual hearer the broken, parenthetic style. The speeches of Iachimo in the last act[1] show the same trait more extravagantly still. Altogether, the style of *Cymbeline* probably demands closer attention than that of any other work of Shakspere.

This almost perverse complexity of *Cymbeline* is not confined to details of style. To understand the structure of the play you must give it preposterous attention. Until the very last scene, the remarkably involved story tangles itself in a way which is utterly bewildering. At any given point, overwhelmed with a mass of facts presented pell-mell, you are apt to find that you have quite forgotten something important. Coming after such confusion, the last scene of *Cymbeline* is among the most notable bits of dramatic construction anywhere. The more one studies it, the more one is astonished at the ingenuity with which *dénouement* follows *dénouement*. Nowhere else in Shakspere, certainly, is there anything like so elaborate an untying of knots which seem purposely made intricate to prepare for this final situation. Situation, however, is an inadequate word. Into 485 lines Shakspere has crowded some two dozen situations any one of which would probably have been strong enough to carry a whole act.

An analysis of these is perhaps worth while. The

---

[1] V. v. 153 seq.

scene opens with the triumphal entrance of Cymbeline,[1] who proceeds to knight his heroic sons[2] —
neither side suspecting the relation. His triumph is
interrupted by news of the queen's death,[3] and of her
villainy.[4] Before this can much upset Cymbeline,
however, the captives are brought in,[5] and the *dénoue-
ments* are fully prepared for. To realize what they
are, we may remind ourselves that we now have on
the stage not only the mutually unknown father and
sons, but also the following personages whose identity
is more or less confused : Imogen, disguised as a
youth, is known to be herself only by Pisanio, but is
known to her brothers — whom she does not suspect
to be her brothers — as the boy Fidele, whom they
believe dead. Belarius and Posthumus, each in disguise, are known to nobody. Iachimo is present
undisguised ; but his villainy is known only to Imogen, and not wholly to her. Meanwhile, nobody but
the sons of Cymbeline knows that Cloten has been
killed. One's brain fairly swims. The action begins
by Lucius, the Roman general, begging the life of
Imogen, whom he believes to be a boy in his service.[6]
This boon granted, Imogen, instead of showing grati-
tude to Lucius, turns away from him, with apparent
heartlessness.[7] Her real object, however, is to expose
the villain Iachimo,[8] — a matter which so fills her mind
that she has no eyes for her brothers, who half recog-

[1] L. 1.   [2] L. 20.   [3] L. 27.
[4] L. 37.   [5] L. 69.   [6] L. 83.
[7] L. 102.   [8] L. 130.

nize her as Fidele.[1] Iachimo, caught with the ring of Posthumus on his finger, now confesses his villainy.[2] Thereupon Posthumus, at last enlightened, and believing that Imogen has been killed by his command, reveals himself in an agony of rage.[3] Imogen interrupts him, and he, believing her an officious boy, strikes her down.[4] Pisanio then reveals her identity;[5] and in telling her story reveals also circumstances which prove her identity with the boy Fidele.[6] Thus the interest of disguised Belarius, Arviragus, and Guiderius is thoroughly aroused; and when Pisanio goes on to expose the wicked purposes of Cloten, who is missing, Guiderius declares himself Cloten's slayer.[7] Thereupon Cymbeline, who has just knighted him, feels bound to condemn him to death.[8] The execution of this sentence is interrupted by Belarius, who is presently condemned too.[9] He thereupon reveals the identity of the sons of Cymbeline[10] and his own; and his statements are confirmed by conventional stage birth-marks.[11] In the general thanksgiving which follows, Posthumus reveals himself as the missing hero of the battle.[12] Iachimo confirms him;[13] and is thereupon pardoned.[14] Then the soothsayer expounds how all this solves the mysterious riddle,[15] peace is proclaimed,[16] and, in some savor of anticlimax, everybody is happy.

---

[1] L. 120. [2] L. 153. [3] L. 209. [4] L. 229.
[5] L. 231. [6] L. 260. [7] L. 287. [8] L. 299.
[9] L. 310. [10] L. 330. [11] L. 363. [12] L. 407.
[13] L. 412. [14] L. 417. [15] L. 435. [16] L. 459.

In this *dénouement*, we have specified twenty-four distinct stage situations. Over-elaborate as this is, — and tautologous, too, for the audience already knows pretty much all that is revealed, — it is such a feat of technical stage-craft as can be appreciated only by those who have tried to manage even a single situation as strong as the average of these. This last scene of *Cymbeline*, then, which demonstrates the deliberate nature of all the preceding confusion, is very remarkable. Without yielding to fantastic temptation, we may assert that, whatever the actual history of its composition, it is just such a deliberate feat of technical skill as on general principles we might expect from a great artist, stirred to tremendous effort by the stinging consciousness of creative lethargy; and creative lethargy seemed the only explanation of *Timon* and *Pericles*.

In this respect, the last scene of *Cymbeline* proves typical of the whole play. From beginning to end, whatever its actual history, the play is certainly such as we might expect from an artist who, in spite of declining power, was determined to assert that he could still do better than ever. Thus viewed, if hardly otherwise, all its perversities become normal.

Not the least normal thing about the play, too, is the material of which its bewildering plot is composed. Very slight examination will show that *Cymbeline* is a tissue of motives, situations, and characters which in the earlier work of Shakspere proved theatrically effective. There is enough confusion of identity for a dozen of the early comedies; and the disguised characters are headed, as of old, by the familiar heroine in hose and doublet. Posthumus, Iachimo, and Cloten revive the second comic motive — later a tragic one — of self-deception. At least in the matter of jealousy and villainy, too, Posthumus and Iachimo recall Othello and Iago. In the potion and the death-like sleep of Imogen, we have again the death-like sleep of Juliet. In the villainous queen, we have another woman, faintly recalling both Lady Macbeth and the daughters of King Lear. In the balancing of this figure by the pure one of Imogen, we have a suggestion of Cordelia's dramatic value. And so on. If, in some fantastic moment, we could imagine that Shakspere, like Wagner, had written music-dramas, giving to each character, each situation, each mood, its own musical motive, we should find in *Cymbeline* hardly any new strain.

The symphonic harmonies in which the old strains combined, however, would themselves seem new; for the mood of *Cymbeline* has a quality which, except in feebly tentative *Pericles*, we have not found before. *Cymbeline* leads its characters through experiences which have all the gloom of tragedy; but the inexorable fate of tragedy is here no longer, and ultimately all emerge into a region of romantic serenity. In *Cymbeline*, men wait; and in spite of their errors and their follies, all at last goes well.

Looking back at the plays we have considered, only one appears to have been so completely recapitulatory as *Cymbeline ;* this is *Twelfth Night.* In almost every other respect, however, the effects of these two plays differ. Among their many differences none perhaps is more marked than their comparative relations to the older works which they recapitulate. In *Twelfth Night*, the old material is almost always presented more effectively than before ; in *Cymbeline*, it is almost always less satisfactorily handled. To a reader, and still more to an enthusiastic student, Cymbeline has the fascinating trait of at once demanding and rewarding study. On the stage, however, compared with the best of Shakspere's earlier plays, it is tiresome. For this there are two reasons : it contains too much, — its complexity of both substance and style overcrowds it throughout; and, with all its power, it lacks not only the simplicity of greatness, but also the ease of spontaneous imagination. It has amazing cunningness of plot; its characters are individually constructed ; its atmosphere is varied and sometimes — particularly in the mountain scenes — plausible ; its style abounds in final phrases. Throughout, however, it is laborious. Just as in *Twelfth Night*, for all its recapitulation, one feels constant spontaneity, so in every line of *Cymbeline* one is somehow aware of Titanic effort.

In brief, then, *Cymbeline* seems the work of a consciously older man than the Shakspere whom we have known. As such, it takes a distinct place in our study. In thus placing it, to be sure, we must guard against certainty. At best, our results must be conjectural ; and we have no external evidence to confirm us. Always remembering that we may not assert our notions true, however, we are free to state and to believe them.

In *Timon* and in *Pericles* we saw reason to believe that Shakspere's creative power had lapsed. Any courageous artist, thus placed, would be stirred by consciousness of this lapse to an effort hitherto unapproached. We may imagine Shakspere, then, with disdainful technical mastery of stage-craft and of style, sweeping together all manner of old material which had proved itself effective. We may imagine him combining this in a new form, — more comprehensive, more varied, more intricately skilful, and in the ultimate sweetness of its romantic harmony more significant than any form in which he had previously used its components. The result we may imagine to be *Cymbeline*. Though in *Cymbeline*, however, Shakspere's power, compared with any other man's, remain supreme, it does not, for all his pains, rise to its own highest level. Vast though it be, it cannot conceal the effort at last involved in its exertion. In this effort, one feels the absence of his old spontaneity. Here, if nowhere else, *Cymbeline* reveals unmistakable symptoms of creative decadence.

III. THE TEMPEST.

[The *Tempest* was among the plays paid for, as having been played
at court, on May 20th, 1613. It was entered in 1623, and published
in the folio. In that volume it is the opening play, — a fact which has
given rise to a comically general impression that it was the first which
Shakspere wrote.

No unmistakable source has been discovered. Apparently, however,
the *Tempest* was in some degree affected by *A Discovery of the Bermu-
das, otherwise called the Isle of Devils; by Sir Thomas Gates, Sir
George Somers, and Captain Newport, with divers others*, which was
published in the autumn of 1610. The Utopian scheme of Gonzalo —
II. i. 147, seq. — seems to be taken from Florio's *Montaigne*.

Verse-tests place the *Tempest* between *Cymbeline* and the *Winter's
Tale*. It is generally assigned conjecturally to 1610.]

In total effect, the *Tempest* is unique. A comparison
of its incidents with the records of Elizabethan voyages
will show one reason why. These voyages — of which
Sir Walter Ralegh's *Discovery of Guiana* is a good
example — reveal a state of things unprecedented in
human experience, and never to be repeated. The
general outline of the earth was at last known to everybody; the limits of the physical world had finally been
ascertained. At the same time, this world was almost
totally unexplored; what it might contain nobody
knew; behind every newly discovered coast might
actually lurk Utopia or the fountain of eternal youth;
for the moment such an isle as Prospero's was credible. The only place where it could possibly be, however, was in the Western Seas. The Mediterranean
was as well known as it is to-day; and Tunis was what

it remained until our own century, — a notorious nest of Barbary pirates. While the magic isle, then, which now seems the most palpable impossibility of the *Tempest*, was not so in the days of Elizabeth, what now seem the credible parts of the play — the allusions to Milan, Naples, and Tunis — really put the action beyond the bounds of possibility. In laying his magic scene between two such familiar regions as Tunis and Naples, in making the distance between them oceanic, and in serenely disregarding the notorious character of Tunis, Shakspere seems deliberately to have idealized such facts as the records of the voyages gave him. His real topic was human life, in the broadest sense; but just as he idealized the records of the voyages, he idealized everything. In the *Tempest*, more than anywhere else, his work seems deliberately removed from reality.

In the matters here idealized, there is much trace of such formerly effective material as we found more palpably in *Cymbeline*. The tit-for-tat of the shipwrecked courtiers [1] revives in some degree the ingenious verbal pleasantry which began in the plays of Lyly and reached its highest point in *Much Ado About Nothing*. Stephano and Trinculo, the drunken comic personages, similarly revive Sir Toby Belch and Falstaff and the Fools, mingling with all these a suggestion of the old distrust of democracy. The story of Prospero and his brother is somewhat akin to situations in *As You Like It*, and still more to situations

---

[1] II. i.

in *Hamlet*. The idyllic and the magic scenes recall the mood of *As You Like It*, and more still that of the *Midsummer Night's Dream*. Ariel revives the child-actors, who must have been effective not only in the fairy poem, but in *Richard III.* and in *King John* and in *Coriolanus*.[1] The wreck reminds one of *Pericles*, of *Twelfth Night*, and of the *Comedy of Errors ;*[2] the abandoned child is akin to Marina. And so on. In the *Tempest*, however, these old motives are all idealized, refined, subtly varied; they do not, as in *Cymbeline*, reveal themselves at once.

Another cause of the unique individuality of the *Tempest*, however, is very palpable. This is a technical trait which seems wholly new. In the *Comedy of Errors*, to be sure, Shakspere did something like what he has done here ; when translating his classic motive into the terms of the Elizabethan theatre, he so far adhered to the classic model as to preserve unity of time and action, and not to stray far from unity of place.[3] In the *Tempest*, however, there is no suggestion of a classic motive ; no work in English Literature is more romantic ; yet, at the same time, something very like the pseudo-classical unities is maintained throughout. The play would act in between two and three hours ; and between two and three hours would probably include everything which happens ; the time of the *Tempest*, then, is actual. The action, too, is almost continuous ; and while the scene shifts a little, from

[1] See pp. 113, 141 ; and cf. *Coriolanus*, V. iii. 127.
[2] See pp. 207, 347.   [3] See p. 91.

one part of the island to another, it remains virtually unchanged, practically observing also the unity of place. As a technical feat, we have found nothing comparable to this, unless it be the last scene of *Cymbeline*. There Shakspere packed into less than five hundred lines a *dénouement* of unparalleled, deliberate complexity, involving some two dozen distinct stage situations. In the *Tempest*, on the other hand, he expands his *dénouement* into a whole five-act play.

This feat involves a degree of pains escaped by whoever should write in free romantic form. Before the unities can be observed, the material in hand must be not only thoroughly collected, but thoroughly digested. Plot, character, atmosphere, and style, accordingly, must be pretty thoroughly fused; as is the case with the *Tempest*, however, they need not be fused indistinguishably. The plot, in substance such a life-long romance as the plots of *Cymbeline* and of *Pericles*, is put together with great firmness. The opening scene of shipwreck is just such an adaptation of the old induction as we found in *As You Like It*, in the *Merchant of Venice*, and in the *Midsummer Night's Dream*.[1] Alone of the scenes in the *Tempest*, it is minutely true to life. What happens is just what might have happened to any company of Elizabethan seamen whom you had seen sail from Plymouth or Bristol. For all any Elizabethan could tell, too, these very seamen, bound no one knew quite whither in the Western Seas, might actually split on unknown magic

[1] See pp. 110, 146, 159.

islands. No introduction to such matter as was coming in the *Tempest*, then, could have been more skilfully plausible; and from the moment when the castaways set foot on the magic island, all moves straight forward, dominated by the deliberately providential spirit of Prospero. This deliberately providential spirit typifies the treatment of character throughout the *Tempest*. Individual though almost every personage be, all are broadly typical, too. In this respect the *Tempest* again recalls the *Midsummer Night's Dream*. There, however, the characters were hardly individual at all, but were rather collected in three distinctly typical groups;[1] here, on the other hand, individualization is probably carried as far as is consistent with the delicately idealized atmosphere. This atmosphere, as remote from actuality as that of the *Midsummer Night's Dream*, is distinct; its sustained, exquisite dreaminess never becomes palpable unreality. We are in another world than our own, but a world which is only just beyond the limits of the world we all know. On the old coins of Spain were stamped the pillars of Hercules, with the legend *Plus ultra,* — *More is beyond.* The mood into which the *Plus ultra* of old Spain leads one is such as pervades the *Tempest*. After all, these strange events and beings are not a mere mist of fantasy; they are rather a vision of something only just beyond our ken. Even though their place be nowhere on earth, they might well be somewhere within our reach; and

[1] See p. 111.

24

if they were, very surely the language there spoken would be the lovely poetry of the *Tempest*.

At first reading, this style seems very different from that of *Cymbeline;* but a very little comparison will show that the difference is really less marked than the similarity. Take Prospero's most familiar speech : [1] —

> " Our revels now are ended.   These our actors,
> As I foretold you, were all spirits, and
> Are melted into air, into thin air :
> And, like the baseless fabric of this vision,
> The cloud-capp'd towers, the gorgeous palaces,
> The solemn temples, the great globe itself,
> Yea, all which it inherit, shall dissolve
> And, like this insubstantial pageant faded,
> Leave not a rack behind.   We are such stuff
> As dreams are made on, and our little life
> Is rounded with a sleep."

Compare with those last three lines the lines from *Cymbeline* at which we first glanced : [2] —

> " He did keep
> The deck, with glove, or hat, or handkerchief,
> Still waving, as the fits and stirs of 's mind
> Could but express how slow his soul sail'd on,
> How swift his ship."

For all the finer music of the *Tempest*, the metrical structure of the two passages is the same. Again, compare with Imogen's elaborately parenthesized inquiry, — " Pisanio . . . say . . . how far it is to . . . Milford," [3] — Prospero's story of Antonio's treachery : [4]

---

[1] IV. i. 148.   [2] I. iii. 10.
[3] See p. 357.   [4] I. ii. 66.

" *Pros.*   My brother and thy uncle, call'd Antonio—
I pray thee mark me — that a brother should
Be so perfidious! — he whom next thyself
Of all the world I loved and to him put
The manage of my state ; as at that time
Through all the signories it was the first
And Prospero the prime duke, being so reputed
In dignity, and for the liberal arts
Without a parallel ; those being all my study,
The government I cast upon my brother
And to my state grew stranger, being transported
And rapt in secret studies.   Thy false uncle —
Dost thou attend me ?
    Mir.   Sir, most heedfully.
    Pros.   Being once perfected how to grant suits,
How to deny them, who to advance and who
To trash for over-topping, new created
The creatures that were mine, I say, or changed 'em,
Or else new form'd 'em," etc.

Leaving to those who love grammar the task of
parsing these parenthetic excursions, we may content
ourselves with remarking that the simple sentence
which underlies this whole structure is no more than
this : " My brother . . . Antonio . . . new-created the
creatures that were mine." If more grammatically
bewildering than the over-excited speech of Imogen,
this speech of Prospero, to be sure, is more agreeable
to the ear. In structure, however, the two are almost
identical. These examples typify the style of both
plays throughout. Fundamentally similar, they differ
remarkably in effect; for in general, while the style
of *Cymbeline* is harsh, cramped, obscure, the style of
the *Tempest* is sustained, lucid, and easy. In the

Tempest, we may say, the style is not only mastered, but it is so simplified as really to possess the simplicity of greatness.

The *Tempest*, then, is a very great, very beautiful poem. As a poem one can hardly love it or admire it too much. As a play, on the other hand, it is neither great nor effective. The reason is not far to seek : its motive is not primarily dramatic ; the mood it would express is not that of a playwright, but rather that of an allegorist or a philosopher.

The providential character of Prospero, for example, is a commonplace ; nothing could more distinctly mark the divergence of the *Tempest* from the fate-ridden tragedies than his serene mastery both of emotion and of superhuman things, by mere force of intellect. A commonplace, too, is the fresh assertion in the *Tempest* of that ideal of family reunion and reconciliation [1] of which there are traces in *Coriolanus*, in *Pericles*, and in *Cymbeline*. A commonplace, as well, is the ideal solution of the troubles which actual life involves. In the *Tempest* there are no such doubts as Hamlet's or Claudio's, nor any such despair as Lear's or Macbeth's : —

> " We are such stuff
> As dreams are made on, and our little life
> Is rounded with a sleep."

Not quite so familiar, perhaps, but still often remarked, is the comprehensive, prophetic view of social fact, typically set forth in Stephano and Trinculo, and above

[1] See pp. 332, 353, 362.

all in Caliban. The two former sum up the old distrust of the lower classes. They are not a mob,
to be sure; on the magic island there was no chance
for a mob to breed; in Stephano and Trinculo, however, all the folly and the impotence of a mob are
incarnate. With Caliban the case is different; in
him there is a perception of something not hinted
at before.

The single, unique figure of Caliban, in short, typifies
the whole history of such world-wide social evolution,
such permanent race-conflict, as was only beginning
in Shakspere's day, and as is not ended in our own.
Civilization, exploring and advancing, comes face
to face with barbarism and savagery. Savage and
barbarian alike absorb, not the blessings of civilization, but its vices, amid which their own simple virtues
are lost. Ruin follows. To-day European civilization has almost extirpated Maoris and Hawaiians and
Australian blacks. At this moment it is face to face
with the hordes of barbarian Asia and savage Africa.
Humanity forbids the massacre of lower races;
the equally noble instinct of race-supremacy forbids
any but a suicidally philanthropic man of European
blood to contemplate without almost equal horror the
thought of miscegenation. When Caliban would possess Miranda, we torment Caliban, but still we feel
bound to preserve him, — which is not good for the
morals or the temper of Caliban. That savage figure,
then, shows a vision so prophetic that at least one
modern scholar has chosen to study in Caliban the

psychology of Darwin's missing link. Marvellously prophetic suggestiveness, however, is not exactly a condition of theatrical effect.

The very complexity, indeed, and the essential abstractness of the endlessly suggestive, philosophic motive of the *Tempest* is reason enough why, for all its power and beauty, the play should theatrically fail. Like *Cymbeline*, though far less obtrusively, it contains too much. Like *Cymbeline* it reveals itself at last as a colossal experiment, an attempt to achieve an effect which, this time at least, is hopelessly beyond human power. Less palpably than *Cymbeline*, then, but just as surely, the *Tempest* finally seems laborious

It distinguishes itself from *Cymbeline*, of course, by the fact that its construction and its style alike are grandly simple. In this simplicity, quite as much as in its pervading atmosphere of enchantment, and in its general purpose of pure beauty, it rather resembles *As You Like It*, and still more the *Midsummer Night's Dream*. In final effect, however, it is as far from either of them as from *Cymbeline* itself. To a great degree the motive of *As You Like It*, and without qualification the motive of the *Midsummer Night's Dream* is purely to give pleasure; whatever else than pleasure one may find in either of them is incidental. The motive of the *Tempest*, on the other hand, we have seen to be philosophic, or allegorical, or at least something other than purely artistic. The three most familiar quotations from the three plays

will clearly define them. Take Theseus' great speech
in the *Midsummer Night's Dream :* [1] —

> " The poet's eye, in a fine frenzy rolling,
> Doth glance from heaven to earth, from earth to heaven ;
> And as imagination bodies forth
> The forms of things unknown, the poet's pen
> Turns them to shapes and gives to airy nothing
> A local habitation and a name."

Take Jaques' " Seven ages of Man," in *As You
Like It :* [2] —

> " All the world 's a stage,
> And all the men and women merely players :
> They have their exits and their entrances ;
> And one man in his time plays many parts,
> His acts being seven ages ; "

and so on. Compare with these the wonderful speech
of Prospero : [3] —

> " And, like the baseless fabric of this vision,
> The cloud capp'd towers, the gorgeous palaces,
> The solemn temples, the great globe itself,
> Yea, all which it inherit, shall dissolve
> And, like this unsubstantial pageant faded,
> Leave not a rack behind. We are such stuff
> As dreams are made on, and our little life
> Is rounded with a sleep."

The three passages will show what one means
who should call the *Midsummer Night's Dream* spontaneously fantastic, and the *Tempest* deliberately
imaginative.

This quality of deliberation, perhaps, typifies the
fatal trouble. Creatively and technically powerful as

---

[1] V. i. 12.　　　[2] II. vii. 139.　　　[3] IV. i. 151.

the *Tempest* is, — sustained, too, and simplified, and beautiful, — it has throughout a relation to real life which we cannot feel unintentional. In a spontaneous work of art, one feels that the relation of its truth to the truth of life is not intended, but is rather the result of the essential veracity of the artist's observation and expression.[1] In such an effect as that of the *Tempest*, then, one grows more and more to feel that, for all its power, for all its mastery, for all its beauty, the play is really a tremendous effort.

As such, the *Tempest* groups itself where verse-tests place it. In something more than mere form it is akin to *Cymbeline* and to *Pericles*. In these we saw indications that Shakspere's power was waning; here we find them again. In *Cymbeline* we found what seemed a deliberate attempt to assert artistic power at a moment when that power was past the spontaneous vigor of maturity. Here we find another such effort, more potent still. Shakspere not only recalls old material, and re-composes it; he digests his material afresh, until at first glance it seems new. He adds material that is really new, — drawing inspiration from the voyages which at the moment were opening a world of new, unfathomable possibility. All this, old and new, he suffuses with a single motive of serene, dominant beauty. In every detail he composes his work with unsurpassed skill. His motive, however, is not really dramatic, nor even purely artistic; it is philosophic, allegorical, consciously and deliberately

[1] See pp. 103, 171, 397, 399.

imaginative. His faculty of creating character, as distinguished from constructing it, is gone. All his power fails to make his great poem spontaneous, easy, inevitable. Like *Cymbeline*, it remains a Titanic effort; and, in an artist like Shakspere, effort implies creative decadence, — the fatal approach of growing age.

IV. THE WINTER'S TALE.

[The *Winter's Tale* was seen by Dr Forman at the Globe Theatre, on May 15th, 1611. In an official memorandum made in 1623, it is described as "formerly allowed of by Sir George Riche." Though Riche undoubtedly licensed plays before August, 1610, this was the date of his official appointment as Master of the Revels. The play was entered in 1623, and published in the folio.

The source of the plot is a novel by Robert Greene, originally published in 1588 under the title of *Pandosto*, and later republished as the *Historie of Dorastus and Fawnia*.

Verse-tests place the *Winter's Tale* later than *Cymbeline* and the *Tempest*. Taking these in connection with the records mentioned above, most critics conjecturally assign it to the end of 1610 or the beginning of 1611. Mr. Fleay is disposed to place it a little earlier; probably before the *Tempest*.]

The marked individuality of effect which we observed in both *Cymbeline* and the *Tempest* proved on scrutiny chiefly due to the fact that the dramatic structure of each involves a new and bold technical experiment. In each the experiment consists chiefly of a deliberately skilful handling of *dénouement*. In *Cymbeline*, after four and a half acts of confusion, comes the last scene, coolly disentangling the confusion by means of four and twenty cumulative stage situations ; in the *Tempest*, with due adherence to the unities of time, of place, and of action, the *dénouement* is expanded into five whole acts. In the *Winter's Tale* we find an analogous individuality of effect, due to a similar cause. Structurally the *Winter's Tale* is perhaps the most boldly experimental of all. The play is frankly double. The first three acts make a complete independent tragedy, involving the deaths of Mamillius and of Antigonus, and, so far as you can tell for the moment, the still more tragic end of Hermione. The last two acts make a complete independent comedy, which, taking up the story at its most tragic point, leads it to a final *dénouement* of reconciliation and romantic serenity.

Alike complete, the tragedy and the comedy are quite as independent as the separate plays in a classic trilogy or in an Elizabethan series of chronicle-histories. As we saw when discussing *Julius Cæsar*, too, the Elizabethan practice of making consecutive plays on the same subject was not confined to chronicle-history. Such after-plays of revenge as Chapman's *Revenge of Bussy d'Ambois* and Marston's *Antonio's Revenge* we saw to throw light on the structure of *Julius Cæsar* itself. Nor was such prolonged treatment of a subject confined to tragedy ; in Dekker's *Honest Whore* and Heywood's *Fair Maid of the West*, to go no further, we have elaborate romantic comedies in two parts. By its prolongation of popular stories into more than one performance, indeed, the Elizabethan theatre proves, as in other aspects, queerly like the modern Chinese stage. What Shakspere has done in the *Winter's Tale*, then, is to take the plan of a double play — peculiar in itself for being half-tragic and half-comic — and to compress what would normally have occupied two full performances into the limits of one. With little alteration of the conventional proportions of a double play, he completely alters its dimensions. With the slightest possible departure from his models, with characteristic economy of invention, he produces by mere compression a remarkably novel effect.

The very fact of compression, however, naturally produces a trait which, for theatrical purposes, is unfortunate. In both substance and style, the *Winter's Tale* is overcrowded. Take, for example, the passage where Hermione has persuaded Polixenes to prolong his visit and Leontes thereupon becomes jealous: [1] —

> "*Her*. What! have I twice said well? when was 't before?
> I prithee tell me; cram 's with praise, and make 's
> As fat as tame things: one good deed dying tongueless
> Slaughters a thousand waiting upon that.
> Our praises are our wages: you may ride 's
> With one soft kiss a thousand furlongs ere
> With spur we heat an acre. But to the goal:
> My last good deed was to entreat his stay:
> What was my first? it has an elder sister,
> Or I mistake you: O, would her name were Grace!
> But once before I spoke to the purpose: when?
> Nay, let me have 't; I long.

[1] I. ii. 90–120.

> *Leon.*   Why, that was when
> Three crabbed months had sour'd themselves to death,
> Ere I could make thee open thy white hand
> And clap thyself my love: then didst thou utter
> ' I am yours for ever.'
>   *Her*.   'T is grace indeed.
> Why, lo you now, I have spoke to the purpose twice:
> The one for ever earn'd a royal husband;
> The other for some while a friend.
>   *Leon.*   (*Aside*) Too hot, too hot!
> To mingle friendship far is mingling bloods.
> I have tremor cordis on me: my heart dances;
> But not for joy; not joy.   This entertainment
> May a free face put on, derive a liberty
> From heartiness, from bounty, fertile bosom,
> And well become the agent; 't may, I grant;
> But to be paddling palms and pinching fingers,[1]
> As now they are, and making practised smiles
> As in a looking-glass, and then to sigh, as 't were
> The mort o' the deer; O, that is entertainment
> My bosom likes not, nor my brows! Mamillius,
> Art thou my boy?"

In more ways than one the passage is typical of the
Winter's Tale.   During less than twenty lines, to begin with, Leontes is carried through an emotional experience which in the case of Othello had been prepared
for by above two acts, and when it came occupied
nearly two hundred and fifty lines.[2]   Again, while in
Othello every one of these lines is clear and fluent,
this passage from the *Winter's Tale* is both obscure
and crabbed.   The verse is more licentiously free than
ever before, and at the same time overpacked with

---

[1] Cf. *Hamlet*, III. iv. 185.   [2] *Othello*, III. iii. 35–279.

meaning. After Shakspere's regular fashion, too, this scene from the *Winter's Tale* proves both in substance, and to a less degree in phrase, reminiscent. In all these traits, which pervade the *Winter's Tale*, the play resembles *Cymbeline* and the *Tempest* as clearly as it resembles them in its boldly experimental structure and its serenely romantic motive.

The overcrowding of the style is what most distinguishes these three last plays from what precede. In Shakspere's earlier work, almost to the end of the tragic period, one generally felt that, when composing plays, he always endeavored to present his material, however serious, in such form as should be acceptable to an audience. In these last plays, one is aware of a radically different mood. The playwright, despite his vigorous technical experiment, has at last become a conscious poet. He cares about substance rather than style. Thoughts crowd upon him. He actually has too much to say. In his effort to say it, he disdainfully neglects both the amenity of regular form, and the capacity of human audiences. The only vehicle of expression at his disposal, meanwhile, was the public stage; and this vehicle his artistic purposes — now rather intellectual than emotional — had finally outgrown. In the *Winter's Tale* this trait is more palpable than anywhere else; Shakspere's style is surely more decadent than ever before.

In the *Winter's Tale*, too, the old trait of recapitulation is quite as palpable as in *Cymbeline*. Shakspere, to be sure, keeps fairly close to Greene's novel; but

Greene's novel itself deals chiefly with matters which Shakspere's earlier plays had proved effective; and what Shakspere adds — Paulina, for example, and Autolycus, and the Clown — is almost always directly taken from his old repertory. How recapitulatory the *Winter's Tale* is, any one can see. In the tragic part, the jealousy of Leontes, clearly akin to that of Posthumus, revives also the jealousy of Othello; and at the same time dispassionately revives a distinct phase of such overwrought self-deception and unbalance of mind as pervaded the great tragedies. Hermione, in her undeserved fate, resembles Imogen, and Desdemona, and Hero; at her trial she is like Queen Katharine. Paulina, a character introduced by Shakspere, has obvious analogies to Emilia in *Othello*, and to Beatrice, so far as Beatrice is concerned with the troubles of Hero. Mamillius, like Ariel a child-actor, is like the Duke of York in *Richard III.* and Prince Arthur in *King John.*[1] To pass to the comedy of the last two acts, the very entry of Autolycus is reminiscent:[2] —

"I have served Prince Florizel and in my time wore three-pile; but now I am out of service: . . . My traffic is sheets; when the kite builds, look to lesser linen. My father named me Autolycus; who being, as I am, littered under Mercury, was likewise a snapper-up of unconsidered trifles. With die and drab I purchased this caparison, and my revenue is the silly cheat. Gallows and knock are too powerful on the highway: beating and hanging are terrors to me: for the life to come, I sleep out the thought of it."

[1] See p. 367.   [2] IV. iii. 13–32.

Here, in the cramped dialect of this period, is a plain statement of such a situation as Falstaff's when the Prince had discarded him. The relations of Polixenes to Florizel are another clear reminiscence of *Henry IV*. Again, the Shepherd and the Clown revive not only the conventional boors of the early comedy,[1] but the relations between Falstaff and Shallow,[2] a bit of the absurdity of Sir Andrew Aguecheek, and incidentally the old distrust of democracy. The recovery of Hermione resembles those of Æmilia in the *Comedy of Errors*, of Hero in *Much Ado About Nothing*, and of Thaisa in *Pericles*.[3] In the great pastoral scene[4] there is not only abundant confusion of identity — the chief trait of all the early comedies — but an atmosphere which recalls the open-air scenes of *Love's Labour's Lost*, of the *Midsummer Night's Dream*, of the last act of the *Merry Wives of Windsor*, and of *As You Like It*.

All but the last of these reminiscences call to mind passages which, at least in vitality, are better than those in the *Winter's Tale*. Compare, for example, the characters of Falstaff and of Autolycus: Falstaff, though presented in a more archaic manner, is drawn from the life; Autolycus, though sympathetic and amusing, is so compressed and idealized, that he is like one of those finished pictures whose every detail somehow reveals that they are drawn from memory or from sketches. Better still, compare the final en-

---

[1] IV. iii. 702 seq.   [2] Ibid. and V. ii. 134 seq.
[3] See pp. 91, 195, 353.   [4] IV. iii.

lightenment of Othello[1] with the similar enlightenment of Leontes.[2] This is generally typical of the *Winter's Tale*. Tolerably effective in conception, it is at once too compressed for full effect, and perceptibly less spontaneous, less simple, less plausible, less masterly, than the greater work which it instantly recalls.

This is not unduly to dispraise the *Winter's Tale*. In many traits — in composition of plot, in firm grasp and contrast of character, in variety and precision of atmosphere, in freedom and pregnancy of phrase — the *Winter's Tale* is constantly above any power but Shakspere's. Compared with his own work elsewhere, however, the *Winter's Tale* rarely shows him at his best. The only passage, indeed, which may fairly be deemed better than similar passages which have come before is the pastoral scene.[3] Here for once, amid all the added ripeness of feeling which pervades this romantic period, we find something like Shakspere's full, spontaneous creative power. With it comes such a whiff of pure country air as calls to mind the actual harvest homes of rural England, and as sets critics who seek Shakspere's " inner life " to saying wise things about the effect on the man's morals of his return to Stratford. Such guesses as this are unprovable vagaries; all that one can safely say is that, unlike any scene which we have considered since *Antony and Cleopatra*, this pastoral scene, though full of romantic unreality, is plausible.

---

[1] *Othello*, V. ii. 102–282.

[2] III. ii. 132–173.   [3] IV. iii.

With all its lack of realism, all its cunning stage-craft, all its lovely poetry both of conception and of expression, the scene seems so spontaneous, so racy, so inevitable, that the old mood of the best time steals on you unawares. Again and again you yield to the illusion, feeling as if once again all this were true.

In the *Winter's Tale*, however, there is at least one touch which tends to show that Shakspere would deliberately guard against any such impression of reality. Greene's novel makes Bohemians sail to sea-bound Sicily; Shakspere deliberately makes Sicilians sail to sea-bound Bohemia. At this period, as we have seen again and again, the decay of spontaneous impulse gives good reason for believing Shakspere to have been constantly deliberate. If, then, his wanton departure from geographic fact be deliberate, its reason should seem to be that Shakspere meant to place all this romance in no real world, but rather in such a world just beyond the limits of reality as he created in the *Tempest*,[1] — a world where Tunis was no longer the lair of Barbary pirates, but a chivalrously romantic kingdom, a world where the Mediterranean expanded into an ocean as limitless as the Western Seas, a world where close to the spot in which from earliest times geographers have rightly placed Sicily, a King of Naples might be cast away on the magic isle of Prospero, there to find — in full agony of race-conflict — the savage Caliban. Such romances as we are now dealing with, this deliberate

[1] See p. 369.

fantasy seems to say, are never real. They are the dreams, the ideals which, fancied in a world alien to ours, make tolerable the inexorable facts of our own. Inexorable fact, despairing sense of fate, expired with *Coriolanus*, or at latest with *Timon*. The plays which follow breathe instead an atmosphere of idealism, wherein the troubles of actuality may all merge in the delights of free fancy.

Free, at any rate, beyond *Cymbeline* or the *Tempest*, we may fairly call this *Winter's Tale*. Less complicated in plot than the one, it is less elaborately artificial than the other. More varied in character than either, it is at once more firmly individual than the *Tempest*, and less laboriously so than *Cymbeline*. Its atmosphere is all its own. Its style has the carelessness of disdainful mastery. For all this freedom, however, one can hardly feel that theatrically the *Winter's Tale* could ever have been much more satisfactory than the unsatisfactory *Cymbeline* or *Tempest*. The structural experiment of deliberate duality is perhaps the boldest of the three. In every technical detail the work shows complete, disdainful mastery of power. Again and again, however, except in the great pastoral scene, this mastery lacks the final grace of unconscious spontaneity, just as the style lacks final simplicity. Throughout the play, in short, one is aware of a self-consciousness, of a deliberation which makes one hesitate before guessing the full intention of this touch or that. This conscious deliberation reveals just such trace of growing age as we found in *Cymbeline* and in the *Tempest*. Conscious deliberation means effort; effort means creative exhaustion. Here, perhaps, the effort is more masterly, less palpable, than before; here still, however, the effort cannot conceal itself; and the effort tells the final story, — Shakspere's old spontaneous power was fatally gone.

V. Henry VIII.

[*Henry VIII.*, as we have it, was first entered in 1623 and published in the folio. Various records prove, however, that a play on this subject was given at the Globe Theatre on June 29th, 1613. Carelessness in the discharge of a gun set fire to the theatre, which was totally destroyed. Quite what relation this play of 1613 bore to the *Henry VIII.* we possess is uncertain.

The sources of the present play are Holinshed, Hall, and Foxe's *Martyrs.*

The famous criticism of Mr. Spedding — summarized in the introduction to the *Leopold Shakspere* and in the *Henry Irving* edition — virtually demonstrated that a considerable part of this play is by John Fletcher. Mr. Fleay [1] believes that much is also by Massinger; and that the only scenes really by Shakspere are I. ii.; II. iii.; and II. iv. Certain critics go so far as to question whether any of the play is genuine.

If Shakspere's at all, this play is probably later than any other. It may be conjecturally assigned to 1612 or 1613.]

In most editions of Shakspere, *Henry VIII.* is printed immediately after *Richard III.* Thus placed, its maturity of detail makes it seem thoroughly ad-

[1] *Life*, 250–252.

mirable. Here, one exclaims, is no tissue of impossible villainy and operatic convention; here, rather, is real life. How any one could for a moment deem such work not Shakspere's own is hard to see.

Coming to *Henry VIII.*, on the other hand, as we come to it now, where modern chronology places it, one finds its effect strangely different. When one has considered all the masterpieces of comedy, of history, and of tragedy, when one has considered, too, the tremendous efforts made in the three great romances which we have just put aside, *Henry VIII.* seems comparatively thin, uncertain, aimless. Instinctively one's sympathies take a different turn. Instead of wondering how work like this can be ascribed to anybody but Shakspere, one finds one's self at a loss to see how work like this can rationally be ascribed to Shakspere at all. Of course there are masterly touches in *Henry VIII.*; of course, too, at least Queen Katharine and Cardinal Wolsey are very notable characters. After all, however, is there anything in either the style or the characterization of *Henry VIII.* which should make one surely affirm any part of this undoubtedly collaborative work to be by Shakspere's hand? May not one rationally doubt whether this is anything more than what John Webster stated his *White Devil* to be,[1] — a play to be judged by the standards of the masters?

For our purposes such questions need no answer. The very fact of their existence is more instructive

[1] See p. 20.

than the most definite of answers could possibly be;
for it proves that, whoever wrote or collaborated in
Henry VIII., the play is broadly typical of what the
English stage was producing when Shakspere's writing
ended.

At the very beginning of our study, we met a similar state of things.   Like *Henry VIII.* the two plays
to which we first gave attention — *Titus Andronicus*
and *Henry VI.* — were ascribed to Shakspere in 1623,
and have recently been doubted.   For our purposes,
however, we found the doubt more instructive than
any certainty could have been.   Whoever wrote *Titus
Andronicus* or *Henry VI.*, we found, the plays were
admirably typical of the theatrical environment amid
which Shakspere's work began.

What this environment was like we may remind
ourselves by a glance at the opening scene of *Henry
VI.*   In Westminster Abbey are assembled the funeral
train of King Henry V.; and this is how his brothers
and uncles begin to discourse: —

> "*Bed.* Hung be the heavens with black, yield day to night!
> Comets importing change of times and states,
> Brandish your crystal tresses in the sky,
> And with them scourge the bad revolting stars
> That have consented unto Henry's death !
> King Henry the Fifth, too famous to live long !
> England ne'er lost a king of so much worth.
>   *Glou.* England ne'er had a king until his time.
> Virtue he had, deserving to command:
> His brandished sword did blind men with his beams ; "

and so on, for six lines more.

> " *Exe.* We mourn in black : why mourn we not in blood ?
> Henry is dead and never shall revive:
> Upon a wooden coffin we attend,
> And death's dishonourable victory
> We with our stately presence glorify ; " —

there are six more lines of this.

> " *Win.* He was a king bless'd of the King of kings.
> Unto the French the dreadful judgment-day
> So dreadful will not be as was his sight.
> The battles of the Lord of hosts he fought:
> The church's prayers made him so prosperous."

So far goes the opening quartette of lament, which nowadays would take the form of grand opera. Gloucester now breaks in, beginning the strain of discord which is to be silenced only with the other Gloster — Richard III.

> " *Glou.* The church ! where is it ? Had not churchmen pray'd,
> His thread of life had not so soon decay'd :
> None do you like but an effeminate prince,
> Whom, like a school-boy, you may over-awe."

This is more than enough to remind us of all the archaic, operatic conventions which beset the stage when Shakspere began writing. Whether his or not, these lines are such as in the beginning he might have written.

Turn now to the opening scene of *Henry VIII.* : the Dukes of Norfolk and of Buckingham meet in an antechamber of the palace, and the following talk ensues : —

> " *Buck.* Good morrow, and well met. How have ye done
> Since last we saw in France ?

> *Nor.*   I thank your grace,
> Healthful; and ever since a fresh admirer
> Of what I saw there.
>   *Buck.*   An untimely ague
> Stay'd me a prisoner in my chamber when
> Those suns of glory, those two lights of men
> Met in the vale of Andren.
>   *Nor.*   'Twixt Guynes and Arde:
> I was then present, saw them salute on horseback;
> Beheld them, when they lighted, how they clung
> In their embracement, as they grew together;
> Which had they, what four throned ones could have
>   weigh'd
> Such a compounded one?
>   *Buck.*   All the whole time
> I was my chamber's prisoner.
>   *Nor.*   Then you lost
> The view of earthly glory : men might say,
> Till this time pomp was single, but now married
> To one above itself ; — "

and so on to a brilliant description of the Field of the Cloth of Gold. The calm rationality of this dialogue, its almost prosaic modernity, its profound acknowledgment of the actual conditions of fact combined with a free, breaking use of blank-verse and of not too extravagant metaphor, are more than enough to remind us, if we needed reminding, of the conventions which beset the stage when Shakspere's work ended. Whether his or not, these lines are such as in the end he might have written.

From the doubtful *Henry VI.* we have proceeded through a long series of indubitably genuine works to the equally doubtful *Henry VIII.* Nowhere on the

way has any work seemed very unlike those about it.
The contrast between the first doubt and the last,
then, is startling; nothing could more clearly demonstrate how Shakspere marks the progress of English
Literature from a state which seems wholly of the past
to one which seems almost like the present. For our
purposes, we need look no longer at *Henry VIII.*

VI. SHAKSPERE ABOUT 1612.

For our purposes, too, we need pause very little to
summarize our impression of the last works of Shakspere, as they have appeared in this chapter. Details
of their dates can never be decisively settled. There
is every reason to believe, however, that, in some order
or other, the plays we have here considered were all
written after those which we considered before, and
that they virtually complete Shakspere's work.

Allowing them the widest chronological range admitted by any consenting criticism, we find them to
belong to the years of Shakspere's life which carried
him from forty-five to forty-eight, and from the
twenty-second year of his professional work to the
twenty-fifth and last. In all three of the unques-
tioned plays, and quite as much in the doubtful *Henry
VIII.*, we found constant traces of declining creative
power, which even the tremendous technical efforts of
Cymbeline and the *Tempest* and the *Winter's Tale*

were powerless to conceal. What impulse was left
the man, after the complete break of his spontaneous
power in *Timon* and *Pericles*, was an impulse rather
of philosophic thought than of artistic emotion. For
such a purpose there are few worse vehicles than
the public stage.

Compare with these plays, now, the general records
of publication during the years in question.[1] In 1609,
the year to which we conjecturally assigned *Cymbeline*, Beaumont and Fletcher's *Maid's Tragedy* is said to
have been acted, and among the publications were not
only the *Sonnets*, *Troilus and Cressida*, and *Pericles*,
— the last three works of Shakspere which originally
appeared during his lifetime, — but the final version
of Daniel's *Civil Wars*, Dekker's *Gull's Hornbook*,
Drayton's *Lord Cromwell*, Jonson's *Epicœne* and *The
Case is Altered*, and the Douay translation of the
Bible. In 1610, the year to which we conjecturally assigned the *Tempest*, Beaumont and Fletcher's *Knight
of the Burning Pestle* and Jonson's *Alchemist* are said
to have been acted; and among the publications were
Bacon's *Wisdom of the Ancients*, twelve books of
Chapman's *Iliad*, Donne's *Pseudo-Martyr*, Fletcher's
Faithful Shepherdess, and the final edition of the
Mirror for Magistrates. In 1611, the year to which
we conjecturally assigned the *Winter's Tale*, Beaumont
and Fletcher's *King and No King*, and Jonson's *Cati-
line* were acted; and among the publications were
twelve more books of Chapman's *Iliad*, Coryat's *Cru-

[1] Ryland: *Chronological Outlines of English Literature.*

dities, Dekker and Middleton's *Roaring Girl,* Donne's *Anatomy of the World,* Speed's *History of Great Britain,* Tourneur's *Atheist's Tragedy,* and the Authorized Version of the Bible. In 1612, the year to which — more conjecturally still — we assigned *Henry VIII.,* came the second edition of Bacon's *Essays,* two plays by Beaumont and Fletcher, Hall's *Contemplations,* and John Webster's *White Devil,* whose preface, as we have seen, mentioned Shakspere as an honored tradition.[1]

The hasty list is enough for our purpose. At this time, when Shakspere's power showed plain signs of weakening, English Literature was at once more modern and more fertile than ever. Of the riper dramatists, whose work is full of effective invention, all but the distinctly decadent Ford and Massinger were in their prime. There is small wonder, then, that Shakspere wrote no more. Competition was stronger than ever; and, at the same time, his purposes had outgrown his vehicle, and his spontaneous impulse had ceased. Both as an artist and as a man he had more to lose than to gain.

[1] See pp. 20, 408.

XII

WILLIAM SHAKSPERE

WE have now reached the last stage of our study. We have glanced at the facts of Shakspere's life; we have briefly considered the condition of English Literature when his work began; and, with what detail has proved possible, we have considered, in conjecturally chronological order, all the works commonly ascribed to him. The few remaining works which are probably more or less his — *Edward III.*, the *Two Noble Kinsmen*, and a few lyrics — are not generally included in the standard editions. Less accessible, then, than what we have considered, they are also less interesting; nor do they contain anything which should alter our conclusions. Our conclusions, however, may well be affected by another matter at which we have glanced, — the English literature, in general, which came into existence between 1587 and 1612, during which interval, in some order or other, the works of Shakspere were certainly produced. We are ready, then, finally to review our impressions.

In looking back over our course, perhaps nothing is more notable than its limits. We are so far from having covered the whole subject of Shakspere, that we have neglected parts of it important enough to make our neglect seem almost a confession of ignorance. Not to speak of endless details, we have hardly touched on the range or the quality of his genius; we have thought little about the subtleties of his art; we have hardly glanced at the scope and the character of his philosophy; nor yet have we discussed at all the surprising range of his learning. And so on. The truth is that the subject of Shakspere is inexhaustible. Whoever would deal with it, must perforce neglect much of it. At any moment, then, those phases may best be neglected which happen at that moment to have been best discussed elsewhere.

Such a phase, clearly, is Shakspere's genius. In the fine arts, we remember, a man of genius is he who in perception and in expression alike, in thought and in phrase, instinctively so does his work that his work remains significant after the conditions which actually produced it are past. The work of any man of genius, then, is susceptible of endless comment and interpretation, varying as the generations of posterity vary from his and from one another. Such interpretative comment is always suggestive. The most notable example of it concerning Shakspere may perhaps be found in the writings of Coleridge. Foreign alike to Shakspere's time and to our own, the mood of Coleridge was not long ago vitally contemporary. While to-day what Coleridge says about Shakspere often seems queerly erratic, it must always be interesting, both as an important phase of human thought, and as lasting evidence of how Shakspere's genius presented itself to one who came near being a man of genius himself. In some such manner the genius of Shakspere, like any other, must present itself, with ever fresh significance, to men of our own time and of times to come. Like Nature herself, the work of the great artists must always possess a fresh significance for every generation which comes to it with fresh eyes. As we have seen, however, this significance is generally implicit. It is there because, by the very laws of his nature, the artist worked with instinctive fidelity to the greater laws which govern actual life. In a course of study like ours, then, whose object is chiefly to see the artist as he may have seen himself, we may well neglect those aspects of his work which are visible only after the lapse of centuries. On these, as the centuries pass, there will always be emphasis enough. The danger is not that Shakspere's genius will be forgotten; but that, in admiration for the aspects in which, from time to time, that genius defines itself, people may fatally forget the truth that Shakspere's work really emanated from a living man.

Again, there is a great deal of criticism about the art of Shakspere, — discussion as to how conscious it was, how deliberate, how essentially fine. One still hears much debate as to whether the free, romantic form of his dramas be a nobler thing or a meaner than the more rigid form of the classics, and of their modern imitations. Such discussion is interesting;

and so far as it deals with the precise artistic methods of Shakspere might well have found place in our study. Here and there, indeed, as space permitted, we have touched on it, — most notably, perhaps, in showing how the finished form of the *Midsummer Night's Dream* grew at once from old motives and from old and crude conventions.[1] So far, however, as such discussion deals with general matters,— questioning, for example, whether classic art or romantic be the finer,— it is foreign to our purpose, and in some aspects akin to the less famous discussion as to whether shad or custard be the greater delicacy. For our purposes, we may be content with knowing that Shakspere, an Elizabethan playwright, was as much bound by the conditions of his time to write in the Elizabethan manner as was Sophocles of Athens to compose his tragedies after the manner of the Greeks. Whoever, then, would finally or intelligently criticise the art of Shakspere must first master, as hardly anybody has yet mastered, the conditions of Shakspere's theatre. Much of the extant criticism of Shakspere's art resembles that of Gothic cathedrals which prevailed when pseudo-classic architecture was all the fashion ; much of what remains resembles that criticism of the same Gothic churches which refers the origin of their aisles and arches to the trunks and boughs of forest alleys. Partly for want of space, then, partly for want of sufficient knowledge as yet, we have studied Shakspere's art only so far as was

[1] See pp. 107, 110.

necessary to make clear the general conditions of his time.

Concerning Shakspere's philosophy,—his deliberate teaching,—the state of affairs is much like that concerning his genius. Earnest students innumerable have read between his lines endless lessons, some of which are doubtless very wise and valuable. Just how far he meant to put them there, however, is another question. We have seen enough of Elizabethan Literature to recognize that much of its aphorism is nothing intentionally more serious than a fresh combination of language. In the very prevalence of its aphorism, however, we must have recognized a symptom at once of a general appetite for proverbial philosophy, and of that generally ripe state of practical experience which at intervals in history gives more or less final expression to a state of life about to pass away. The aphoristic wisdom of Elizabethan Literature, so far as it is more than verbal, broadly expresses the experience of mediæval England. To this aphorism Shakspere added much. Very probably, though, what he added was no system of philosophy; it was rather a series of superbly final phrases, now and again combining to produce a complete artistic impression, — such as the pessimism of *Macbeth*, or the profound idealism of the *Tempest*, — which to him would have seemed rather emotional than dogmatic. In one sense every artist is a philosopher; but as philosophy is commonly understood, artists are apt to be unconscious philosophers, — philosophers rather by the inevitable law of their nature than by any deliberate intention ; and, whatever else we have done, we have never allowed ourselves to forget that from beginning to end Shakspere was an artist.

Another matter, much discussed nowadays, we have hardly glanced at. Nothing more surprises such readers of Shakspere as are not practical men of letters than the man's apparent learning. To one used to writing, the phenomenon is less surprising. To translate technical matters from a book merely glanced at, into such finished terms as the uninitiated suppose to imply years of study and research, is within anybody's power. Whoever will take a few Elizabethan books,— North's *Plutarch*, for example, Paynter's *Palace of Pleasure*, Foxe's *Martyrs*, Holinshed, and Coke on Littleton,— and, with the help of stray passages from all, translate some narrative from one of them into blank-verse dialogue, will produce an effect of erudition which shall profoundly impress not only his readers but himself. Whoever has a few compendious works at hand and knows how to use them, in fact, can make himself seem a miracle of learning to whoever does not know his secret. In Elizabethan England almost all books were compendious; so was the common talk of all intelligent men, — for learning was not yet specialized. Given these facts, and given the exceptionally concrete habit of thought and phrase native to Shakspere, and Shakspere's learning is no longer a marvel, except to those who insist on finding it so.

To pass from matters neglected to a matter purposely reserved, nothing is more notable to a student
of Elizabethan Literature than the fact that Elizabethan
Literature presents a remarkably typical example of
artistic evolution.   Art, of any kind, in nations, in
schools, even in individuals, progresses by a rhyth-
mical law of its own.   At certain epochs the arts of
expression are lifelessly conventional.   Born to these
conventions, often feeble and impotent, the nation,
the school, or the individual destined to be great, will
begin, like those who preceded, by simple imitation,
differing from the older conventions only in a certain
added vigor.   By and by, the force which we have
called creative imagination will develop, with a strange,
mysterious strength of its own, seemingly almost inspired.   Throbbing with this imaginative impulse, the
nation, the school, or the individual artist will begin
no longer to imitate, but instead, to innovate, with an
enthusiasm for the moment as unconscious of limits
to come as it is disdainful of the old, conventional
limits which it has transcended.   After a while, the
limits to come will slowly define themselves.   No creative or imaginative impulse can stray too far.   The
power of words, of lines and colors, of melody and
harmony, is never infinite.   If slavish fidelity to conventions be lifeless, utter disregard of conventions
tends to the still more fatal end of chaotic, inarticulate
confusion.   One may break fetter after fetter; but one's
feet must still be planted on the earth.   One may move
with all the freedom which the laws of nature allow;

but if one try to soar into air or ether, one is more lost
even than if one count one's footsteps. So to nations,
to schools, to individuals alike a growing sense of
limitation must come. There are things which may
be achieved ; there are vastly more things and greater
which remain fatally beyond human power. Experience, then, begins to check the wilder impulses of
creative innovation. Imagination is controlled by a
growing sense of fact. Finally, this sense of fact,
this consciousness of environment, grows stronger
and stronger, until at length all innovating impulse
is repressed and strangled. Again art lapses into a
convention not to be disturbed until, perhaps after
generations, fresh creative impulse shall burst its
bonds again.

As elsewhere in nature, so in art, creative impulse
is a strange, unruly thing, tending constantly to variation from the older types, but not necessarily to
improvement. While the general principles just stated
are constantly true everywhere, their result is often
abortive, often, too, eccentric or decadent. At rare
moments, however, creative impulse surges for a while
in a direction which carries art irresistibly onward to
greater and better expressions than men have known
before. Such impulses as this the centuries find marvellous. When a great creative impulse has come,
when the shackles of old convention are broken, when
the sense of the new limits is developed at once so far
as to tell instinctively what may be accomplished, and
not so overwhelmingly as to crush imagination with

the fatal knowledge of all which is beyond human power, then, for a little while, any art is great. The moment of ultimate greatness comes when a true creative impulse is firmly controlled, but not yet checked, by a rational sense of fact.

These general phenomena are nowhere more concretely shown than in the growth, development, and decay of English Literature during the period which we call Elizabethan. Really beginning before the reign of Elizabeth, this literary evolution really survived her, lasting indeed until the unhappy times of Charles I. The central figure of the period during which it took place, however, was undoubtedly the great queen, who, above any other English sovereign, was once the central fact of national life. The literature, then, which we may assume to have begun with Wyatt and to have ended with Shirley, may safely enough be named Elizabethan. In this literature the earlier work — such as that of Wyatt, of Surrey, of Roger Ascham, of Foxe, of Paynter — was chiefly notable for its eager breaking away from old conventions. In substance and in form alike its chief motive was to present to English readers other and better things than English readers had known before. Its method was to imitate the thought or the manner of greater or more polished peoples or times. Then came a fresh group of writers, — Sidney, Lyly, Spenser, Hooker, and the earlier dramatists. All alike, these bold, spirited linguistic innovators were busy chiefly in proving, with constantly freshening impulse, what the newly found English language might do. Then came Marlowe and Shakspere, and the great Elizabethan drama, — the one thing which at that moment the language and the race might best accomplish. Then, very swiftly, came the decline, when such men as Bacon and Drayton, and Davies, and Chapman, and lesser ones, — actually contemporary with the greatest, but tending rather toward limitation than toward innovation, — began to use the tamed language for purposes more and more special. The old impulse was a thing of the past.

Such generalizations must seem nebulous. A glance at a half-forgotten, but still great work of the period, may perhaps define them. During the reign of Queen Elizabeth no Englishman lived a more complete life than Sir Walter Ralegh. Country gentleman, student, soldier, sailor, adventurer, courtier, favorite and spoilsman, colonizer, fighter, landlord, agriculturist, poet, patron of letters, state prisoner, explorer, conqueror, politician, statesman, conspirator, chemist, scholar, historian, self-seeker, and ultimately a martyr to patriotism, he acquired through the latter half of Elizabeth's reign the most comprehensive experience ever known to an Englishman. Almost with the accession of King James his prosperity came to an end. He was imprisoned in the Tower, where for above ten years he busied himself with writing his great *History of the World*. To this task he brought a rare equipment; for not only did he nobly conceive history as the visible record of God's dealing with mankind, but he had actually experienced more wide variety of such matters as make history than has any other Englishman before or since. With above ten years of enforced leisure and concentration, with the best scholarship of the time to help him collect material, with a very beautiful stately English style of his own, he set about his task. In 1614, as much of his work as he ever finished was published. The *History of the World* has so long been obsolete that except for its name it is almost forgotten. It is traditionally supposed to be queer and fantastic, with occasional fine bits of rhetoric. Really, it is among the most nobly planned books in the world. History, as we have seen, Ralegh conceived to be the visible record of God's dealing with men. Its value, then, lay chiefly in the fact that to whoever should study it seriously and reverently, it taught truths not elsewhere accessible concerning the nature and the will of God. In the language of his time this meant what to-day would be meant by a philosophic historian, who should find in his subject not merely stirring narrative or plain record of fact, but the visible teachings of human experience, which, properly understood, should govern future conduct. Not only was Ralegh's effort a grandly philosophic one, too, but, as we have seen, he brought to its accomplishment an almost unique equipment. Besides all this, the man had a wonderfully cool, clear, rational head; his mind was among the most prudently and judiciously critical in all historical literature. Yet, as we have seen, his great *History* has proved of so little value that people nowadays mostly suppose it to be merely quaint.

The reason for this failure clearly defines just what the chief limit of Elizabethan Literature was bound to be. Human nature has always open to it a wealth of experience which may indefinitely develop individuals; and in the time of Elizabeth the possible range of individual experience was probably wider than at any other period of history. Whoever would write, like Ralegh, however, in a profoundly philosophic spirit, needs more experience to work with than can ever come to any individual. No individual can master the material world, even of his own day; still less can he extend his experience beyond the limits of his own life. To deal with history, then, on such a scale as Ralegh planned, a man must have recourse to endless records which, to avail him, must have been subjected to generations of patient scientific criticism; and in Ralegh's time — in Elizabethan England — there were no records which he could safely trust. In history, in science, in all things alike, the gathering of valid material was still to make. All that was ready for anything like final expression, then, was on the one hand the actual experience of individuals, and on the other a plain assertion of some method by which, in generations to come, serious study might safely be guided.

In the ripeness of Elizabethan Literature, both of these things were finally expressed. Whatever its error of detail, the philosophical writing of Bacon has done more than any other work of modern times to guide in the road which they have travelled the thought and the scholarship of the future. More notably still, the Elizabethan Drama — whatever its artistic peculiarities, or faults, or vagaries — expressed with a power and a range never surpassed the infinitely varied possibility and intensity of individual experience. Of these two final achievements the drama, if not the more lasting in its effects, was for the moment the more complete. Nothing less than the lapse of centuries could have demonstrated the value of Bacon's philosophy. By the very nature of things, on the other hand, the power of a great dramatic literature must be evident to the public which first welcomes it. With an approach to truth, then, we may say that Elizabethan Literature reduces itself finally to the Elizabethan Drama.

In the work of Shakspere we have studied this drama somewhat minutely. Incidentally, too, we glanced at the state in which Shakspere found the stage, and also at the work of his greatest predecessor and early contemporary, — Marlowe. Before Shakspere had really begun to show what power was in him, Marlowe was dead. Since Marlowe's time, we have considered the drama only as it appears in Shakspere. More clearly to define his position, we may now to advantage glance at another dramatist who seems, like Marlowe, greater than most of his contemporaries.

This is John Webster. While Mr. Fleay[1] shows

---

[1] *Chronicle of the English Drama,* II. 268.

reason to believe that Webster collaborated with
Drayton and Middleton and others as early as 1602,
there seems no doubt that his first independent work
was the *White Devil*, — the play, published in 1612,
which he expressly hopes shall be read in the light of
Chapman's work, and Jonson's, and Beaumont and
Fletcher's, and Shakspere's, and Dekker's, and Heywood's.[1] Just as the work of Marlowe typifies what
the stage was like when Shakspere's writing began,
then, the *White Devil*, — a fair type of Webster's power,
— coming after Shakspere's work was done, may be
taken as an example of what the stage was like when
Shakspere's writing ceased.

The story of the *White Devil* is virtually historical; what is more, it was almost contemporary. The
events therein detailed occurred, about 1585, in that
Italy which to Elizabethans was much what the Second
Empire in France was to the Americans of thirty years
ago — at once their model of civilization, the chief
source of their culture, and at the same time the sink
wherein they learned, along with much polite accomplishment, to what depths of depravity human nature
may fall. The story, in short, bore to Webster's audience such relation as might be borne to a modern
audience by a play which should deal with the career
of Louis Philippe's Duc de Choiseul-Praslin, or with
that of Louis Napoleon's Countess Castiglione. Webster, to be sure, took his artist's privilege, and altered
certain characters for dramatic effect: Camillo, the

[1] See p. 20.

injured husband, for example, he made a wittol, and Isabella, the murdered wife, a highly respectable person, — which was far from the actual case. On the whole, however, he preserved enough fact to claim the protection of historical authority.

As he tells the story, Vittoria Corombona, the daughter of a poor Venetian family, is married to Camillo, a Roman numskull. Her brother, Flamineo, an utterly corrupt soldier of fortune, induces her not unwillingly to become the mistress of the Duke of Brachiano. This infatuated voluptuary finally determines to marry her; whereupon he has his faithful wife, Isabella, poisoned, and meanwhile Flamineo manages to make Camillo break his neck. Francisco de Medicis, brother of the murdered Isabella, and the Cardinal Monticelso suspect foul play, and have Vittoria arrested on a charge of murdering her husband, Camillo. Although the crime cannot be proved, sufficient evidence is adduced to send Vittoria to a Roman Bridewell. Francisco, meanwhile, has privately convinced himself that the real murderer of Isabella was Brachiano. In pursuance of revenge, then, he takes advantage of the confusion attending the election of Monticelso to the papacy,[1] and enables Brachiano to steal Vittoria from prison, and to carry her, with all her family, to Padua. For this impious

---

[1] Historically the man whom Webster calls Monticelso was named Montalto, and was made pope by the name of Sixtus V. Webster makes him take the name of Paul IV. — historically that of a Caraffa This licentious treatment of historic fact is typically Elizabethan.

escapade, the fugitives are excommunicated. Francisco, still bent on vengeance, follows them in disguise, accompanied, among other ruffians, by a certain Count Lodovico, who had hopelessly loved the murdered Duchess. At a tournament, they managed to poison Brachiano's helmet. As he lies dying in agony, Lodovico, disguised as a priest, pours into his ears, under color of extreme unction, all the curses his revengeful brain can devise. Then, while Flamineo and Vittoria are quarrelling over what Brachiano has left, Lodovico breaks in and kills them —only to be killed in turn by Francisco, who would cover his tracks.

The first thing which impresses one in the treatment of this morbidly horrible story is that, within the now established traditions of dramatic form, it is studiously realistic. The characters throughout are considered as living human beings. The atmosphere is so veracious that the play can teach us, almost historically, what Sixteenth Century Italy was like. This Italy — the country which produced Machiavelli — was remarkable for such bewildering complexity as always pervades an over-ripe period of society. Of this complexity, Webster, with his realistic purpose, was so profoundly aware that throughout the play, despite all his power of imagination, you feel him constantly hampered by a sense of how much he had to tell. Great as he was, in short, his subject and his vehicle combined almost to master him. Every scene, every character, every speech, every phrase, seems deliberately studied; every line shows painful thought; yet for all these pains the play remains in total effect rather a tremendous sketch than a finished work of art. At first sight, with all its complexity of detail, it is puzzling. As you study it, you begin to feel its power more and more, until, compared with any other power except Shakspere's own, it seems almost supreme. Constantly, however, you feel that at an earlier period in the drama such power might have exerted itself not with painful effort, but with spontaneous ease. As matters stand, though the construction of scenes and the development of character prove Webster a great dramatist, and though phrase after phrase prove him a great poet, you feel him paralyzed by a crushing sense of his limitations. A wonderful stroke of character stands by itself, then comes a startling situation, then an aphorism, then a simile, then some admirable interjected anecdote; and so on. Nothing is finally fused, however; you feel none of that glowing heat of spontaneous imagination which, unchecked by adequate sense of fact, kept still half-inarticulate the aspiring poetry of Marlowe. If one would know what the force of creative imagination is like which awakens a great school of art, one cannot do better than turn to Marlowe; if one would realize the sense of limitation in which a great school of art finally declines, one cannot do better than turn to Webster.

Between them stands Shakspere, actually contemporary with both, and throughout his best period, fusing the chief merits of each. Between them, too, in artistic evolution, if not always in actual dates, comes the great group of ripe dramatists with whom, during the most vigorous period of his work as well as during its laborious decline, Shakspere competed for public favor. We can glance at them only very hastily; but a hasty glance is worth our while. Ben Jonson was the greatest master of eccentric "humour" — a trait always dear to the English — who ever wrote for the English stage; probably, too, he was the most consummate master of mere stage-business. Marston, though coarse, was an admirable writer of sensational tragedy. Dekker was unique for a joyous, off-hand spontaneity of feeling and of phrase. Middleton, but for a fatal coldness of personal temper, might almost have rivalled Shakspere in the handling of character, tragic and comic alike. Heywood, untroubled by such traditions of courtly grandeur as made Shakspere, to the end, habitually head his *dramatis personæ* by the figure of a sovereign, was thorough master of romantic sentiment. Chapman, if inarticulate, was a constantly impressive and weighty moralizer. Tourneur was almost modern in his impious recklessness. Beaumont and Fletcher, though palpably decadent, were superb masters of fascinatingly sentimental, always mellifluous, constantly interesting romance. Nowadays, of course, any one can see that neither these nor any of their fellows can compare, for range or power, with Shakspere. None of them, nor indeed any Eliza-

bethan but Shakspere, was contemporary at once
with Marlowe and with Webster. One and all,
however, have merits which, by any contemporary
standards, might well have been confused with
his. Generally spontaneous, their work has continual flashes of insight; it is often very beautifully phrased; and it is rarely overburdened with
anything which should fatigue or repel a popular
audience. In the full flush of their power, these
men had popular merits, as well as merits which
have proved lasting. From the outset, too, their
merits were patent.

In several ways, however, these later men differed
both from the earlier group which preceded Shakspere,
and less palpably from Shakspere himself. As we
saw in the beginning, the first Elizabethan playwrights were closely connected with the actual stage,
at a time when the stage was socially disreputable.
They were men of fine poetic gifts and of tolerable
education; but they were the Bohemians of a society
which admitted no distinction between reputable life
and such professional crime as is lastingly pictured
in the tavern scenes of *Henry IV*. The later playwrights, on the other hand, were men of higher
rank and of far more reputable habit. Beaumont,
for example, was the son of a judge; Fletcher was
the son of a bishop; Webster's father was a London citizen of the better sort; and so on. In their
own private life the traditional Mermaid Tavern,
which foreshadowed the clubs and the coffee-houses

of the Eighteenth Century, took the place of such squalid surroundings as saw the end of Marlowe and of Greene. Many of these men, too, were merely poets or dramatic authors; they were not actors. The stage, in short, was growing into such better repute as was bound to come with the increasingly definite organization of society. A true Bohemia was coming into existence.

The work of these more reputable men, at the same time, was less reputable than that of their predecessors. As the stage grew established, it grew more and more licentious. The work of Marlowe needs little expurgation; that of Beaumont and Fletcher, for all its grace and beauty, is full of abominations. As will often be the case with any school of art, the beginnings of the Elizabethan drama had a simple, spontaneous purity which vanished when the development of the school made over-refinement of effort, take the place of such broadly general motives as underlay the work of Greene and Peele and Marlowe.

Another distinction has been admirably defined by Mr. Fleay : [1] —

"I may perhaps at this point note how greatly the playwrights who were also actors excelled the gentlemen authors . . . We have first on the actor-poet list Shakspere, more than enough to counterpoise all the rest; then Jonson, the second greatest name in our annals; then Heywood, Field, Rowley, Armin, Monday. On the other side are great names also: Beaumont, Fletcher, Web-

[1] *Chronicle History of the London Stage*, p. 167.

ster, Massinger, Shirley, Chapman, and many others, all
great as poets, but none (except Massinger perhaps) equal
to even the lesser men in the other list in that undefinable
quality which separates the acting play from the drama for
closet reading; the quality which makes Goldsmith and
Sheridan successful, but the want of which condemns
Henry Taylor, Browning, and Shelley to remain the delight, not of the crowd, but of the solitary student. My
opinion in this matter is no doubt open to much qualification, but there is in connexion with it one fact beyond
dispute, viz., all actor-poets of any great note began their
theatrical careers before the accession of James."

These brief notes must suffice to define the historical position of Shakspere as the central figure, and the
most broadly typical, in the evolution of perhaps the
most broadly typical school of art in modern literature. Quite apart from its lasting literary value,
apart, too, from its unique personal quality, the work
of Shakspere has new interest to modern students as
a complete individual example of how fine art emerges
from an archaic convention, fuses imagination with
growing sense of fact, and declines into a more mature convention where the sense of fact represses and
finally stifles the force of creative imagination.

To repeat in detail the summaries of his work already made were tedious. It is enough merely to
glance at the four periods into which we divided his
career. The first — from 1587 to 1593 or thereabouts
— we called experimental. He contented himself
with widely versatile imitation, revealing two personal

qualities: a habit of mind by which, to a degree unique in English Literature, words and concepts were identical; and later, a power of enlivening the conventional figures of his original sources by no end of little touches derived from observation of life. Throughout this first period, however, his work never so differed from that of his contemporaries as to be free from the palpable archaism amid which a great school of art begins.

During the second period of his career — from 1593 to 1600 — the force of his imagination, first revealing itself in the artistic completeness of the *Midsummer Night's Dream* and almost simultaneously in the vivid characterization of *Romeo and Juliet*, pervaded and altered whatever he touched. His command of language almost constantly strengthened, until — as throughout his career — one felt half insensibly that while his native habit of mind, fusing phrases and concepts, never altered, he tended constantly to consider thoughts more and words less. Meanwhile his power of enlivening character by the results of observation so persisted and strengthened that at last — as in the case of Falstaff — his characters began to have almost independent existence. At the same time, with all this power of creating character and of uttering ultimate phrases, he displayed more and more palpably a sluggishness, if not an actual weakness, of invention. He repeated, to a degree unapproached by any other writer of his time, whatever device had proved theatrically effective, — confusion of identity, for example, and later self-deception. Apart from these traits, this second, purely artistic period revealed little. He created a small army of living individuals, he displayed a constant artistic impulse, but he revealed no profound personal sense of fact. During this period, then, his own peculiar power of imagination and of artistic impulse was at work almost unchecked. The most marked peculiarity of his power, however, — that it was confined to such matters of detail as character, phrase, or atmosphere, — meant that his natural sense of fact was strong. The growing vitality of his personages indicated meanwhile a superb fusion of imagination with this sense of fact.

During the third period of his artistic career — from 1600 to 1608 — we found again this superb fusion of his own peculiar creative power and his own strong sense of fact. During this period, however, we found something far more significant than the merely artistic impulse which had preceded. Up to this time his plays had expressed nothing deeper than the touch of irony which underlies *Much Ado About Nothing*. Now, in place of the old versatility first of experiment and then of concentration, we found a constant, crescent expression of such emotion as should come only from profound spiritual experience. He began to use his thoroughly mastered vehicle for the dramatic expression of such motives as we had seen to underlie his wonderfully finished *Sonnets*. In these motives we observed first a profound and increasing sense of

27

irony, of fate, of the helplessness of human beings in the midst of their crushing environment. Then came, with endless variations, a profound sense of the evil which must always spring from the mysterious fact of sex. Finally, perhaps as a result of these two causes, came a state of mind so over-wrought that, had it not been balanced by his supreme artistic sanity, it might almost have lapsed into madness. At the height of this period, when he produced his four great tragedies, his imagination was working with its fiercest power, and his sense of fact meanwhile controlled it with ultimate firmness.

One by one, the profound traits of this period began to disappear. With *Macbeth* we saw the end of the morbid excitement of mind; with *Antony and Cleopatra* we bade farewell to the evil of woman; with *Coriolanus,* where at length eccentricity or " humour " began to replace inevitable character, came the last complete expression of despairing irony. In other words, the power of his imagination, perhaps exhausted by the very intensity of its exercise, began to weaken under the pressure of a crushing sense of fact.

In *Timon* and *Pericles* we found a moment of artistic transition. The spontaneous power was gone. All that remained of the old Shakspere was the marvellous command of language, palpable even in his earliest work, and crescent with him to the end.

Finally, in the fourth and last period of his career — which extended at most from 1609 to 1612 — we found a colossal series of technical experiments, where, with all his unequalled mastery of art, and with a serenely ideal philosophy, he was struggling, in vain, to enliven with something like the old spontaneous imaginative power, the crushing sense of fact which was fatally closing in not only on him, but on the school of literature to which he belongs. The more one studies Shakspere's work as a whole, the more complete becomes its typical historic significance.

This typical quality, however, is not the trait which has made it survive. Just now the study of literary evolution happens to be the fashion, or at least to appeal to the temper of the day. The temper in question is new and probably transient. Shakspere was a supreme figure long before it existed; he will remain such long after it has taken its place among the curiosities of the past. What makes him perennial is that, above any other modern poet, he was a man of genius, — one who in perception and in expression alike, in thought and in phrase, instinctively so did his work that it remains significant long after the conditions which actually produced it have vanished. In our admiration for this genius, for this constantly fresh significance, we are apt to forget all else, and in our forgetfulness to be lost in stammering wonder.

Nowadays the form which this wonder most aptly takes is, perhaps, first amazement, then incredulity, then frank doubt as to whether all this wonderful poetry could conceivably have been produced by a middle-class Englishman, the record of whose life is so calmly commonplace. Such doubt can no more be dispelled by any process of argument than can religious scepticism. Like religious scepticism, too, such doubt has small effect on anything but the temper of people who are not disposed to share it. To the doubters, such views as have been set forth in this study may perhaps seem pathetically erroneous. To believers, on the other hand, certain obvious coincidences between these views and the recorded facts may perhaps seem fortifying if not convincing.

In the first place, of course, we must assume that William Shakspere happened to be what many another man of humble origin has been before and since, — a man of genius. In the second place, as we saw perhaps most clearly when we studied the *Sonnets*, the man's temperament, for all his genius, was strongly individual, — different from that of any contemporary, or indeed of anybody else at all. In the third place, as our whole course of study has shown us, his artistic development from beginning to end was perfectly normal. In the fourth place, his two most marked traits as an artist are both unmistakable and persistent: from beginning to end he displayed a habit of mind which made less distinction than is generally conceivable between words and the concepts for which words stand; and his imaginative power, in many aspects unlimited, always exerted itself chiefly in matters of detail, — most of all in the creation of uniquely individual characters. In mere invention, in what is vulgarly called originality and what really means instinctive straying from fact, he was weaker than hundreds of lesser men.

Given these facts, there is a marked correspondence between the conjectural chronology of his work and the recorded facts of his life. What little is known of him up to the time of Greene's allusion in 1592 indicates that, in country and in city alike, he had during the first twenty-eight years of his life rather unusual opportunities for varied experience; and a distinct motive for making the most of his chances to better his condition. The experience of these experimental years began to bear fruit with the *Midsummer Night's Dream.* At the time to which we assigned the *Merchant of Venice* and *Henry IV.*, the process of fruition had gone far enough to establish him as for the moment the ablest dramatic writer in England. Here, on the one hand, the records show him beginning to re-establish his family at Stratford; and a little later Meres's allusion proves, what any one might have inferred, that he had actually won professional recognition. With the exceptional publication of 1600 came the climax of his career. Later we found him no longer merely an artist, but a poet deeply stirred by such emotions as should normally have come to him had the conjectural story of the *Sonnets* been substantially true. Meanwhile he produced the great tragedies; and all the time, with the growing prosperity which such work should have involved, he kept strengthening the position of his family in their country home. About 1609 came the break in his creative power, at a moment when professional competition was stronger than it had ever been before. After that, the actual records show him no longer connected with professional life, but retiring more and more into the comfortable ease of a country gentleman. And so came the end.

At first glance, of course, the two records still look incompatible. They have in common, however, a trait which to many minds may well seem the most profoundly characteristic of all. Throughout Shakspere's career his imagination, for all its power, was concentrated on matters of detail. He created a greater number and variety of living characters than any other writer in modern literature. He made innumerable final phrases. Ever and again, by patient and repeated experiment with familiar motives, he combined old materials in constantly fresh and lastingly beautiful artistic effects. To a degree hardly paralleled, however, he was free from vagaries. Throughout his career, one may almost say, what he really and constantly did was this: instead of soaring into the clouds or the ether, he looked calmly about him, took account of what material was at hand, and with the utmost possible economy of invention decided what might be done with it and disposed of it accordingly. Among imaginative artists he is unique for practical prudence.

In the conduct of his life, as the records reveal it, precisely the same trait is manifest. The problem before him, as a man, in 1587, was one which most men find insoluble. The son of a ruined country tradesman, and saddled with a wife and three children, his business at twenty-three was so to conduct his life that he might end it not as a laborer but as a gentleman. After five-and-twenty years of steady work this end had been accomplished.

Grossly material it is the fashion to call such aspiration and such success as this. No doubt there is much to warrant such a contemptuous slur on self-made men. Personally such people are often unlovely, scarred and seamed by the struggles of a contest for which their critics are more than often too feeble. Even though the self-made man of petty commerce seem a prosaic fact, however, the real trait which has raised him above his fellows is a trait which his critics as a rule so lack that they honestly fail to appreciate its existence. What the successful trades-man has really done is to perform a feat of constructive imagination every whit as marvellous, if not so beautiful, as the work of any artist or poet. Facing the actual world as he sees it, all against him, he has made in his mind, perhaps unwittingly, an image of some state of things not yet in existence: a popular demand for some new commodity, it may be, or a sudden shift of values. Acting on this perception, to which less imaginative people are blind, he has outstripped others in the race for fortune. To put the matter perhaps extravagantly, what vulgar criticism would call grossly material success really involves a feat of creative imagination in certain aspects more wonderful than any other known to human experience; for while the creative artist is bound only to imitate the divine imagination which controls the universe, the man who achieves practical success is bound so to share that divine imagination as for a while even to share, too, the prophetic foresight of divinity.

Such a material achievement as Shakspere's, then, involves an imaginative feat quite as wonderful, if not so rare, as the imaginative feat involved in the creation of Shakspere's works. Granting this, as all who honestly appreciate it surely must, we may see in the peculiar concreteness of Shakspere's artistic imagination a trait which instead of contradicting the record of his life goes as far as any one fact can go to confirm it. Applied to the stage by which he was forced to make his way, his peculiar imaginative power produced the marvellous characters and phrases which make his work almost a part and parcel of the divine creation. Applied to the material facts of life, this same concrete imagination so controlled and grouped and composed and mastered them that a life-time of honest work resulted in just such achievement as throughout English history has been the general ideal of honest, simple-hearted Englishmen.

Life and work alike, then, if we will but look at them together, tell the same story. Both begin simply, carelessly, trivially. Both pass through a period of growing impulse and aspiration. To both alike — if for a moment we may pass from records and take for granted that, whatever the actual story of the *Sonnets*, the *Sonnets* are spiritually true — come fierce buffets. Both alike, after years of struggle and of conquest, fade into peace.

AUTHORITIES, ETC.

THE standard text is that of the *Cambridge Shakespeare.* This is virtually reproduced in the single-volume *Globe Shakespeare,* to which all the references in this book are made. The type of the *Globe* edition, however, is too small for general reading.

For such purposes as are considered in this book — purposes not concerned with textual criticism — any well-printed edition will serve.

The photographic reproductions of the quartos are convenient.

Furness's *Variorum Shakespeare* is beyond criticism, as far as it has gone.

Rolfe's notes are convenient and compendious ; so are those of the *Henry Irving Shakespeare.*

Schmidt's *Shakespeare Lexicon* is the standard dictionary.

Mr. John Bartlett's forthcoming *Concordance* will doubtless supplant all others.

The commentaries directly used in composing this book are referred to in the notes.

To present anything like an adequate bibliography of Shakspere would require a large volume. Whoever wishes to study the subject in detail will find an admirable guide in the printed catalogues of the Barton Collection in the Boston Public Library. These may conveniently be supplemented by the exhaustive bibliographies published from time to time in the *Shakspere Jahrbuch.* Taken together, these authorities will direct attention to almost all books on Shakspere and his times which are accessible to the general public.

INDEX.

———•———

IN this Index no attempt has been made to analyze the regular discussions of the separate works of Shakspere, to which any one desiring knowledge of them would naturally turn. All mentions of these works, and of characters therein, which do not occur in the regular discussions, have been noted.

The works of Shakspere are entered alphabetically under the head of *Shakspere ;* and the characters are entered alphabetically under the heads of the plays in which they occur.

When works of other authors are mentioned, they are similarly entered alphabetically under the heads of their writers.

The term *seq.* is used to indicate that the matter in question is mentioned on more than two consecutive pages.

————